THE YEAR OF THE
ROBIN

THE YEAR OF THE
ROBIN

Watching It All Go Wrong
for Charlton Athletic and the World

Jen Offord

ICON

Published in the UK and USA in 2022 by
Icon Books Ltd, Omnibus Business Centre,
39–41 North Road, London N7 9DP
email: info@iconbooks.com
www.iconbooks.com

Sold in the UK, Europe and Asia
by Faber & Faber Ltd, Bloomsbury House,
74–77 Great Russell Street,
London WC1B 3DA or their agents

Distributed in the UK, Europe and Asia
by Grantham Book Services, Trent Road,
Grantham NG31 7XQ

Distributed in the USA
by Publishers Group West,
1700 Fourth Street, Berkeley, CA 94710

Distributed in Canada by Publishers Group Canada
76 Stafford Street, Unit 300
Toronto, Ontario M6J 2S1

Distributed in Australia and New Zealand
by Allen & Unwin Pty Ltd, PO Box 8500,
83 Alexander Street, Crows Nest, NSW 2065

Distributed in South Africa
by Jonathan Ball, Office B4, The District,
41 Sir Lowry Road, Woodstock 7925

Distributed in India by Penguin Books India
7th Floor, Infinity Tower – C, DLF Cyber City,
Gurgaon 122002, Haryana

ISBN: 978-178578-757-7

Typeset in Sabon by Marie Doherty

Printed and bound in Great Britain by
Clays Ltd, Elcograf S.p.A.

For Lyra
I love you even more than Alan Curbishley.

Jen Offord is the co-host and producer of the hugely popular *Standard Issue* podcast, for which she has interviewed many leading sports stars. She writes and broadcasts for many other high-profile outlets on issues of sport, equality and mental health. She lives in East London.

CONTENTS

The Warm-up

This is my story of the 2019/2020 season as experienced by me, my family, Charlton Athletic Football Club, and the world (in that order). As we went through everything those absolutely brutal months threw at us – boardroom meltdowns! a worldwide pandemic! an unexpected pregnancy! a nil-nil draw with Fulham! – I found myself wondering what it was that kept us going. Like, *literally* what kept us going back to those rainswept seats in the North Stand just to watch our team struggle through a midweek match in January – but also figuratively, what kept us going as a club and a community when everything seemed stacked against us (repeatedly)?

So I began to talk to the people who made the club what it was – the star striker with his knack for controversy, and the manager who'd turned everything around, but also the people in the background: the men who ran the club museum on barely a shoestring; the woman who looked after young players away from home for the first time; the community workers tirelessly tackling discrimination at grassroots level; the fans who had led protests and campaigns to save the club from oblivion more times than they cared to remember.

And maybe it was because I was sharing my season ticket seats with my brother, or maybe it was because I was in fact about to extend my own family, but everything I learned about CAFC that year told me something about family.

Everyone thinks their club is special, but Charlton Athletic actually IS special. You'll see.

The Play-offs – or how my brother and I returned to the Charlton Athletic fold

In mid-March 2019, Charlton Athletic were fifth in the League One table. It was the third of four tiers of the English Football League, and one I hadn't been able to muster much interest in since Charlton's spiral into the abyss from the glory days of the Premier League.

There had been some near-misses in recent years as we'd yo-yoed in and out of the Championship. A few years ago, we'd even come close to challenging for a place back in the Premier League. It was the Charlton way to come close to moderate success yet still fail, and I'd not even cared very much about it when it had happened. The fact of the matter was, I'd not really cared much about what was going on at Charlton for a while now.

But there was something different about the club this year.

'So Michael,' I'd said to my older brother on the phone. 'Do you want me to get us tickets to Charlton for your birthday, since there's a chance we might actually win?'

'Hmmmmmm,' Michael had made a low noise, the implications of which were negative. 'Thing is, sis, I'm boycotting them, so I can't.'

Like many others, Michael was unhappy about Charlton's owner, a Belgian billionaire by the name of Roland Duchatelet who bought the club in 2014. It was under Duchatelet that the tone of the club had changed to something not just unsettled and unhappy, but downright unsavoury as fans turned up to – curiously – lob packets of crisps onto the pitch, or just didn't bother to turn up at all.

Duchatelet appeared to us to be running something of a rabid dictatorship at The Valley, enacted one bonkers press notice at a time. It's impossible to talk about Charlton without talking about Roland and his reign of terror, but we'll come back to him.

'Really?' I asked him. 'Are you sure?'

'Yep, sorry, sis, but I can't go until he sells the club.'

Fast-forward a month, as we hurtled towards the end of the season and the very real possibility of a place in the play-offs, and Michael found himself in quite the moral maze.

'So, I've been thinking,' he told me one day, 'that *IF* we make it to the play-offs ...'

The emphasis had been on 'if', as with so many Charlton supporters, still refusing to allow himself to dare to dream, despite having been firmly rooted at the business end of the table for months.

'... I'm not sure it would technically mean I'd broken my boycott, so long as you bought the tickets,' he continued. It was classic Michael maths, I had to hand it to him.

'So you know you said you would buy me tickets for my birthday ...' I absolutely had, and these would certainly be considerably more expensive than those *if* we made it that far.

'What I'm saying is,' he went on, 'should you buy me tickets for the play-off final *if* we make it that far, I'd have no choice but to go.'

'OK, Minks,' I responded, addressing him by his family nickname, 'Then I *absolutely won't buy you tickets to the play-off final *IF* we make it that far.'

'Good stuff,' he nodded. 'Appreciate that.'

●

By the end of the season I was gripped with excitement.

Charlton had, beyond all hope and expectation, made it to the play-offs, having finished the season third.

Now just two matches from the crushing inevitability of failure on a televised stage for the first time in years, we were due to face Doncaster away, in the first leg of the semi-finals, and I was ready for it. In fact I was even prepared to be a big brave girl and watch it in the pub alone, had my mate Dave not stepped in.

'I can't let you do that,' he'd said, himself a Manchester United supporter, concluding, 'it's too tragic.'

•

On 12 May, Charlton beat Doncaster 2-1 in the first televised match I'd seen them play in since 2006. I had texted my brother some waffle in the early hours of the morning about being nervous. He understood the nerves, he said.

The pub had been most amenable to switching the channel from the Old Firm match that had been playing out. After all, this was London. Though the barman had initially been sceptical.

'Is that even on telly?' he asked, a quizzical expression on his face.

'It's Sky Sports blah, at blah,' I told him firmly, feeling like J.R. Hartley himself.

'Yeeeeaaaaaah,' the barman started, in a tone that was familiar to me – it was the same tone used by anyone reacting to the news that I support Charlton Athletic: 'I *like* Charlton.'

'Got a mate actually,' he continued. 'Used to play in Charlton's youth academy.' It was a long-held theory of mine that everyone knew someone who either had played in Charlton's youth academy, or at the very least *nearly* played in it.

'The thing you forget about Charlton,' I began, 'is that a lot of big names have come from their academy,' citing the three names I could immediately recall, vowing to get better pub chat. After the victory I called Michael to discuss the match.

'For all his failings,' Michael commented wistfully, 'you can't deny Lee Bowyer has brought the club together again,' before adding something negative about the probability of getting tickets *if* we got to the final.

I silently rolled my eyes at him for the first of many times over the next couple of weeks.

•

A week later and I was at dinner with a group of friends. The second leg of the play-off semi-final was under way and it's fair to say I was distracted from my dinner. It was a long-standing commitment that I had felt unable to un-make, given that the majority of the party members had arranged a night off from mothering for the sake of our meal.

'Does anyone actually give a fuck about Charlton Athletic?' one friend asked me, as I checked my phone for the 50th time.

I was confused, since my dedication to SE7 was well documented.

'Oh,' she said as I justified my distraction, 'I sort of thought that was a joke.'

Dinner finally came to an end and we made our way to a pub, one less amenable to showing third tier English football, and so I brought up the club's Twitter feed on my phone as my fellow drinkers chatted amongst themselves, knowing now that they had lost me. Somehow – *SOMEHOW* – having won the first leg against Doncaster, we had found ourselves level pegging against the visitors, after extra time. Penalties it was.

Penalties. Well, that was that, then. Brought down by *fucking Doncaster* before we'd even had the chance to waste money on tickets to see them lose at the home of English football, Wembley Stadium. Brought down by the team who'd finished in *sixth place* to our third.

'Fuuuuuuuuuuuucking hell,' I texted Michael.

'What a nightmare!' he responded.

Or not.

Oh ye of little faith. And indeed, I had forgotten that my little club had some pedigree in the business of penalties in the play-offs, having beaten Sunderland via the very same arbitrary mechanism in the play-off final of 1998 – widely regarded as one of the greatest play-off finals of all time.

Unbelievably luck was to be on our side again that fateful Friday night, as I waited with bated breath for the Twitter feed to update. Suddenly images of euphoric fans invading the pitch at The Valley began to flood my timeline as Charlton beat Doncaster 3-2 on penalties.

As the news came in that old foes Sunderland had beaten Portsmouth, and Charlton would face them for a second time in a play-off final, Michael messaged me again.

'Got to get tickets! I'll be checking for sales announcements pretty much every 30 secs from now on!'

Warmed by victory and more than a few glasses of wine, I sat grinning on the number 149 as I travelled through the drizzle on Kingsland Road, not even caring if anyone could hear that I was listening to 'Bamboleo' by the Gipsy Kings, in celebration.

We were going to Wembley – for the first time in 21 years.

•

The day of the play-offs arrived, and I met my brother, his girl-friend Kerry and childhood friend Jamie at a pub near Liverpool Street station. I was hung-over and late, and they'd somehow managed to sink two pints before I arrived.

With Michael still technically boycotting the club and busy 'working' on the morning tickets went on general sale, I had been on ticket-buying duties. In the days prior to this, I had been receiving almost hourly texts from my brother imparting either some sort of negative energy about the improbability of actually securing the tickets, or tactical wisdom on how to ensure that we did.

'Don't think it will be easy,' he told me.

'Approx 38k tickets each, 25k at The Valley for the semis. Each of those can get up to six tickets ... who knows ...'

'Loads of people rushing to get tickets tomorrow ... Crack on as close to 9am as you can ...'

The burden of being on ticket-buying duties had actually led to a sleepless night in the run up to the event, but I had done it. And I had racked up some major sister points, a delighted Michael conceded.

•

The night before the play-offs themselves I had been at a friend's bar, close to home in Hackney, chatting excitedly about the upcoming clash.

'Oh, right,' he said. 'My friend Mike's going to that as well,' introducing me to a member of his staff.

Mike and I regarded each other with caution, before a pathetically British, good-natured chat ensued, neither party prepared to slag off the other, or accept the possibility of victory, both so desperately wanting it.

Mike, who I thought was probably about ten years older than me, had been at the play-off final in 1998 and witnessed the heroics of hat-trick-scoring Clive Mendonca, a Mackem himself, now a Charlton Athletic legend.

I had been just fifteen years old at the time, and not even able to watch the match in the pub with my brother, but Mike spoke with genuine warmth of a great day and a wonderful match. He must surely have thought this time would be his time?

'It was such a great match – such a friendly atmosphere,' he told me. 'Let's hope for more of the same tomorrow.'

Indeed, I thought, as we shook hands and finally went our separate ways.

Back in the pub, there was a sense of foreboding in the air as it occurred to me, and not for the first time, that there was a very real possibility we would not win this.

I had never been to a Charlton match and seen them win, and though I knew realistically this was not my fault, I had wondered if I was a football jinx. At almost any time I nailed my colours to the mast on Twitter, any team I affiliated myself to would promptly turn their fortunes around to lose. And let's face it, if ever a team were capable of this, it was Charlton.

There were a few other football fans in the pub, and Michael quickly sought out one with a North East accent, sitting alone, who he offered to buy a pint for. I found his sportsmanlike gesture both classy and heart-warming. He was a good lad really, my brother.

Alas, he explained in a hushed tone, he had seen some Sunderland fans on the train to London, helping an old lady with her suitcase. Buying a Sunderland fan a pint, he thought, would redress the balance of karma in Charlton's favour.

Shortly after the transaction was made, it transpired the

man was in fact a Newcastle fan, on his way to Stansted airport for a flight, and his presence in London completely unrelated to the game. If anything, I assumed he would probably have preferred a Charlton win, but hoped karma would appreciate the gesture, nonetheless.

●

It was a warm day in late May, and I had never seen a Tube carriage so densely populated with sunburned faces, as our Metropolitan line train to Wembley Park filled up at Baker Street. Standing room only for those now piling on, red shirts filled the carriage, clashing wildly with the various hues of pink.

Sunderland fans to our right, Charlton fans to our left, the chanting started between the two. One woman took her phone out to film the two tribes as they – in what seemed a relatively good-natured battle – began to shout at one another from across the Tube.

'*We've seen you cry on Netflix, we've seen you cry on Netflix! La la la la, la la la la!*' began the Charlton fans, referencing a now infamous documentary supposed to chart the phoenix-like rise of Sunderland back into the Premier League after their recent descent, but ultimately telling a very different story.

The Tube shuddered with the weight of the men at either end, stomping their feet with excitement as the cries continued: '*Lyle Taylor, baby! Lyle Taylor whoooooooooaaaah!*', to the tune of The Human League's 'Don't You Want Me'.

The young couple with a small child sitting next to me seemed to take it in their stride as the train erupted into song again: '*And now we've got Lee Bowyer, we're fucking dynamite!*'

●

As we arrived at Wembley Park, all I could see stretched ahead of me on Wembley Way was a sea of red and white – a sprawling mass of synthetic red fabric pulled taut across rotund bellies. Charlton would play in their home colours, as the higher placed team at the end of the season.

There were older men, in their fifties, sixties and seventies, and plenty of people around my own age in their mid-thirties. But also children, teenage boys, presumably tied to this unglamorous South East London club by local connections, as I had been. There were young girls with their dads, perhaps drawn in by the recent groundswell of support for women's football. There were more women than I had expected, which I discovered with some regret as I joined the queue for the ladies'.

It was good-natured – joyous even – as we all united with the hope of winning. It was the hope of your team winning rather than the other losing. There were no London faces here, avoiding eye contact or visibly balking at the prospect of speaking to a stranger, but you couldn't escape the lingering tension of knowing just shy of 40,000 people would leave the stadium in a couple of hours' time, without that feeling of hope. My stomach knotted at the prospect of being one of them.

In our seats right up in the gods of Wembley Stadium, we watched on. We hadn't quite arrived in time to neck another pint before kick-off, and I couldn't have felt more sober compared to the five or six men in the row behind us. Without exception, they appeared the absolute epitome of anything bad you had ever thought about football fans, their faces an extraordinary shade of puce, slurring their words and jostling into the back of our seats as the excitement began to build.

'Wonderful,' I thought to myself as I grimaced at Kerry.

The stadium roared as the match got under way, in the anti-climactic way that all football matches begin. Having watched a lot of football by now, I had concluded everyone was a bit shit in that unremarkable early stage of a game, as teams find their feet and seek to establish the dynamics of their impending power play.

I was unprepared for just how shit a team could be.

Disaster struck in the fifth minute as Charlton defender Naby Sarr passed the ball back to the keeper Dillon Phillips. It appeared to unfold in slow motion as the ball rolled – and not at great speed, it must be said – towards Phillips, a little way out of his goal area. As we watched, it didn't even occur to us that there could possibly be anything to worry about.

'It's OK, he's going to get that,' I began to think over the few seconds that seemed to stretch out for an eternity. 'He'll get that,' I repeated to myself.

'He's going to …' Somehow, he didn't. There was an audible gasp as the ball rolled across the line and into the goal. Charlton were 1-0 down after five minutes thanks to the stinkiest of *all of the stinkers*.

Sharing my match-day experience via Twitter, I typed: 'Shitting hell.'

Dillon Phillips echoed the reaction of every Charlton fan in that stadium as he brought his brightly coloured, gloved hands to his face, and closed his eyes.

'You still have time!' one of my followers piped up.

I wanted to go home. That was it, I thought to myself. How could we come back from that?

There was silence, for a time, even the mob behind us seemed to say nothing, but Phillips made a decent save shortly thereafter, and we sighed collectively in relief.

'Thank Christ for that,' Michael said. 'He's got the home crowd behind him now, but they're going to give him so much shit at the away end in the second half – thank God he made that save now.'

And Michael was right; it seemed to be just enough to give them that edge of confidence – perhaps, *perhaps*, they might be able to do something with this game after all.

After a cagey period, it was of course Lyle Taylor baby himself who made the low cross to Ben Purrington to tap the ball in the net in the 35th minute, and at last we were back in the game. The crowd roared with excitement, and the men behind us screamed.

By this point, the only discernible words coming from our friends were various slang words for intimate parts of the female anatomy. Everything else was just a long, scratchy rasp of vowels.

'ooooooooooooooooooooooo scorrrrrrrrrrrred?' one of them screamed.

It went on for the best part of the rest of the half, oblivious to the ball icon sitting next to Purrington's name on the giant screens.

'Yoooooooouuuuuu fahhhhhhhhhkin puuuussssssssssy!' one of them rasped, looking perilously close to death as he did so, the puce of his face deepening to a sort of aubergine hue. He was also apparently unaware that it was in fact one of our own players on the ball.

One of them tipped his bucket of popcorn on top of his head, exclaiming the act was in tribute to Lyle Taylor's bleached curly hair, and everyone within approximately ten people of said man visibly winced, not for the first time – was that … was that a bit *racist*?

As the half-time whistle blew, I was relieved when after

falling into the back of Michael for the second time, they shuffled off to the bar.

'I wonder,' pondered Jamie, referring to our fellow supporters, 'what do you think they actually do? You know, in their day-to-day lives? Like, what do you think their jobs are?'

I had noticed a couple of obvious weaknesses in our game, I told Michael and Jamie as Kerry went to the loo. We weren't very good at set pieces, I commented, adding: 'Or keeping the ball in – they're quite bad at keeping the ball on the pitch. It's almost as if they don't really understand how big the pitch is?' It was a big pitch, after all.

Still, there were promising elements to the game and hope was still alive; they were nothing if not doggedly determined.

The match went on. After some decent chances in the first half, Charlton seemed revived, but the break would not come.

The atmosphere grew more tense and the men behind us more drunk, by this point having twice lurched into the back of me as well. Ordinarily, I would have been the kind of person to get a bit lairy about such things, but sensing these might not be the most reasonable characters, I bit my tongue, not wanting Michael and Jamie to have to deal with the fallout.

'Please be *careful*,' I hissed.

'Aaaaahhhh, sorrrrrrrrrry, love,' he slurred, trying to hug me, which was almost as offensive as the barging, to be honest.

As we approached the end of the second half, I felt I wouldn't be able to bear another 30 minutes of the tension, should the match go to extra time. I had already clapped my hands to the extent that I could see purple bruises swelling under the surface of my skin.

'How *on earth* do you clap?' Jamie asked me. Aggressively, apparently.

When the giant screens announced four minutes of stoppage time, my heart sank. It was enough time for one team to score, but in all probability, not both teams.

We watched on, teeth gritted, jaws jutting, praying *just to stay in the game*. We could not have predicted what was to follow.

Suddenly all bodies were in front of the Sunderland goal. There was a shot on goal and we groaned as it deflected, but in what would be almost the last kick of the game, it was leapt upon by captain Patrick Bauer – and somehow, magically, we had taken the lead.

The crowd erupted, as Lee Bowyer began to celebrate and players ran off the bench. *Blow the whistle. Blow the whistle.*

The whistle blew just seconds later.

The noise in the stadium was deafening as the players ran up and down the pitch, sliding across it on their knees. Preparations began for the trophy presentation and the crowd roared. I felt a lump rise in the back of my throat as Bowyer embraced Charlton legend Alan Curbishley – the man Bowyer had played under himself as a youngster at the club.

My phone began to vibrate as friends sent congratulatory messages – they understood what it meant.

I looked at the giant screens and they declared 'Charlton Athletic: WINNERS!' and I took in the atmosphere around me. To my right was just a barren wasteland of empty seats – I had never seen 38,000 people evaporate so quickly. But here, in the thick of it we were jumping up and down, singing, shouting, screaming even – a football match had never meant so much to me.

In that moment I remembered the day – it was the fifteen-year anniversary of the death of our older brother, Stephen, and if the tears weren't there already, they began to prick painfully at my eyes. Through the tears, in the corner of my right eye, I could see Michael also looked a little choked, and I wondered if the same thought had occurred to him.

I remembered how it had been the Euros in 2004, shortly after Stephen died. I remembered going back to Sussex University and watching England play Portugal in that tournament, the penalties, and the unbearable prospect of failure.

I remembered silently telling myself as I left the bar unable to watch those penalties, and in the way that one makes arbitrary rules or judgements in the face of losing all control over their own life, that if England could just score those goals, it would *mean* something. It would mean that Stephen was somewhere, and I genuinely believed if they could just win the game, it would in some small way be indicative of some sort of higher power. But England did not score those goals. It was stupid, superstitious – I wasn't a superstitious person and I didn't even believe in any specific higher power, but it stayed with me, and was always in the back of my mind during important international games.

Stephen hadn't actually supported Charlton – somewhat contentiously, he had been a West Ham fan – but he loved football more than any of us. It would have been a match he almost certainly would have come to, and a victory he could easily have got behind, for his siblings and because Charlton were the kind of club you could get behind. I began to sob quietly as finally, a game had actually meant something, and I could allow myself for that brief moment in time to believe this victory was *spiritual*, even.

It was spiritual, at least, until two of the puce-coloured men from the row above fell on top of me.

In the Beginning

I first went to see Charlton Athletic play in 2002. I cannot remember who we were playing against, if I'm entirely honest, but looking at the fixtures list now, I feel it could have been Southampton. It was late in the Premier League season, against a team you could easily get tickets for, it had been at The Valley, and we had drawn. It had been underwhelming and exhilarating all at the same time, to a large extent because earning the right to be there in the first place had been hard won.

Michael – the only other person I knew who wanted to see Charlton Athletic play – had been reluctant to allow me to go with him. His mate Ben had sort of adopted Charlton as his team, so he didn't need my company and, he said, I would 'ask too many questions'.

Looking back on it now, and knowing Michael not to be, nor having ever been a misogynist, I wonder if this stance might have been more to do with feeling Charlton was 'his thing'. We had always got on well, but I had muscled my way into almost every friendship group he'd ever had, and perhaps he'd just wanted something for himself. As much as he had pissed me off at the time, perhaps retrospectively I could have been a little more sympathetic.

The fateful day had come about by unfortunate accident. It had been Michael's birthday in late March, and back then – before he was 'boycotting' the club, he had always wanted Charlton tickets as presents for birthdays and Christmases. Knowing that our mum had done as asked and procured these, and it being his 21st, I had wanted to buy him something special

– an experience he could remember, not just a CD or DVD as was customary.

So I bought him two tickets for the London Eye.

Yes, with hindsight it was perhaps not a *great* present, but there was a method to my madness – why not have a lovely day out in London when he went to see Charlton? The Eye was relatively new at the time, so who *wouldn't* want to check it out?

'I hate London and I hate heights,' he told me as he stared bewildered by the contents of the envelope I had handed him.

He had never told me he hated either, but the disdain was nonetheless palpable and I was crestfallen. I had genuinely considered it a thoughtful and inspired gift.

To this day, I don't know what happened next – whether he took the decision himself, or whether he had been leaned upon by our mum, unimpressed by his reaction. Whatever inspired the gesture, in the week that followed, Michael apologised unreservedly and – to show he meant it – offered to take me with him to both the Charlton match *and* the London Eye, and I had enthusiastically accepted. After all, who *wouldn't* want to go on the London Eye?

We would both travel from our respective universities – his in Canterbury and mine just outside Brighton – to meet on the day. The London Eye first, then to The Valley

The night before I had been mortally drunk and snogged a boy in the campus club, The Hot House. He was the cock of the Sussex University walk and had told me with an air of superiority that he was invited to Dean Gaffney's birthday party – *and* that his brother played for Crystal Palace's youth academy. He wasn't even lying as there had been a T4 documentary series at the time, *The Players*, and sure enough the brother had been on it.

'Urgh,' I scoffed, keen to put him in his place while

establishing myself as a woman of niche footballing tastes. 'I don't even *like* Crystal Palace. I support Charlton – I'm going to a match tomorrow.'

I was excited and proud to be attending my first football match, and I wanted everyone to know about it.

In the event, when I arrived in London I had been desperately hung-over, having sobered up somewhat on the journey into Victoria.

'Oh look,' Michael said, his face pressed against the glass of the capsule, while I sat with my head in my hands as we reached the Eye's zenith. 'You can see the Tower of London.'

We ended up having a good day, although perhaps Michael's had been slightly better than mine, but this wasn't just my first Charlton match – it was my first football match outside of the ones I'd watched my brothers play at school.

The Valley seemed huge with its capacity of 27,000, and the atmosphere had been epic. We had chuckled along with the young family next to us, as a man effed and blinded, before realising his error and clasping his hand to his mouth in horror. However, it never seemed scary or intimidating in the way that one imagines a football match might be – it had always seemed like a warm place to be.

Desperate to be allowed back, I bit my tongue throughout, and ultimately Michael had to concede I had not asked too many questions. One or two, he thought (lies), but not an untenable amount. Perhaps he would extend this privilege to me again one day, after all.

We did in fact return to The Valley together several times, and I cannot remember who we played on any occasion, apart from Arsenal in October 2003, although we had not won any of the matches we had been to together.

I mostly remember the Arsenal match because it was the era of the 'Va-va-voom' Renault adverts and Thierry Henry had been playing. Incredibly, we ended up with pitchside tickets. Michael had been quite reasonable, as my commentary consisted largely of things like 'Get off him!' when someone pulled Henry's shirt.

'This is the closest you will ever legally be to Thierry Henry,' he had shrugged with what seemed a genuine degree of understanding.

We didn't win, but we didn't lose. It was a big match, and Paolo Di Canio had scored an audacious penalty for us. It ended 1-1 and Henry had scored the Arsenal goal, so there was a lot to be happy about, from my perspective.

•

In the weeks that followed our victory in the play-off final, I became increasingly interested in the fate of my team, again. I wouldn't say I was a fair-weather fan, rather that my love of Charlton had been reignited, and that for the first time in a *long* time, there had been a positive vibe about the club.

'I think we should get season tickets,' I told Michael, upon learning that the cheapest tickets only cost £220.

Michael took a more cautious approach. Not living in London himself, he wasn't sure he'd be able to make the pilgrimage often enough to warrant the expense. He was also concerned about the likely impact of promotion on the squad, and the possibility of haemorrhaging our good players. Our budget was going to be tiny and it might not be the great fun I was imagining, but my head was already full of Leicester City's 2016 season, great sporting triumphs and the possibility – no matter how small – of a return to the Premier League glory days.

I mulled it over, despite his reluctance, and found myself three pints and no dinner down on a date, a week or so later, explaining my dilemma.

'You'll see some good football in the Championship,' my date had reasoned.

By the time I got home I was suitably merry enough to whip out my credit card and make the purchase, with really very little idea about what I was doing in terms of seat selection, but I picked two, signing one over to my brother.

I broke the news to Michael as he received a surprise email from Charlton congratulating him on becoming a season ticket holder. I half expected him to be a bit annoyed that I had effectively gone against his wishes, so I played it down and stressed that there was no pressure on him to make all the matches, I'd take friends with me, and so on, but he was about as happy as I'd ever seen him.

'Honestly, sis, this is the nicest thing anyone has ever done for me,' he said. 'I'm actually crying a bit.'

His reaction, in turn, made me a little weepy myself. Buying him that season ticket, and the absolutely *first-class* sistering on my part, became my proudest moment in life.

The CAFC Museum

Over that summer – those heady weeks between winning the play-offs and starting our first Championship season – I thought about that funny little corner of London at great length. I had spent the first six years of my life there, and could remember our old house on Delafield Road – almost directly opposite Floyd Road and just a stone's throw from The Valley.

It was the house where family legend had it that Michael had coined the term 'gommow' for trains. Apparently this had come about because every time my dad had exclaimed at his tiny son, 'Look, a train!' pointing at the tracks at the end of our garden, Michael would react at just the point Dad sighed, 'Ahhh, it's gone now.' Until one day he had shrieked 'GOMMOW! GOMMOW!' as he finally got a glance of the shuddering beast.

I could remember Fossdene Primary School, where I had attended nursery and reception infants' class; our neighbours Lou and Bill; and a cat called Sheba who lived on the other side and was said to have been about eighteen years old when we lived there. I had a sense retrospectively that a lot of the people on our road were working class, but these were not really the things a five-year-old thought very much about.

Though I had been to The Valley a fair bit, I'd not wandered around Charlton for years and years, but I got the feeling from things people said to me that the area was 'a bit Brexity', and largely untouched by the gentrification many other formerly working-class areas of London had experienced. Indeed, a quick Google search revealed that a five-bedroom house in

Stoke Newington was apparently worth almost double that of its Charlton equivalent.

'Go and look at the Village,' my mum had suggested when I'd asked her about it, referring to what must have been considered the more 'upmarket' end of town. 'At the top of Charlton Church Lane – that's probably where you'll find your artisanal breads.'

In a bid to immerse myself back in all things SE7, I was keen to have a nose around the land from which we hailed, and to visit the Charlton Athletic museum – a place I had only recently discovered the existence of, nestled in a back room within the grounds of The Valley. The museum only opened on Saturday match days for a couple of hours, and one Friday afternoon each month.

On this drizzly Friday, I found myself wandering past the usual turnstiles and the photos of Charlton greats adorning the outer walls of the North Stand. The heroes of 1998 were all there: Clive Mendonca brandishing his hands in what would later become the universal sign for 'brrrrrrrrrrrrap'; the resplendent Saša Ilić, who saved the match-winning penalty on that fateful day and was now apparently running a detox retreat in Montenegro; and of course a beaming Alan Curbishley himself (player, manager of fifteen years, and the legend who took us from the brink of bankruptcy to TWICE promoted to the Premier League) holding the trophy aloft – they were all here.

Following the car park round, I found a sign welcoming visitors to the museum which could be found, it said, on the third floor. Tentatively, I pressed a buzzer and awaited the response of a disembodied male voice, inviting me to take the lift inside.

I was welcomed by what would probably rather generously be called a mural, depicting the robin and knight mascots on a wall of a dark corridor. To my knowledge I had never been in this part of the stadium before. It didn't look like *anyone* visited this part of the stadium too much, I thought, as I entered a lift straight from the 1980s, with its rudimentary operating mechanisms.

And then I was there, in the Charlton Athletic museum itself. A row of busts sporting Charlton shirts through the ages lined the long window running across the space. The old Woolwich Bank logos were emblazoned across the chests, as the sponsors of yesteryear, and the Viglen shirts I remembered from the late nineties – these were, according to Michael, akin to the old Arsenal JVC shirts in terms of iconic prestige. To my left, there was a table with a visitors' book and a small box welcoming donations. Along the wall ran a timeline of the club's history.

I was approached by a man who appeared exactly as I imagined an elder statesman of the game to look – perhaps it was the remnants of a summer tan, but he was not unlike Alan Curbishley, only with heavier eyebrows. His name was Nick.

I shook his hand and told him I was there to find out more about the history of my beloved club. He gestured around him, explaining some of the exhibits available. A small room playing a video about the club's history and some books of newspaper cuttings; shirts, trophies and other paraphernalia.

They were not, he added, funded by the club, though former CEO Katrien Meire, Roland's right-hand woman who had fallen foul of fans for, among many reasons, referring to them as 'customers' in ill-advised communications, had found this room for them.

'Really, no money at all?' I asked, surprised.

'To be honest, it's a blessing really,' Nick told me with a wry look creeping across his face. 'Means we don't have to toe the party line too much.'

I liked Nick. He had the air of a man who had seen many Charlton games in his time – committed, wary, but ultimately not without a decent sense of humour.

I explained my interest in the club and the area, and how my naughty scamps for brothers had somehow sourced old programmes from the then-abandoned box office in our youth.

(To be honest, I had always questioned this story – Stephen having only himself been ten and Michael seven when we left, and I remembered we weren't allowed to even play on the street, so there was no way they'd have been breaking into anything. I figured someone else's big brother must have been the benefactor of these items. But for the purposes of my conversation with Nick, I went with the legend rather than the probable truth.)

'Ah, then you probably need to talk to this guy,' he told me, leading me further into the museum where another chap stood astride a large Sainsbury's bag, full of books.

I was introduced to Alan – not Curbishley; turns out there are many Alans in the story of Charlton – a bespectacled man of robust build, who I judged to be probably in his sixties. He eyed me with some suspicion as we shook hands.

'Oh, right,' he said as I started to explain myself again, seemingly underwhelmed by my story.

'Look, full disclosure, I'm a journalist,' I told them, sensing their hackles immediately rise.

'But not a horrible one,' I added quickly. 'I love Charlton and I'm just trying to find out a bit more about the history of the club for a project I'm working on.'

Their questions came in thick and fast – What kind of project? What did I want to know? What was I hoping to find? – as they began to gesture to cupboards and cupboards full of information.

This tiny museum was run by volunteers – just a bunch of old boys who loved the club and wanted to see out their retirement obtaining obscure artefacts like a court summons evicting travellers from an abandoned Valley in 1989 – and it was sitting on an absolute treasure trove of information about days gone by of the beautiful game. I was particularly interested in one seismic period in CAFC's history – our time out of The Valley, and how we came back to it.

On 8 March 1983, the club – on the brink of financial ruin – had been set a deadline of 5pm by the Football League to obtain approval for a rescue package to be put before the High Court. With 25 minutes to go before they faced being wound up completely, the High Court gave its approval. Though the club had managed to hold off the ultimate disaster, their fortunes did not improve much in the years that followed and they played their last home match at The Valley on 21 September 1985, before a lengthy spell at Selhurst Park.

The Valley had effectively been left to rot for the rest of the 1980s, with all of its contents still in it. After the return to The Valley in 1992, the museum had salvaged minutes of board meetings and accounts of the financially ravaged club among other items available for its visitors' perusal.

'This is an *amazing* archive,' I told them

'And this was all just *here*?'

They nodded, as they began to tell me about those bygone days.

Alan Dryland was born 33 days after Charlton's much spoken of 1-0 victory against Burnley in the 1947 FA Cup final. He liked to think of himself as not only a lifelong fan, but an antenatal one, too.

He came to the club in the traditional way – his dad had

been a fan and took him to his first match on 30 April 1955. It was the last game of the season, but Alan counted it as the whole of the 1954/55 season, because it gave him an extra year of fandom, he said – 67 seasons, in total. He still had the programme, which he would later show me as evidence of this. Charlton had lost 4-0 that day to Preston North End, but seven-year-old Alan fell instantly in love, nonetheless.

'They say that you don't choose your club, your club chooses you,' he told me. 'Once you're hooked – you're hooked.'

Back then, Alan lived with his family in Borough Green, mid-Kent, and was dependent on lifts to The Valley until he was considered old enough to make the journey by himself, at which point he began attending matches more regularly. As with many families and football, it was a tradition that Alan had in turn passed on to his two sons, and his grandson had been at the epic playoff final against Sunderland, that summer.

These days, he said, 90 per cent of his interest in coming to The Valley was social.

'You still go,' he told me, 'because of course, what happens at three o'clock is irrelevant to all the talking rubbish and having the drink that you had before.'

'And there's the stadium – we're very proud of it,' he added. 'Rightly so, it's a good place to come. It's not some soulless shed.'

He'd lived for 25 years in a flat overlooking The Valley, he told me, and he remembered well the first time he'd shown his sons, who'd been ecstatic by the proximity to the stadium.

In his 66 (or 67) years of supporting the club, he'd seen some things. This current turbulence with Roland was nothing new, really. Though a bit before his time, the tensions between Duchatelet and Bowyer, recently exposed through a series of bonkers press notices about the failure to agree terms of a new contract, were not unlike those between former manager and owners Jimmy Seed and the Gliksten family. Though fortunately for the Glikstens, they'd had neither Twitter nor the *Voice of The Valley* fanzine to contend with back in those days.

The conversation meandered wildly as the two fans held court, opining on everything from those tensions to the current prospects of the club. 'It's all built on sand,' Nick sighed, lamenting the absence of any substantive signings over the summer transfer window – on to one of Alan's favourite Charlton anecdotes.

'I'll tell the story which always makes my sons roll their eyes in disbelief,' he began, describing how his then partner, while planning a holiday, had accidentally chosen a hotel that happened to be the England camp at the 2000 Euros, hosted by Belgium and Netherlands.

1966 England hero Geoff Hurst had been part of the FA's coaching setup at the time, and during a chance encounter with him, Alan told him he'd been at Wembley in '66, but his was the *second* best hat-trick he'd ever seen at Wembley.

'"Second best, who was the best?"' Alan repeated. 'I said Clive Mendonca.'

'Oh Charlton,' had apparently been Hurst's response, with a sigh.

In 2005 at Charlton's centenary celebrations, Alan had the chance to recall this moment to Mendonca himself.

'"What did he say? What did he say?"' Alan mimicked Mendonca's response in a North-East accent.

'It was a brilliant moment,' he chuckled, adding, 'so Charlton gives you this. I mean, you might have to wait twenty years for the next one, but they're worth it when they come.'

Eventually, we settled on the meaty subject of the club's return to The Valley back in 1992, a moment I had been keen to learn more about. The club had a long history of protest, it seemed, and Alan was visibly excited as he told me all about it.

'We formed a political party,' he told me, referring to the fans' attempts to return to The Valley in the early nineties.

By this point, Greenwich Council was not keen on the club returning to SE7, because of a feared impact on the local community. In 1988, the club's first protest group of sorts was formed, by way of Rick Everitt's *Voice of The Valley* – it was, as far as I could tell, the 1980s version of *Arsenal Fan TV*, and probably about as popular with Greenwich County Council as AFTV with Arsène Wenger.

In 1990, Greenwich Council rejected a planning application made by the club to rebuild its derelict grounds – but shit was about to get extremely real for them, as CAFC fans, much like their beleaguered players, would not take no for an answer. As Bowyer himself would say – and *frequently* did in post-match interviews – 'They don't know when they're beaten.'

Fielding candidates in the local elections on 3 May 1990, The Valley Party polled almost 15,000 votes – an astonishing 10.9 per cent of the vote. It wasn't enough to usurp the very safe Labour council who took 43.6 per cent of the vote share, but it *was* enough to split the vote of Councillor Simon Oelman, chair of planning, and for the local politicians to start taking Charlton's fans seriously. But not before a punch-up between Oelman and The Valley Party's photographer that evening, outside the town hall.

As they continued with their story, Alan and Nick chuckled to themselves retelling this moment of glory.

'We were going to stand for election in Belgium,' Alan told

me. I was not sure they'd actually have been allowed, not being Belgian and all that, but I appreciated the gesture.

'So they just settled for graffitiing Roland's yard instead?' I asked.

'I don't think that was our fans,' Alan told me. 'The language was all wrong.'

'If you're researching, you'll need this,' he said, handing me a copy of a book called *Back to The Valley*, by Everitt, now himself the Labour Party leader of Thanet District Council.

'Do you take cards in here?' I asked, explaining 'I don't have any cash on me,' as they chortled at the prospect of such technological facilities.

'No, no, have that,' Alan said, handing me another book, *Charlton Athletic: A Nostalgic Look at a Century of the Club*, apparently part of the curiously named *When Football Was Football* series.

'This is embarrassing,' I said

'No, no,' Alan said again. 'If you're going to spread the word, we'd like you to have them.'

A little lump rose in the back of my throat, because *this* was what it meant to be a Charlton fan. *This* you could not expect to find on a tour of the Emirates.

'I'll come back,' I said, promising a future donation, as Nick became distracted by another visitor in the museum.

'He's in here all the time,' he said, gesturing at a man in a tracksuit and baseball cap, loitering by some shirts. He had missed an unfeasibly small number of home games in the last few years, they told me.

'I'd like to talk to you some more about your project,' Alan told me. 'I live in Woolwich and I've been in this area for a long time.'

And so I wrote my email address down for him and bid him good day, about to head off in search of artisanal bread in the Village. They both looked a little uncomfortable as I gushed earnest – and really very sincere – gratitude for their time and the books.

●

Less than 24 hours since my trip to the museum, and several discussions with disinterested parties about how Charlton was *even more* interesting than I had imagined, I received an email from Alan.

'Jennifer,' he wrote. '*It was a great pleasure to meet you in the Museum yesterday. I'm sorry if I hijacked your visit, but meeting a delightful lady Addick in such heady surroundings easily starts me off!!*'

He informed me he could be found in the fans' bar ahead of most home matches, and asked me to keep in touch, thus starting an exchange that would continue for much of the rest of the season.

THE SEASON BEGINS

August:
Charlton Athletic v Stoke City

Contrary to all expectations, we began the 19/20 season with victory – 2-1 away to Blackburn. I was feeling tentatively hopeful.

'Dude, 3pts!' I texted Michael.

'I know! Totally wasn't expecting that!' he replied.

The following week was our opening home fixture, against Stoke City, and a first outing for the Offord family season tickets.

Having to go to the Edinburgh Fringe for work, I had to miss this one, so Kerry went in my place. It followed the end of a particularly stressful week leading up to deadline day in the transfer window, the first I had cared about for well, ever, I suppose.

Working in sports journalism it was impossible to care beyond finding Sky Sports News' apocalyptic coverage of it amusing, along with the occasional 'Lionel Messi spotted in Bognor Regis!' type tweet. Or that time Moussa Sissoko ghosted Ronald Koeman on deadline day. Which was genuinely funny

The problem with transfer rumours is that 99 per cent of the time, you just knew they were utter bollocks, crafted to drive valuable clicks on tabloid websites. They were the kind of thing you really hated yourself for having to cover, simply because everyone else was covering them, also knowing it was bound to be in no way reflective of reality. In all probability, there was little chance of Pep Guardiola taking the helm at Macclesfield Town, and we all knew it.

This year transfer deadline day actually meant something, following two days after I received a message from fellow Charlton fan, Joel, a podcast producer who I had previously worked with but only recently discovered our shared interest in SE7.

'Jen, I literally cannot deal with these Lyle Taylor rumours.'

'WHAT RUMOURS??? He's not leaving? I can't believe this.' It was a disingenuous response, because like all other Charlton fans, I very well could.

MVP didn't quite cover it when it came to Taylor. Of course he could get more money elsewhere, and he was perilously close to the end of his contract.

'Maybe don't search his name on Twitter if you're planning on having a nice day.'

Taylor had been linked with Brentford, an attractive club so thought Joel, and one with £20 million knocking around after the recent sale of a decent player. Duchatelet was known for trousering a quick buck if it was offered for a decent young player who'd come through the academy, and of course, the thing you *forget* about Charlton is ...

Taylor was not young – 29, in fact, and had never played in a league above Championship level. This could be his Jamie Vardy moment, the stuff of sporting fairy tales, catapulted from the abyss to Premier League hero and an England call-up in just a couple of seasons. This was his moment, and he would take it, the Twittersphere, my brother and Joel echoed around me.

But he could have his moment *here*, I thought to myself. And somehow, a little voice in the back of my mind genuinely believed it. *Charlton could be the next Leicester City, and I would cry as Lee Bowyer gestured for the fans to pipe down and respect the artistry of Kasabian, as Claudio Ranieri had for Andrea Bocelli.* I knew this, and concluded that Lyle Taylor knew this, as it transpired he had *not* left.

He probably hadn't known this, rather he'd had absolutely no choice – he was under contract until the end of the season. Beyond all hope and expectation, Duchatelet had been persuaded that the financial value of the club staying up this season was higher than the rumoured £4 million Brentford had offered for him.

After a tense week and a minority of Charlton fans utterly shaming themselves on social media, Taylor announced he was taking a short break from Twitter.

'On the level … I will be taking time away from Twitter especially because the last few days have been unacceptable. I wish you all well and you'll see me in due course.'

He was back five days later.

•

I texted Michael on the morning to wish him a good first match as a season-ticket holder.

'Hoping for three points and that Taylor doesn't get a whole load of shit from the fans!' he replied.

At 3.26pm he texted me again: 'He is forgiven ☺'

'I think my team's winning, as I just got a text from my brother,' I told my interviewee excitedly.

'Who's your team?' she asked me.

'Charlton Athletic,' I replied.

'Awwww,' prize-winning author Malorie Blackman said, as she tilted her head to one side in the familiar fashion.

August:
Charlton Athletic v Nottingham Forest

Michael couldn't make it to the next game, a midweek fixture, so I instead took my friend Steve with me on my first visit to The Valley as a season ticket holder. I had worked with Steve in the Civil Service – we met as temps in Defra's Customer Contact Unit in 2006. And by 'Customer Contact Unit' I mean the place where letters were sent by people angered by their neighbour's cat shitting in their garden, or who were furious about water shortages and hosepipe bans but mostly still thought climate change was a load of old cobblers.

It was a World Cup year, and cast aside by the department, over in Vauxhall in a building (later condemned) where it was said a security guard had lost a finger trying to open a window, we were not heavily policed.

The BBC Sport website had, that year, produced 'make your own' masks of prolific England characters, available for download. It was a GOLDEN AGE of English football, the year of the WAG, Peter Crouch's robot dance and, curiously, a teenager called Theo Walcott. No, we didn't know, either.

It was to become the year of Wayne Rooney, red cards, and a wink that would forever make me despise Cristiano Ronaldo, if his penchant for inexplicably distressed jeans hadn't already sealed the deal – there was a lot not to like, to be honest. But before all that, there was hope, as was so wretchedly often the case with England, and indeed, Charlton Athletic.

Charlton had finished thirteenth in the Premier League that season thanks to the heroics of top goalscorer Darren Bent, though he had not made the England squad, to the *sort of* surprise, of many.

Back in our squalor in Vauxhall, we had readied ourselves for England's opening fixture against Paraguay by fashioning what we would call the 'Crouchbot' from a printout of BBC Sport's Peter Crouch mask, some plastic cups from the water cooler, and some bits of polystyrene we'd found knocking around in a cupboard. The Crouchbot made it to the pub next door to our office for the match, an 'effigy' as Steve had called it, which gave it an entirely undeserved sense of grandiosity.

England had won 1-0 thanks to an own goal by Paraguay, a disappointing result, but we'd take the three points regardless. No one could remember what had happened to the Crouchbot the next day, but Steve pointed out: 'Someone else has found him. And you know whoever that was will have absolutely loved him.'

•

Football is a means of bonding between men in a world where it's still not massively acceptable for them to express emotions. I had seen men almost as robotic as Crouch's famous dance weep in response to a beautiful goal or unexpected managerial resignation (yes, I'm talking about Alan Curbishley). I had dated men who were so emotionally repressed they had literally ended all communication between us rather than explain themselves, but openly admitted to crying over an epic comeback in the Champions League. It was baffling.

Liking football made me feel as if I had been granted access to a secret society that not everyone had been welcomed into – as a teenager I knew very few girls my own age who enjoyed football or had even a passing interest in it. To be honest,

I still don't, though I have actively sought some out in recent years.

By the time I was a teenager I was actively seeking out football. Charlton matches were not usually televised before they were promoted to the Premier League and we didn't have Sky TV anyway. ('Just an excuse to watch more telly!' as my dad would always respond to pleas for a televisual upgrade.)

So Michael and I would sit in the living room, him doing his A Level coursework, me my GCSEs, while listening to 5 Live and watching Teletext. I developed a fondness for the way commentators would fill the time when not very much was happening.

'It's a cream affair today,' the pundit would say, describing Charlton's away kit right down to the detail of their socks.

The gentle background roar of the crowd became soothing. When I inherited the old black-and-white TV which you literally tuned in with a dial on the front of it, as my brothers graduated one by one to proper TVs, I would keep it on overnight, tuned in to channels showing weird, niche sporting tournaments in the wee hours to help me sleep.

As a teenager and young woman, I found there had been a suspicion by men of women and girls who enjoyed football. They were either gay, or doing it to cross enemy lines and gain access to their world in order to ruthlessly get off with them. Either way, it firmly put those men at the centre of a narrative about what women would or wouldn't do for their penises. It was probably a valuable lesson to learn at a young age.

The reality was that I grew up with two older brothers and, as the youngest and the only girl, the hierarchy was well established and I had absolutely no say in what we watched on TV or what games we played in the park. So it was join in or go and do something on your own, and the latter was not massively appealing. And so many an afternoon was spent standing between makeshift jumper goalposts being pelted by balls, or reading a copy of *Shoot!*, simply because that was all that was on offer. But also, as a kid, I loved being around my brothers. To say I idolised them would be a bit much, not least because Michael will probably read this one day, but your older siblings are the first people in life whom you desperately want to impress.

As well as being resigned to going along with whatever my brothers wanted to do, I was also constantly surrounded by their various male friends who were often in the house, and so it was a language I had to learn, and a world I had to be socialised in. Football was part of that and it had stood me in good stead.

I reject the notion that women learn about football in order to get laid – if for no other reason than men usually don't require an excuse for such things ('Oh, she supports *Spurs* – go on then, why not?!', said no man, ever). But I can't deny knowing about football has frequently given me an instant 'in' with men in social situations. Be that at work, trying to endear myself to a new boss, or at a party if a conversation has dried up. I have seen the relief in a person's eyes when I've asked them if they follow a team.

Of course not all men like football and not all women dislike it, and plenty of people are capable of talking about other things, but in the same way that I bonded with my brothers and their friends all those years ago, I have bonded with a number of male friends, too. Football can do that.

•

On this occasion, it was Steve who had benefited from my newly acquired commitment to Charlton, and we were having a cracking first half against Nottingham Forest. We were probably playing the best I'd ever seen us play – making a mockery of them, almost.

We scored before half-time and as the ball came to our end of the pitch I missed whatever it was Michael was referring to in his text, described as 'possibly the best tackle I have ever seen'. Steve agreed with his analysis.

The Valley seemed smaller and quainter than it had all those years ago, the capacity somewhat dwarfed by stadiums I'd recently been to: Wembley, the new White Hart Lane, and even OGC Nice's Allianz Riviera stadium for the Women's World Cup that summer, which had a capacity of 36,000.

There was no fancy microbrewery at The Valley for the half-time pint, just a choice of Heineken or Foster's and some signage indicating a Christmas party that made the mind boggle.

Steve emerged from the toilet to tell me he'd encountered a man decanting his pint into a Bovril cup, in the gents. Asking him what he was up to, the man explained this was what he'd always done.

'What is Bovril?' Steve pondered. 'Sort of beef tea?'

'Yeah, like, basically beef stock,' I said, though I was pretty sure my vegan granddad used to drink it.

I eyed up the crowd directly around us trying to ascertain who might be our new 'neighbours'. There was a woman in front with a shirt with 'Peggy' emblazoned on the back. A family sitting to our left comprised of a couple with two young boys. There was a young Asian man with a baseball cap and a long beard sitting just over the aisle, also to our left, though the crowd was a lot less diverse than, for example, at a Tottenham match.

The Valley was absolutely rocking and I was astounded by how loud it was. But Forest seemed to be having the better second half. It was a low point in my spectatorship as I asked Steve: 'But why are they shouting?'

'Um, they scored.'

I very much hoped no one around us had heard my question.

I began to feel anxious in that second half as Forest raised their game considerably. The crowd continued to roar but I couldn't help feel that the fans were giving the team something to play for, right now. The team were riding high on the goodwill of the fans, but the situation was so fragile. They could lose that goodwill if we lost this match, I thought, and then what would they have? The fact of the matter was, between short-term contracts and loan deals, this team *was* built on sand, as Nick had lamented.

Nonetheless, the game ended 1-1, and there was still everything to play for as we remained unbeaten in the Championship.

August:
Charlton Athletic v Brentford

Just days later I was back in SE7 for the next home game, against would-be Lyle Taylor thieves, Brentford. Surely this would be the test?

Kerry returned again with Michael – she was properly in the Charlton fold now, this being her third match and, unlike me, she had only seen them win, thus far. She was, said Michael, a good-luck charm.

'Kerry, do you actually like this?' I asked her, wondering if she was just tolerating Michael's hobby.

'Yeah,' she said. 'I've watched loads of football recently. I watched quite a lot of the Women's World Cup over the summer, and whenever he has it on the telly, I end up watching it.'

It was not that dissimilar to my own experience of getting into football.

It was a hot day, 32 degrees hot in fact, and I had rocked up wearing a dainty Topshop sundress. The withering look on Michael's face as he spotted me outside the fan shop was one that screamed, 'What on earth have you come as?' It was *hot*, I protested.

I was showcasing the matching scars on both of my shins, from where I had been pushed into the seats in front of us as the full force of two grown men fell on me, on that fateful day at Wembley. I had almost fallen into the next row myself, but Michael had pulled me back to prevent this, leaving me splattered on the concrete floor and both men on top of me. But not before I had sent an elderly man in front of me flying as well.

Oh how they laughed as I was crushed under the weight of the pair of them. I had been rather less impressed.

'Please get off me,' I had whimpered. 'You're actually really hurting me.'

'I didn't really know what to do,' Michael had later said. 'Instinctively I wanted to punch them, but I thought it would probably be more helpful to get them off you.'

The charity 10k I had been committed to the next day had not been fun, the black bruise on my arse, the size of my hand, jiggling each time a foot landed.

'Jesus Christ,' Kerry said as I pointed out the burgundy welts on my legs.

•

Sitting in our seats, I noticed Peggy, the family and the bearded chap were back. So they *were* our neighbours, after all.

As I squeezed past the young family next to us, I apologised to the young man I assumed was at the head of it.

'Sorry,' I said.

'You're not though, are you?' he responded, abruptly.

Slightly taken aback, I began to protest.

'I am a *little* bit,' I said honestly.

'AHHHAAAAAAHHAAAAA!' he wailed, 'I'm *JOKING*!'

It didn't stop him from saying it to me almost every match day for the rest of the season, however. It wore thin after maybe the second match.

When we got to our seats, the team were warming up, taking shots at the goal, and they were right in front of us. I could actually make out their facial features, they were so close. I had done a good job with the seats, I silently congratulated myself, wilting in the heat. Though I wondered how much fun it would be to be out on this limb during the winter months, when it would doubtless be hammering down with rain.

'I fucking hate those things,' Michael said, gesturing towards the mascots, enjoying japes on the side of the pitch – one was a robin, and one was a knight, a valiant knight, presumably, reflecting two of the club's nicknames.

'I don't think they're aimed at you,' I replied, a little taken aback by the force of his feelings.

'They're not for anyone,' he said. 'You know whoever's in there is some prick who's not even getting paid to be here, they just love it. Who'd want to be doing that in this heat?'

•

It was a tough game, and we were not the better side. Brentford threw everything they had at us, and I couldn't pretend it was particularly enjoyable to watch. We were on the edge of our seats hoping, once again, just to stay in the game, until Conor Gallagher's goal came for Charlton in the 41st minute.

'I wish he'd scored a bit earlier,' I said. 'The whistle's going to go in a minute – it would have been good if they kept this momentum up for a bit longer.'

'Urgh,' Michael scoffed at me. 'If there's a goal, we'll take it.'

He was right, but, you know, so was I.

Brentford continued to pose an almost constant threat in the second half, but it wasn't enough, and they couldn't get past the mighty Addicks. In the additional time of four harrowing minutes, we all screamed '*Blow the whistle!*' as Charlton players literally threw themselves in front of the relentless shots on goal. It had been enough, and we won 1-0.

I reckoned Brentford had had over 60 per cent of the possession. Turned out it was 68 per cent.

It had not been a pretty win, but one goal was all it took, after all, and if Brentford's finishing had been shit – and it had – well, sorry, that's the price you pay.

I couldn't believe it; we had played six games in the Championship and not lost one. I turned to look at Michael as he returned the applause of the players to the fans. The atmosphere was incredible and I chuckled at his beaming face.

'What?' he asked, noticing I was laughing at him.

'Nothing,' I said. 'Just ... look how happy you are.'

•

After the match we wandered to Greenwich for an overpriced pint in the shadow of the *Cutty Sark*, a landmark which I estimated we had been taken to approximately 9,000 times as children, Pappa Offord being a fan of ships, and actually any form of transport. And apparently the Thames Barrier, which could probably rival said ship in terms of number of visits by the young Offord family.

Michael was reflecting on the remarkable turnaround in Charlton's fortunes.

'When I first started supporting Charlton, we'd come out of losing The Valley,' he said, referencing the club's spell at Selhurst Park.

'We got Curbishley, but we were always punching above our weight,' he said. 'We were always the underdog, and that's what we've rediscovered.'

I wasn't sure I followed.

'It's different under Lee Bowyer,' he went on. 'We don't go into every match thinking "we WILL win", but we go into every match thinking "we COULD win". Bowyer has recaptured that underdog spirit that Curbishley had.'

We were a few pints down by this point, but it seemed it wasn't just Charlton's fortunes that had seen a rapid turnaround.

'I *love* them again,' said the man who had, until around April the same year, been vowing not to return to the club until it had been sold.

'The fans are connecting again. We feel like we're fighting against something! We had three shots on goal today – that's all, and we *won*!'

Charlton was a club with a history of fighting, he was quite right. Perhaps they were at their best when they were fighting something? Perhaps we all were.

September:
Charlton Athletic v Birmingham City

It was 14 September – the day before my birthday – and Michael and I met outside the fan shop on Floyd Road.

'Here you go, sisqo,' he said as he handed me a battered pink envelope with my nickname 'Gwen' scrawled across the front.

'I was nearly late getting that,' he said as if I should somehow be grateful, nodding at the envelope now in my hands.

'No present then?' I asked, passive-aggressively – it wasn't like I'd just bought him this season ticket *not even for his birthday*, was it? Oh, wait.

'Errrrrr, I had to pay for my *train fare*,' he replied, again as if I should somehow be grateful.

Much to my disappointment, he had also point blank refused to tweet the club for the half-time birthday roll call, not least because of an incident during the Brentford match in which I had accidentally caused a photo of our mugs to be shown on the big screen. In fairness, the 'big screen' was one, solitary screen at the far corner of the pitch, not much bigger than the TV in Michael and Kerry's living room. It sat next to the always vacant letter 'Y' in 'Valley' which ran across the seats in the East Stand.

'I'm not doing any of that shit,' he had told me several weeks previously when I suggested it.

The next day, I would turn 37, and The Valley, Floyd Road, home of our beloved Charlton Athletic, turned 100 the very same weekend. All the club royalty would be out in force.

'Curbishley and Darren Bent are going to be here,' I told

Michael as we settled in our seats after the tense birthday exchange.

Darren Bent, of course, was one of our more famous players, who enjoyed Charlton's brief dalliance with the Premier League, before moving to Tottenham for a then club record fee. It had been more than Barcelona had paid Arsenal, up front at least, for Thierry Henry.

Before his move to Spurs, Bent had ruled himself out of the beginning of the 2006/07 season for six weeks after severing a tendon while preparing a 'celebratory meal', so the newspaper reports* had said. That the meal in celebration of having just renewed his Charlton contract had been a sandwich, said *everything* about our club.

Back in the Championship, we were about to play match number seven of the season against Birmingham City – a former team of Lee Bowyer's that he had seen relative success with as well as, in 2010, a record 98th Premier League yellow card.

'So, what do you think about today?' I asked Michael, and we both agreed, still unbeaten in the league, we were well overdue a loss. We had done so well thus far that I was actively suspicious. We were also without our star striker, Lyle Taylor, who had ruled himself out for several weeks after picking up an injury on international duty for Montserrat. *Montserrat.*

'Bowyer has been nominated for Manager of the Month, Taylor has been nominated for Player of the Month, it's The Valley's centenary – all the omens are bad,' Michael said, and I nodded sagely, secretly believing we would defy the odds once more.

....

* https://www.dailymail.co.uk/sport/football/article-396869/Bent-slice-bad-luck.html

You got a bit of a vibe about your opposing club by travelling in – as I did – from central London with the away fans. To say that the vibe I got from Birmingham City fans was on the lairier side would be an understatement. I did not look forward to the journey back from The Valley if we lost.

On another scorching day in South London, Charlton were looking good: we'd had some shots, the lion's share of possession and the scoreline remained 0-0 for the half-time centenary pageantry, though my mood soured somewhat as Charlton royalty, including the great Alan Curbishley himself, filed on to the pitch to the sound of far-away booing from the visitors' end.

'HONESTLY!' I raged. 'Who pays to come to a football match to boo a bunch of old men?'

At eighteen months younger than me, Darren Bent might have taken umbrage with being labelled 'old'. Nor perhaps could someone who had moments earlier gleefully chanted that the opposition were, in fact, just a 'shit Aston Villa', take the moral high ground on this occasion.

The sense of occasion was short-lived with Birmingham's 'wonderkid' Jude Bellingham snatching a goal shortly after half-time, and despite Charlton looking the better side, they failed to respond. Tensions ran high and a flurry of bookings ensued as the end of the match played out.

Hours later and a few post-match pints down, Michael and I consoled ourselves that, despite today's loss, we were still second in the league – at least until Sunday.

'I get very emotional when I'm at Charlton,' Michael said, beginning the story that I had heard at least ten times before.

He had first been to Charlton without adult supervision aged seventeen, with his friend Ben. It was a big deal – they'd never even been to London without adult supervision. Legend has it that Ben's dad, who worked at Liverpool Street station, had actually arranged for their train home to be delayed by five minutes, lest they cock it up somehow.

This was the olden days, before online ticketing and emails, and our mum had had to phone Charlton's ticketing line and make a card payment for the match tickets. Things were not immediate back then, as Michael discovered when he went to collect said tickets.

'I'm sorry, love, but the payment bounced,' the woman at Charlton's ticket office told him. Obviously, seventeen-year-old Michael didn't have that kind of cash on him; £50, or whatever it was, was the stuff that birthday dreams were made of. He didn't even have a mobile phone to call home on – this was the 1990s, after all.

'You can imagine,' he told me, again. 'I was devastated. So, I mean it's a bit embarrassing – but it was a big deal, right?'

I nodded.

'I started crying a bit. Not much – I mean I wasn't *bawling* or anything, I was just a bit upset.'

'It's OK, Michael, I remember, it was a big deal.'

'So she says to me, "I tell you what, here are the tickets anyway, but tell your mum to give us a call when you get home," and she let us in.

'Then when I get back, Mum is obviously embarrassed, so she sends a cheque and a letter to the club, saying, "Thanks so much for letting my son in anyway," etc. Then *she gets a letter back from the woman* which says "I'm glad he had a nice time – he had an honest face."'

'Honestly,' he continued, 'I well up a bit every time I see that ticket office.'

It was the stuff of Offord family folklore, if such a thing existed – like the time I allegedly ate a piece of horse shit in the back of one of our many red Ford Sierras, as a child, apparently having mistaken it for a biscuit – albeit a more charming tale. It was a story that never failed to make me feel warm and fuzzy inside, regardless of how many times I had heard it.

'I just wanted to watch a game and I didn't want any sideways stares' – Bhavisha and the Proud Valiants

The Proud Valiants are the official group for Charlton supporters who identify as members of the LGBTQ+ community. Formed in 2015 with the intention of providing a network and support for LGBTQ+ fans, as well as campaigning alongside other organisations such as Kick It Out and Football v Homophobia, the Proud Valiants were led by chair Rob Harris and co-vice-chairs Gary Ginnaw and Bhavisha Ravji. I wanted to know more about what life was like for other fans at Charlton, and Bhavisha had agreed to talk to me about her experience.

Thirty-six-year-old Bhavisha worked as a cardio physiologist in her day job, she told me. She had lived in and around the London area, hailing originally from Harrow, for most of her adult life, but was not born into a Charlton-supporting family. In fact, as with many people growing up in the 1980s and '90s, she'd supported Liverpool, having been 'indoctrinated', she said, by her older cousins, and with whom she had made occasional pilgrimages to Anfield.

As a youngster, she had loved sport – watching and playing it, 'feasting' on it, she told me, on anything she could get her eyes on. She described her athletic ability as 'average', but nonetheless thoroughly enjoyed her own participation in sport. When Bhavisha went to university, she'd even worked with the Scottish FA on her dissertation.

'I really loved it,' she told me. 'I just found all of those classic benefits that they talk about from doing sport.'

'It's given me those lessons in life that sometimes you don't really learn anywhere else,' she added.

When she left university, she'd wondered if she might work in football somehow, but couldn't see a place for herself within it. Further into adult life, Bhavisha had found it harder to fit in trips to Anfield, and easier to access sport on TV, though she'd missed the atmosphere and camaraderie of a live football match. She found herself working in Tunbridge Wells around twelve years ago, and one of her colleagues was an older woman who had supported Charlton all of her life and would make every home game with her 80-or-so-year-old aunt.

'I don't know if you've ever noticed those grandmas who go to football with a thermos of coffee and they bring out their sandwiches at half-time?' she asked me. 'I have,' I told her, as she chuckled warmly.

Bhavisha's colleague invited her to a Charlton match with her one day.

'I don't even think I realised that I was missing football at the time,' Bhavisha said, but nonetheless she decided to go along, and never looked back.

'There was something so magical about just walking up to the stadium. There's a bit of a buzz, and then that feeling of watching the ground sort of open up under the floodlights.'

Bhavisha came to Charlton after the glory days of the Premier League, but she said there was something about the atmosphere that drew her in.

'I just loved the atmosphere. The football was just a bit more rough and ready. The fans were just a little bit more ...' she trailed off, pondering.

'I wouldn't say there was a rawness to the fans, but they felt like those true fans, not like the fans that you would see at Premier League games.'

She ended up going to about half the home games that season, and before she knew it, she was a fully fledged Addick. In fact, she had gone to way more matches than I had in the last twelve years.

'Can I ask what made you come back?' she asked me.

'It stopped being miserable,' I replied, honestly.

It was true that the promotion had been the catalyst for that, but for that brief window at the end of the 2018/19 season and the beginning of the next, there had been hope for the first time in a long while – and what were football fans really, if not just big soppy dreamers?

A name that hadn't always felt particularly comfortable, dropped alongside the romanticism of football, was Lee Bowyer's. I'd certainly had more than a few negative thoughts about him taking over as manager, but nonetheless, it was Bowyer who had achieved the impossible, and given Charlton fans reason to smile again – reason to *dream*.

I wondered how much Bhavisha had known about Bowyer's background and how she felt, as a British-Indian woman, about his appointment?

'Vaguely,' she said, nonchalantly. She had heard of Bowyer's past, though she came to know more. 'As a player, my memories of Lee Bowyer was just that he was a bit of an idiot,' she said. 'He was always a bit mouthy, two-footed challenges, always trying to stir shit up.

'And actually,' she went on, 'the first thing that came to mind when I thought about Lee Bowyer, was a bust-up he had on the pitch with Kieron Dyer.

'I was already a bit sceptical because I was like, "This guy's an idiot. Do we really want him?" But you know, there's a part of me that thinks we have to allow people to grow as well. I think he was probably a very different man – a very different young man to the man that he grew into.'

I completely agreed with her.

It was an interesting thing about football and moral codes, I thought. I was speaking with Bhavisha in the week that the so-called 'Top Six' (though at the time of writing, in fact, they were six of the Premier League's top nine), had announced their intention to break away from the Champions League and form their own European Super League. It was *a bit* like the Champions League, except places were not secured through merit, and conveniently, it guaranteed an additional annual revenue stream of around £300 million.

It was deplorable, symbolic of everything football fans had come to hate about the late-stage capitalism surrounding the beautiful game and, indeed, it was deplored. In fact it was so unpopular with fans that by the end of the day in which the announcement was made, Manchester City and Chelsea were already backtracking, and within a couple of days the league had folded altogether, before it had even begun. You almost felt sorry for them for having gone to the bother of setting up the new website, except, obviously, you didn't.

Morals were not applied with any consistency in football. Collective outrage had not put an end to discrimination in football. While it was obviously far harder for football to make the wholesale societal changes required to eliminate racism, sexism or homophobia from the game, collective outrage hadn't even been applied to a World Cup which we knew was being built by people working as modern slaves. As a bare minimum,

I thought, it would be nice to feel assured that the heads of governing bodies and leagues weren't corrupt, racist, sexist or homophobic.

'I think the upper echelons of football don't necessarily care about wider issues,' Bhavisha told me. 'I do think that there's a connection there between understanding the power and the impact of football and the relationship just with society in general.

'So if we think, let's say, that the standard of person that we hold ourselves to is a cis, straight, white man, and everyone else has to get to that level – who predominantly goes to watch football?' she continued.

'Sometimes a straight, cis, white man has to talk to another straight, cis, white man about issues that aren't about straight, cis white men, and that's where they'll listen to you.

'Football could be so powerful when it comes to changing society, but sometimes it just has to get the conversation going. I think it comes all the way from the top to the bottom, and there has to be an investment and a buy-in right at the top. Because otherwise you just get all the lip services paid, and nothing ever happens,' she said, describing the currently much-discussed situation with racism in football *perfectly*.

'We hear about the same issues over and over again; how many times football players have to be abused on social media before anything gets done about it. But yet, social media comes out and says, "We're really sorry that this happened," and football comes out and says, "Oh, this is terrible." I don't think anyone's taking any responsibility for it.'

One of the recent tactics employed by the football community to try to combat abuse was to stage a weekend-long boycott of social media in protest. Presumably the idea being that if social media platforms lost footfall and, consequently, money, they'd be forced to do something about it. But Bhavisha was absolutely right, I thought – what was football doing in its *own* house? It was the classic mentality of exceptionalism that we saw every time a racist incident occurred against English players in foreign matches.

'I enjoy social media,' Bhavisha began. 'I don't want to boycott social media. Why should *I* have to temper *my* behaviour and the things I do to prove a point? I find those types of solutions problematic.

'I just think that sometimes, as a member of the LGBT community, I am fully aware that my most powerful allies are my straight allies, or the straight community who will have those conversations with their peers. And I don't really know why, but those conversations between those groups have a much bigger impact than say, for example, me talking about these issues.'

It was depressing, but it was true, that to create lasting societal change, you needed to take the people in the positions of power with you, I thought. It was about changing hearts and minds, and it felt difficult, sometimes, changing the hearts and minds of unaffected people who didn't see discrimination as their problem.

As a 'brown, gay woman', Bhavisha was a triple threat, and I wondered, did she feel more acutely aware of this at a football match?

Bhavisha's facial expression was both intent and sort of quizzical as she responded to my questions, and her responses were thoughtful and considered.

'I sometimes think if I was brown but straight, and I was at the football with my white husband, how would I feel? And it's so difficult because I don't know how I would feel,' she said.

And how could she, she elaborated, she had never not been a brown, gay woman.

'I don't have to disclose my sexuality to anyone. I would sort of call myself someone that can pass as a straight person. Depending on what day it is and how strong I feel mentally, there are times where I just want to fly under the radar. I don't want to have confrontations with people. I just want to go out on a Saturday, watch football, enjoy the game, cheer my team on and come home – I don't want to have to make a big statement about who I am and what I stand for and all the rest of it.

'I just want to go out and have a nice day like everyone else there and the colour of my skin is something I cannot hide, and my gender is something that I can't hide,' she continued. 'I think intrinsically people know how to behave when they see a brown woman but sometimes, if they see a brown gay woman, I'm not sure. Even little things like people being surprised when I talk about my wife.'

These were the tiring moments when Bhavisha said she felt she did not fit.

'I think the majority of women on this planet are constantly risk-assessing as they go, as they navigate their way through the world. And I think all the other intersections are just an extension of that.'

It was because of this that Bhavisha had been reluctant to take her wife with her to a Charlton match when she expressed an interest in coming to see what all the fuss was about, despite not being particularly interested in football herself. Her automatic response, she said, was to deflect. She did not want to have to explain who she was.

'If I was there with my boyfriend, I wouldn't give a shit

about holding his hand, but now with my girlfriend, I do give a shit about holding her hand. It's just little things where someone looks at you – slightly, not badly – but just makes a point of looking at it. You know, it's not even that anyone necessarily has to say anything, but then you become aware that you're making other people feel uncomfortable, which is not how it should be, but that's not how it works in reality,' she explained.

'I just wanted to watch a game and I didn't want any sideways stares. I didn't want to feel like I'd have to moderate my behaviour around her.'

Nonetheless, Bhavisha must have – at some point – grown more comfortable, as she eventually became involved in Proud Valiants. This involvement, she said, changed her perception of what football could actually be. She also took her wife to The Valley.

'I was just a bit like, "Fuck it, here's my wife, who is 100 per cent willing to come to the football, purely just to share in something that I feel passionate about. Why would I not want to take her along?" And I did, and it was totally fine. There was no problem, there was no issue.'

Bhavisha said she *did* feel more conscious of her difference at a football match.

'Especially in the lower leagues of football,' she explained. 'The lower down the leagues you go, I feel like you lose diversity. I hardly ever see any non-white people at Charlton.'

Bhavisha agreed with me that racism seemed to be taken more seriously than homophobia when it came to football, but this was because of visibility, she thought. Again, you could *see* which players were black, for example, but you could not see which players were gay. But the absence of openly gay players in English men's football was something Bhavisha lamented.

'Something I've experienced myself is that the mental strain it takes to be in the closet is really fucking *hard*,' she said, echoing my thoughts about the statistical improbability of the complete absence of openly gay footballers in the English Football League.

'You start to moderate what you're saying,' she began. 'People ask you, "What did you do at the weekend?", and you tell them what you did at the weekend, but you just omit who you're doing it with.

'You're then having to be like, "I wonder if this person caught on to something that I might have said?" And then you build lie upon lie upon lie, and then you're trying to keep up with your lies, and the mental burden that it takes to, to keep on top of that kind of stuff.

'I have quite often wondered about those kids in the academies,' she said. 'If you've got a coach down there that's possibly making the odd homophobic comment to a young, talented player who thinks he might be gay, does he just then walk away from football, because again, he just doesn't feel like there's a place for him there?'

Because of this, as she'd got older, Bhavisha had become more of an ambassador for equality, diversity and inclusion because she didn't want to see other people suffer in the same ways that she had done.

'Everything that I do, when it comes to this kind of stuff will always be for that young, gay, brown woman that just doesn't see herself reflected anywhere,' she told me. 'That space needs to exist, as I never felt like it existed for me, and I wanted it to exist for everyone else out there.'

It was a commendable attitude, but I could also see why you might just get sick of putting yourself in the line of fire.

'I will never ever judge anyone for not being out,' she agreed with me.

'Not in a football context, but I have found myself being on the receiving end of racism, and in those moments, you feel so paralysed that you don't do anything because you feel humiliated, you feel little, you don't feel safe, and you feel threatened,' she told me.

'So, of course, your instinct is not to charge after it and try to fight it in that sense,' she added.

I loved that Bhavisha had adopted Charlton, and that Charlton had welcomed Bhavisha in return. Given what she had said about the lower leagues and the sometimes lack of visible diversity, I wondered if Charlton seemed like perhaps a slightly surprising ally?

Funnily enough, Bhavisha told me, while Katrien Meire had been alienating the vast majority of the fan base, she could not have been more welcoming to the Proud Valiants.

'She really championed the Proud Valiants,' she told me, as if she anticipated my surprise.

'She was like, "Whatever you need, we'll try and facilitate it." And I don't know if that was something she felt might have some commercial benefit or whether she really bought into it, but she was incredibly supportive.'

For a long time, she said, it had been just her, Gary and Rob who had carried the Proud Valiants until the club became actively involved, but since that time, the group had evolved exponentially.

'There's a football versus homophobia month, and within that month, a lot of the teams across all leagues will have a game dedicated to it,' she explained. 'I feel like with Charlton, they were like, "What do you want to do? We'll do as much as we can."'

Even in Premier League clubs, she said, LGBTQ+ fan groups didn't always find it easy to engage the powers that be with their cause, and they would end up going 'as far as the club would let them'.

With Charlton, she said, they were always ready to help in whatever way they could, and there were always people behind the scenes – even when the club had been struggling – who were prepared to go above and beyond for them.

'I think that just speaks to the culture of the club,' she added.

It certainly rang true with what everyone else had told me about Charlton – that it was a community as much as it was a football club.

'Charlton will always be a club that's there for its fans and its community. And sometimes I think it doesn't matter how far up the leagues you go, I don't think that it will ever lose its heart with the people that go there and support their team, week in, week out,' she said. 'Like the old school gentleman of football.'

September:
Charlton Athletic v Leeds United

By the time Charlton would face another of Lee Bowyer's former clubs, Leeds United, two weeks later, we were no longer second in the league. By this point, we had experienced our first *convincing* loss of the season – 2-0 away at Wigan – and slid to seventh. But who cared? The season was young and my terminal hope still knew no bounds.

On another sunny day at The Valley, Kerry had joined us again. They were talking about Michael's difficult relationship with the FIFA PlayStation game.

'I don't know if it's good for me,' Michael said, speaking of the rage he had experienced while playing, before eventually admitting under Kerry's withering rolled eyes, 'I had to walk out – I had to leave it.'

Referring to another piece of Offord family folklore, I raised the thorny subject of 'The Time I Beat Michael at FIFA 98'. That year, 1998, was possibly the most significant year in the history of my relationship with football. Charlton, a team I had realistically only been particularly interested in for a year and a half, if that (I'd dabbled recreationally with Man United prior to this. Mark Owen had supported them, after all, so what was a teeny bopper of the 1990s to do?), had been promoted to what was then known as the Premiership that summer after the legendary play-off final, and just fifteen days later, a World Cup started.

I had definitely been interested in the 1996 Euros, but this was the first World Cup I had been particularly bothered about, and I went all in. I watched Baddiel and Skinner's *Fantasy*

World Cup programmes and laughed along as they mocked Alexi Lalas, despite having had absolutely no idea who he was prior to this. I still chuckle about the alleged small percentage of respondents to a phone-in who were said to have answered 'don't know' to the polled question 'Does Pele shag around?' I listened to Del Amitri's mournful plea to the Scotland team, *Don't Come Home Too Soon*, taping it on cassette during the *Chart Show* on a Sunday, and I even went as far as actually buying Echobeatz' version of *Mas Que Nada*, as featured on the Nike advert of that year, the Nike adverts historically being one of the iconic and enduring moments of any World Cup.

Of course, we had watched the England matches together, including David Beckham's infamous red card, the penalty shoot-out, and the sadness, anger and acceptance at the end of The Dream. But much more than that, I recall the three of us sitting in Stephen's room to watch the final between France and Brazil, drawing pictures of the various players, coming up with 'comedy' nicknames for them. It was also here that Stephen and Michael explained to me the offside rule using an apple core and a yoghurt pot (it really wasn't all that complicated, I concluded) while I fawned over a pitchside David Ginola on the BBC's commentary team, doing terrible impressions of his L'Oréal advert.

With our parents away that summer, in the run-up to this, Michael had done what any sensible seventeen-year-old would do, and moved his PlayStation into the lounge, challenging me to a tournament on FIFA 98. Michael was England, obviously, and so I chose who I knew to be The Best, and the subjects of the Nike advert, Brazil. I was not a gamer and so any attempts I made were a case of pressing as many buttons as I could in a frenzied speed while staring at the screen, holding the pad as far away from my body as possible in my completely rigid arms. In all honesty, it was an exhilarating if not quite stressful experience.

Michael had helped me through each round so that we might face each other in the final. At the time I thought it quite sweet but with hindsight realised he simply wanted to win a computer game, and recognised me as the unworthy opponent I truly had been. It was unlucky for him, then, that by some bizarre fluke, I had ended up beating him.

'You were furious,' I laughed, though still not quite sure if he had actually forgiven me yet.

'I've told you before about the rubber band theory,' he began, and indeed he had. 'The better you get at a game, the harder the computer makes it for you.'

It wasn't a good game for Charlton. Leeds had the vast majority of possession and nineteen shots to Charlton's three, but one of those three made it into the back of the net before the end of the first half for Macauley Bonne.

As was often the case with Charlton matches, the rest of the game was spent on the edge of our seats while the man behind us stammered 'Dirty Leeds!' about eight times in a variety of different tones – angry, sad, accusatory, mystified even. In the closing moments of the match Charlton players launched themselves against the line as Leeds desperately pelted balls at the goal, looking to go top of the table, but they were denied.

On the way home, I must have said 'It doesn't matter – it only takes one goal. If they couldn't finish then they didn't deserve to win!' almost as many times as the man behind us had cussed out Leeds. Charlton were up a place to sixth, and I'd take a play-off spot.

October:
Charlton Athletic v Swansea City

Just four days later I was back in SE7, albeit without Michael. It was a trek to Charlton from our home town, Harwich, and a midweek kick-off was almost out of the question if you wanted to make it back in time for work the next day.

As soon as I knew I had a spare ticket, the obvious person to fill the void was old friend and South London native, Ed, aka Conman. Conman had famously once had a sit-down meal at the Wimbledon dogs, which was, he had said, 'pretty Brexit'. I'd known immediately he was exactly the man to appreciate what the club's Twitter feed had indicated would be curry night at The Valley.

Conman himself was a Spurs fan and we had watched a number of matches in their runaway Champions League campaign earlier in the year, culminating in a trip to watch the final against Liverpool on a big screen at the new Spurs stadium. We'd not particularly enjoyed the outcome but you couldn't argue with a stadium complete with a wanky hipster microbrewery on-site.

'I think Heineken at The Valley is a fairly new development,' I had warned him, but Conman was keen.

'I'd love an autumn midweeker at The Valley against a team from the Valleys! The last time I was in that part of the South East it was a bit budget *Mad Max*, which makes The Valley the Thunderdome.' I had to admire his optimism.

Conman had been to The Valley before, back in the halcyon days of the Premier League. But it was not as he remembered it, as this time he found himself enjoying a pre-match drink with me in the North Stand.

'It's … kind of old here,' he remarked as we tucked into our drinks. It had never occurred to me before, but as I looked around at the sea of ruddy faces, he wasn't wrong – the vast majority of the fans were older than us, in our mid-thirties. It was also a surprisingly white demographic, for a London club. This was explained perhaps by the disproportionately high numbers of white people – compared to the London average – living in the neighbouring boroughs of Bexley and Bromley.*

The conversation turned to the Palace v Charlton beef, a rivalry I saw little point in, having played each other all of four times in the last decade. One of the four occasions had been a particularly low point for Charlton fans, after one was later found guilty in a criminal court of attempted damage after trying to punch Palace's mascot – a bald eagle named Kayla.

While debating who was likely to come off worse in a fight between a grown man and a bald eagle (my argument, for what it's worth, was that eagles have quite small faces), we missed the first goal of the night. Unbelievably, Charlton had gone a goal up as loanee Jonathan Leko scored in the second minute, and we downed the last of our drinks to hurry out to our seats.

In scenes that were starting to look familiar, though I wasn't sure if it was a pattern yet, despite conceding a goal after seventeen minutes, Charlton genuinely looked all right in the first half. Yet somehow we had managed to clutch defeat from the jaws of victory after the Swans scored again in the second half.

....

* https://data.london.gov.uk/dataset/ethnic-groups-borough

And lo it came to pass that, as I bid Conman farewell at the end of the match, Charlton had slipped out of the top six, never to return.

The Pride of South London – Gary and Charlton Invicta

As my conversation with Bhavisha had made clear, despite the many issues in football being discussed more widely in recent years, homophobia remained something of a taboo. There were no openly gay footballers in the top four leagues of English football. It was a statistical improbability, which implied that it was still not a comfortable – or even safe – place to be a gay man.

This was, in my opinion, something tied up very much in gender stereotypes, as well as homophobia. While it was apparently completely unacceptable to be a gay male player, it was almost *expected* that a female player would be gay.

I remembered many years ago having been to Chelsea's Cobham training ground to interview women's team manager Emma Hayes and a couple of her players for an International Women's Day piece. They had just turned fully professional, proof that the women's game was beginning to be taken more seriously.

'Were they all *lesbians*?' I was asked lustily by a man I had gone on a date with, later that week.

'I mean, I didn't *ask* them,' I had responded, bored.

My feeling was that this narrow view of the world came down to the even narrower opinion that gay men were somehow not *real* men, and gay women were not *real* women.

While homophobia – at least outwardly – was deemed increasingly unacceptable in wider society, there seemed to have been far less progress in football. That said, the rainbow laces campaign by Stonewall, one of the UK's leading LGBTQ+ rights charities, as well as another charity, Football v Homophobia, were becoming better known within the game.

It was interesting to me that one of the clubs recognised as doing good work around the issue of homophobia was, in fact, Charlton Athletic. Charlton had won the Football v Homophobia Professional Game Award in 2021, and a photo of Lee Bowyer proudly clutching the award had been plastered on the club's website.

It may have sounded like a very small gesture, but I actually thought there was huge value in someone with a bit of a hardman reputation in his time, such as Bowyer, promoting that work.

One of the reasons Charlton was seen as progressive in this area was because of its Charlton Invicta team, the first ever LGBTQ+ team to be officially affiliated with a professional club.

The team was originally set up back in 2011 under the name Bexley Invicta to offer local LGBTQ+ people a safe, friendly and inclusive environment in which to play football. Now the player-manager, Gary Ginnaw had joined the team in 2014, having not really played football for around twelve years prior to that, he told me.

'I didn't feel comfortable being an openly gay man and being in that football environment,' he explained. 'It's OK being at The Valley because when I'm at The Valley, I'm just Gary there.

'I get there at half one or whatever, have a few beers, have a chat with a mate, watch the game. No one will question whether I'm gay or straight. I'm just there watching the football. But *playing* the sport, it wasn't so much during the game. It's the stuff that goes on afterwards, you know, in the changing rooms, going for drinks afterwards, the social side; the closer people get to you, the more questions they start asking.'

Part of the reason for this, he said, was that despite knowing he was gay probably since his teens, he didn't come out until the age of 25, which was a little later than many of his friends. In fact, part of the reason he'd got into football as a teen was because he felt, to a certain extent, it helped him to conceal his sexuality from his peers.

'All the guys at the school were getting girlfriends and going out for drinks on a Saturday night and Friday night or whatever, and there was me wanting to go and play football,' he reminisced. 'It wasn't the only reason why I enjoyed it, but if I was playing football all the time, no one would put two and two together and think, "Well, he's obviously gay," because of that stereotype that you couldn't be gay *and* play football.'

It was kind of heartbreaking to listen to him and think of young Gary, and the stress it must have caused him to feel that he couldn't just be *himself*. The balance of probability told me that there must be players in the top tiers of English football who *still* felt this way, despite the progress made in recent years.

In spite of this, it was a happy ending for Gary, in that he came out, had no problems with any family or friends and the rest, as they say, was history, though he said he had wondered why he had felt so nervous of drawing attention to himself. It was not, however, an uncommon feeling among his peers, he said.

'I had a few chats during lockdown with different people, and they've all sort of touched on going through school life, kind of hiding in the corner, trying not to be noticed. And that resonates a lot with my school life.'

He was now, however, a pretty open person, happy to talk, and happy to put himself out there to try and make a difference to other people. But it struck me if Gary from Bexley had felt this way as a mere mortal, it was easy to see why anyone might feel that way in what could be an extremely toxic environment, such as football.

The big change came for Gary, though, some years after he'd come out, when he hit 30, and – as many people could relate to – he didn't feel his life was where he wanted it to be. He'd broken up with his partner and found he didn't have a very big pool of gay friends and wanted to extend those networks. He came across Bexley Invicta by chance, on Google.

'They were LGBT inclusive,' he said, demonstrating some initial surprise, 'and I'd never heard of anything like it before.'

It took Gary ten months from initially making contact with the team to actually attending a training session.

'You're always a bit panicky until you've got there and you've made a few friends and then you feel like you're part of the team,' he said. 'I've just never looked back from that point.'

After the initial hesitation, Gary threw himself into the team wholeheartedly, and when the manager and chairman both stepped down the following summer, having been at the club for just a year, Gary threw his hat in the ring. He took over as player-manager in 2015.

The team had a difficult time adjusting to this period of change, with many who had been involved for some time deciding it was time to call it a day, for whatever reason, and those remaining struggled, not really knowing how to run a club. Gary had some connections at Charlton's Community Trust, and his partner, Sam, suggested perhaps he could approach them for some help.

In 2016 Gary and some others went for a meeting with representatives of the Trust and had a tour of the Sparrows Lane ground where the Charlton players trained. They were asked what the Trust could do to help, and it evolved from there. The same year, still under the name Bexley Invicta, they were invited to train once a week at the club's training ground *and* to play their home games there – it was a huge improvement on the five or six different venues they'd previously alternated between for matches.

It was important to have a physical – and spiritual – home, Gary said. Not just for the sense of community, but also to feel safe.

'It's not just like playing a football game on a pitch at Hackney Marshes with 80 other games going ahead and you just don't know what it's going to be like. You know you're in a secure and safe and inclusive environment,' he told me.

It was utterly depressing, I thought, that anyone would have to consider the threat of violence or abuse they might face, simply playing a game of football.

After a successful season with an informal relationship with the club, it was decided the following year, in 2017, to formally affiliate Invicta, and bring the team in line with the Trust's other community teams. So Bexley Invicta became Charlton Invicta, and lo, the groundbreaking move was made.

The current team was completely mixed, including cisgender and transgender men and women, and Gary thought that even as a gay man, he'd learnt so much from being on the team. His dad was the chairman of the Invicta team and had also learnt a lot. That was the power, Gary thought, of football: to educate and bring people together. And they were very proud of the fact that their team was mixed, he said. In 2019 the team had attended the European Gay and Lesbian Sport Federation's EuroGames, and theirs was the only team that included women.

I admitted that I didn't know the area – in a modern context at least – particularly well, but as a Londoner, Bexley didn't have a reputation for being particularly cosmopolitan or tolerant. The idea of this groundbreaking team, and the fact that it was affiliated with Charlton Athletic, felt a little incongruous, if truth be told.

Bexley was more Kent than London, he agreed, and there wasn't really a gay culture.

'It's not the most inclusive place. And I totally agree with you. It's not easy to be different whether that's being gay or LGBT or of a different background, and the further out into Kent that you go, it kind of gets a little bit worse. And so it is quite a difficult place to grow up and just be different and be accepted,' he said.

However the Charlton connection was perhaps not as out of place as it might initially have seemed.

'For me personally, when Charlton first suggested we formally affiliate the team, that was them as a club and a Community Trust really, really putting their name to this. And that, for me, as a Charlton fan since the mid-90s, said everything,' he began.

'When you talk about all the work they've done in tackling racism and they do a lot of great community work – I mean, it's *the* Community Trust. They are the ones that lead the way and everybody follows. It *never* surprised me that they wanted to tackle homophobia or LGBT phobia in football and lead with Invicta. That never surprised me at all.'

As well as Gary's experience playing for Charlton Invicta, I was interested in his experience as an openly gay fan. Did people at matches know who he was, from the affiliation, and what kind of impact did it have, if any?

'Sometimes I think on the odd occasion people might look, and think "It's that guy that runs the team,"' he pondered. 'It's weird, isn't it? Like, when I'm at The Valley? I suppose so.'

Gary had always sat in the East Stand at The Valley – he'd only sat in the revered Covered End a handful of times. But he'd decided, feeling bold, that because of the promotion, to soak up the hedonistic atmosphere of Championship glory days, why not get season tickets in the rowdier home seats.

'And you know what? I actually really, really enjoyed it. Obviously, we got relegated and we couldn't watch the last ten games, but other than that, it was just such a buzz.'

Those were heavy caveats, but I largely agreed with him.

Gary said he didn't 'put it out there' that he was gay when he was at the football – in the same way, I supposed, that I didn't put it out there that I was straight, when I was at the football, or indeed anywhere. But he did wear his rainbow laces and pride socks. I wondered if people even noticed.

Gary had never directly faced any homophobia at The Valley, though he had heard a few homophobic words hurled about, he said, specifically on the first home game of last season.

'I sort of looked at my partner. I was like, "Did you hear that?" And he said, "Yeah." And I said, "Well, what do I do?" Because I know people at the club. I literally just dropped a text message and just sort of said, "Look, I'd heard this. I kind of know where it was coming from in that sort of vicinity." I didn't really know what to do because I've never really experienced that, not at The Valley. And I've probably been there for four or five hundred games,' he told me.

The club offered to look at CCTV and see if they could identify the perpetrator, but in the end Gary decided to keep an ear open for the next couple of matches to see if it was repeated. Since then, he said, it had been fine.

It was my opinion that the only way we were going to eradicate racism, homophobia and sexism at football matches – or anywhere – was for it to become socially unacceptable. So fans needed to know that if they were going to shout something, they were going to get – at the very least – pulled up on it by their peers. But it was bloody hard for most people to start a confrontation at a football match and not feel intimidated, I thought. Let alone if the abuse was indirectly aimed at you.

In my day job at *Standard Issue*, I had previously interviewed one of Kick It Out's Professional Clubs Equality Officers, Sarah Train, about homophobia in the sport, so I knew that the charity worked across all forms of discrimination in football. But I wondered how widely known it was that you could report homophobic abuse to them via their reporting app, in the same way that you could report racism?

In fact I had heard homophobic abuse at The Valley once that season, when a burly man had got up and shouted a derogatory term at one of the players, a couple of times.

'*If he does it again, I'm reporting him!*' I had hissed at Michael. But I was slightly ashamed to admit that I had not reported him straight off. I should have, because I felt quite sure I would have done if it had been racist.

Football and social media were places where we were seeing – or at least it was being reported more – a rise in the kind of abuse that Gary and I had witnessed. But football matches were almost unique environments that also enabled that kind of behaviour because of the relative anonymity they gave people, I thought.

'I suppose every club has a section of their fan base that probably *are* a little bit …' Gary checked himself, quickly.

'I'm not saying they're *homophobic*,' he continued. 'They probably just don't see the need for talking about it, and we see that a lot. You know, "We don't need to know if this person is gay – it's got nothing to do with football."'

While Gary said he saw *those* kind of comments a fair bit, he'd never felt there was *anywhere* out of the many stadiums he'd visited as an away fan that he couldn't go to. Save for this one occasion, he'd never experienced any kind of homophobia at The Valley, either. He had never felt that he had to be anything other than himself.

But those comments were still problematic.

'I think there seems to be this perception with gay men as well, that all we're concerned with is sex and we're going to talk about sex,' he lamented. 'But we *can* have a beer, we *can* talk about the weather, we *can* talk about the news or the football.'

It was this perception, he said, that perhaps made it slightly easier to tell the women in the office where he worked that he was gay, than it was the men.

It was an irritating habit which a lot of men had, I thought, that they seemed to just *assume* that *everyone* fancied them. I had spoken to female friends about this a lot over the years. A friend of mine had once mused that perhaps this was based on the way that men felt about other people, although I often wondered if it was just the confidence that our patriarchal society seemed to instil in a lot of straight men.

'I remember there were a couple of guys in particular that I would talk with about football pretty much every Monday morning. You know, what I'd been up to the weekend before,' he continued, detailing an incident that had taken place after a couple of years in his job.

'They knew I was a Charlton fan, and I remember one of my close friends in particular, she was just talking to this guy one day and dropped my name into the conversation and that I was gay.

'And he was like, "What? *Gary*? The one that likes football? No, he *can't* be!" It was as if he couldn't get his head around it because I know *so much* about football,' he laughed.

Gary agreed that straight men did sometimes assume he fancied them simply because he was gay, but in fact, sometimes he tried to talk to them about football *more* so that they would feel comfortable with him.

It was an eye-opening conversation for me. As a woman, some of this felt very familiar to me, from the more serious things he'd described – such as the anticipation of the possible threat of violence – to the minor, but still *irritating* things, such as the assumption of physical attraction. But I couldn't imagine, as a middle-class, straight, white woman, the *tedium* of having to constantly check myself, lest I somehow cause offence to anyone *simply by existing*. It was utterly ridiculous.

While it was clearly daft to assume that gay men *couldn't* like football, in the same way that it was ridiculous to assume the same about women, the fact *did* however remain that the vast majority of gay men I'd known had not been particularly interested in football. Gary agreed that a lot of his gay friends did not, either. I wondered if that was to do with – again – socialisation around gender stereotypes and the notion that gay men were somehow less masculine?

'I was a football fan before I was an openly gay man,' he pondered. 'So, I mean, that's definitely a *reason* behind me feeling confident and comfortable going to football games. But would it have made a difference? I'm not so sure.

'I know a lot of gay guys that have said that they don't feel comfortable coming to a game,' he began. 'And I'm trying to persuade them that it's actually not as bad as you might think it is. But, you know, people have obviously been through personal experiences and one bad experience could put you off for life.'

Certainly, if my experience with those puce-faced drunks at Wembley had been my first ever football match, I doubt I'd have wanted to go back, and that was pretty tame in the great scheme of things.

'There's a lot of LGBTQ people that I know have that perception of football,' he told me, in response to my tale of Wembley woe.

'It's interesting,' he began. 'I've seen quite a few games on the Continent. It's a few years back now, but I used to go with one of my straight mates, and we've been everywhere from Madrid to Paris and games in Munich. And it's just so different.'

'Maybe it's the clubs that we're going to – Real Madrid and Bayern Munich,' he added as examples. 'You can comfortably sit in your seat with a beer.'

He wasn't advocating that we should be able to drink in our seats, he quickly added, but was basically just making the point that in some countries, they managed to behave themselves.

Various international tournaments and games had showed us that indeed, England weren't alone in terms of bad behaviour at football matches, but it did raise the same question politicians and public bodies had been asking for years – why on earth the English didn't know how to rein themselves in when it came to booze, compared to many of their European neighbours.

But besides the culture, one of the other problems was, undoubtedly, a lack of representation – the age-old adage that if you couldn't see it, you couldn't be it. We came back, predictably, to the fact that there were *no openly gay footballers in the top four tiers of English football*. There were also no obvious cultural representations of gay football fans that I could think of, off the top of my head.

Gary was proud, he said, of his club, and the Trust, and the support they had given Invicta, as well as the work Invicta did themselves. He knew that a number of people had joined the team because of the visibility they'd had at The Valley.

'It makes me even more adamant that we have to stand up and be proud,' he said, emphasising the need for visibility and role models for young people, especially given that at the moment there was nowhere in the professional game to get that.

When I had spoken to Sarah from Kick It Out previously, she had said that – in her opinion – there wasn't going to be this 'big reveal' as press reports occasionally alluded to. She believed that the first openly gay top-tier footballer would more likely be a young player who rises up the ranks through the academy system, just always being openly gay, though the absence of anyone already visibly there must have been pretty off-putting for anyone coming up.

In recent times, the concept of allyship had become increasingly associated with so-called 'wokeness', as if not being a bigot was somehow now a terrible insult, although I could understand the criticisms of the performative nature of some of this. My banging on about how terrible this all was, didn't really mean a lot if I wasn't going to step up and report someone, when necessary. But I did wonder, nonetheless, how we could be better allies within the football community?

Gary had thought about this a lot, he said, and had concluded that there was a difference between not being homophobic and actively campaigning for LGBTQ+ rights.

'It's the point I try to make a lot, that when we're all supporting England, we're all friends,' he began. 'But the week after, when it's Chelsea against Man United, everybody hates each other.

'I'm red, you might be blue, but we're all supporters, and ultimately what we want to do is watch our team and see our team win. And it's the same for the LGBT supporter groups.'

There were big things on the horizon for Charlton Invicta. The next thing to strike off their list was to field a team in a mainstream Sunday league – while keeping a team in the LGBTQ+ inclusive league they were already in. This was for two reasons, Gary said. Partly to challenge some of the players in terms of the game itself – the league they were in now was mixed, and, as such, it was necessarily not a particularly physical one, he told me.

The other reason was to change hearts and minds.

'Because we play in an LGBTQ-inclusive league, I suppose predominantly we're always preaching to the converted, because it's what we always call an LGBT bubble,' he said.

'One of the things that we're quite keen on is, we always want to challenge the minds. We always want to make more of a difference. We know that we may face more discrimination on that basis from other teams and players, but I think quite a lot of the team are willing to put themselves in that spotlight and hopefully be more of a role model further out into South East London.'

It was a bold move, I thought, and one that Gary knew some of the players wouldn't want to make, but there were other LGBTQ+ teams he knew of that had a similar arrangement.

Ultimately, Gary thought, it was all about education, and that didn't start and end with the fans – this was a much bigger piece of work.

'People inside clubs are key figures,' he said. 'We're lucky at Charlton that people from the club have taken time out to educate themselves and understand the importance of supporting LGBT equality. Other clubs or other fans of other clubs might not be as fortunate.

'So if people within football and within the FA, within the Premier League, if they can educate themselves, then they'll understand why this is so important and needed.'

As if I needed further proof that despite the bleak headline stat, there was progress being made, Gary told me that the Millwall Community Trust had actually affiliated an LGBTQ+ team the previous summer. The London Romans had become the Millwall Romans, and at some point Charlton fans would have yet another derby match to enjoy.

October:
Charlton Athletic v Derby County

Back in the days when I worked as a civil servant, I had a line manager who, it would be fair to say, had struggled to find much common ground with me. My interest in football had been something of a relief, I think, and he one evening awkwardly approached me as he went to leave the building.

I'm sure he had mentioned football earlier in the day, but if he had I certainly didn't remember as he declared enthusiastically, leaning in towards me: 'And remember – up The Rams!' while pumping his fist. This was all I could think about as Charlton went into match day twelve, against Derby County, and I even felt compelled to remind a couple of my former colleagues about it that morning.

I could only think about that, and the contents of my pants – because having discovered earlier in the week that I was pregnant, something slightly awry seemed to be going on.

●

Putting it all to the back of my mind, I met Michael at The Valley after trying to buy a programme from the street vendor. By this point, after a 2-2 draw at Fulham the match before, the slow slide south of the table had begun, and Charlton were now tenth in the league.

I didn't usually bother to buy a programme, but thought I should on this occasion as Lyle Taylor, who had at this point been injured *forever*, was ramping up his 'Pink October' efforts, Pink October being his annual fundraising campaign for Cancer

Research as part of which he dyed his hair pink, and money from the sales today was to be donated to that fund. I thought I needed some good karma, though the vendor did not accept cards, he informed me after I had queued.

'Here you go,' Michael told me, moments later as he passed me a fiver. 'Happy birthday.'

'My brother lent me a fiver!' I excitedly told the vendor, reaching the front of the queue for a second time. He looked at me blankly as he handed me my two pounds change.

Derby, last season managed by Frank Lampard and very nearly promoted to the Premier League, were having a good season and had been hotly tipped as one of the favourites to win the league already. But they were in a bit of a pickle that week as they came to Charlton, with three of their players involved in a drink-driving incident which saw their captain ruled out for a year – and later sacked – after the trio had crashed.

As we awaited the players' arrival on the pitch, Lyle Taylor was out in force, with his pink hair. He was of course doing a good thing, but something about it grated a little nonetheless.

'Still managing to make it about him, even though he's not playing,' I grumbled.

Taylor had started to irk me a little, and I had grown some-what *suspicious* of his injury – after all, we all knew he wanted to leave. Nonetheless, I had still rushed to his defence when someone I followed on Instagram had slagged his pink hair off, after a Sky Sports appearance the week before.

'Urrrrr, he's raising money for *cancer*, actually,' I had felt compelled to message this quasi-celebrity.

Macauley Bonne, who I rather hoped might usurp Taylor as our top scorer after a run of decent form, found the net within the first ten minutes, and I told Michael: 'We *never* win after we take an early lead.'

'*Don't say that*!' he hissed.

It should have been an enjoyable match, but I couldn't enjoy it, distracted by the stomach cramps I had been feeling for the last few hours. They weren't particularly painful, but they were there nonetheless.

I was listening to the man behind us, with his daughter or granddaughter – I couldn't be sure. He looked quite old to have such a young child, but they were there together, week in, week out. She could not have been less interested in the goings-on, on the pitch, and I felt bad for her, as there never seemed to be any explanation offered as to what was actually happening. It was not enough, I felt, simply to sit her in front of it – he had to give her a reason to care, as my brothers had to me, all those years ago. Perhaps it would come more easily as she got older.

The discovery of my pregnancy had been quite a shock. It had not been planned – and it sounded stupid, but who even knew it was that easy? I'd made it to 37 without getting pregnant, so I was quite unprepared for this momentous news, though by the end of the day I found myself telling a friend, who had joined me to offer moral support as I took a third test: 'I think it's a boy, you know – he'll probably be a footballer.'

•

On that day, Lee Bowyer had been serving the first of a three-match touchline ban for questioning the integrity of the referee after the club's previous loss to Swansea. It had sparked a lengthy conversation between Michael and me.

'I just don't understand who benefits from this?' Michael had said, grumpily.

'Well they can't have him mouthing off at a referee,' I replied. 'I hate it when I see players whining at the ref after he makes a decision they don't like – he's supposed to have some authority over the game. If they see their boss paying him no respect, why would they show him any?'

I was down with the parenting vibes already.

'Yes, but if the referee is shit – where's his comeback? Why does the ref just get to make shit decisions and there be no consequence?'

He had a point.

Despite that touchline ban, it was a good game for Charlton, netting two more goals thanks to Naby Sarr and Conor Gallagher.

'He is,' Michael said of seventeen-year-old Gallagher, a loanee from Chelsea who we were absolutely not going to keep hold of after this season, 'dare I say, *tenacious*.'

We won 3-0 – I had never seen us win by more than one goal before, and I gave my tummy a little rub under my thick winter coat, the crisp autumnal air starting to bite, as the whistle blew.

'*Derby crash and burn at The Valley*', I announced to Michael in my 'sports headline' voice. 'Is that in poor taste?'

•

I had not been sure if I would tell Michael at this stage about my news. I was only five weeks pregnant, after all. It was early days and I had not liked the feel of those cramps at all, but in the end I had not been able to help myself.

'So there's been a bit of a twist in the season …' I began on our usual post-match walk to the *Cutty Sark* to get the DLR.

'Yeah, I know!' he said, excitedly, his head still in the match we had just watched.

'No, I mean there's been a bit of a twist because ...' I hesi-
tated, finding the alien words uncomfortable on my tongue.
'Well, the thing is, I'm pregnant,' I said.

Michael looked at me, wide-eyed.

'Wow,' he replied.

•

After some practical discussions: 'How do you feel about it?
Does the dad know? Is he a bellend?'

And of course, from me, the timeless: 'For *fuck's* sake, don't
tell Mum.'

We moved on to the real issues.

'I don't care,' I said, 'if it's a girl or a boy, if it's gay or
straight, whatever – as long as it's got bantz.'

'*Bantz*?' Michael looked at me with disgust before chuckling, 'As long as it's got bantz ...'

'Yeah, bantz – they'd better have bantz,' I went on, reasoning quickly. 'Well, they are going to be learning from the
master.'

'Thing is, sisqo,' Michael began without skipping a beat, 'I
just don't know how much time I can commit to being around.'

•

On the DLR now, Michael broached the subject of football
clubs.

'You know the dad basically gets to decide who the kid
supports, don't you?'

'No, *no*, I've got this covered,' I told him. 'The kid supports
Charlton. It'll be living almost equidistant between the Emirates
and White Hart Lane, so I'll allow it a secondary North London
team – or both – but it supports Charlton.

'Its dad supports Arsenal, so obviously I'm hoping for Spurs, but that's a decision the kid can make itself.'

'That kid is supporting Arsenal,' Michael laughed at me.

'*Look at who you're talking to*!' I shrieked. 'I'm a sports journalist – *I have a season ticket*! He doesn't have a season ticket. Anyway, we're not going to Arsenal, we can't afford Arsenal.'

'You're fighting a losing battle,' he said.

'It's a tough sell,' I admitted. 'But I'm the one dressing it in a Charlton kit, taking it to Charlton matches, etc. God knows we need some younger fans,' I said.

'So this is its first football match?' Michael almost asked himself the rhetorical question, with a faraway look in his eye and a smile on his face.

'Yeah,' I said. 'I guess so.'

•

During the week that followed, Michael texted me to wish me good luck at a forthcoming GP appointment and told me of Kerry's excitement at hearing the news.

I replied, telling him about some unwanted excitement of my own – that I had had to go for an early scan after some bleeding on the night after the Derby game and again the following day. But that said scan had shown everything to be looking pretty normal, or as normal as the tiny fuzzy blob that would become my baby, could look at that stage.

'Hopefully it's stopped messing around now, and this isn't a sign of a future teenage rebellion,' I texted.

'If it's anything like its mum, it's bound to be a prick,' he quipped, adding, 'They call me Uncle Bantz.'

'I treat them like they're my sons' – Tracey, player liaison officer

The idea of a Charlton Athletic 'family' may have felt close enough to the real thing for many fans – either in the sense of community or a shared appreciation with their actual families. You would, however, be hard-pressed to find someone much more involved in the club's family ties than player liaison officer, Tracey Leaburn. Tracey sat down to speak to me from her office at the Sparrows Lane training ground, wearing an on-brand red jumper, a cascade of wavy blonde hair falling about her shoulders. I commented on the jumper, brandishing my Charlton Athletic mug at the camera as we began our conversation. Tracey chuckled, and I knew almost instantly that I was going to like her.

Indeed, I was not alone in this. Fans seemed to be on first-name terms with most of the members of the backroom staff at Charlton, and Tracey was no exception. She was the wife of Charlton legend Carl Leaburn, who had played for the club between 1987 and 1998, minus one brief loan stint at Northampton Town. Himself a promising footballer, their son Miles had recently joined the Charlton academy.

'Miles was a very energetic little boy, so when he was three I was like, I need to get him into something to wear him out,' she told me. 'He was good at everything – tennis, running – he had great hand–eye coordination. That's definitely from Carl, not from me.'

The Charlton that Tracey described to me was quite literally one big happy family. The Leaburn family were close friends, she said, with a number of players from Carl's era – Chris Powell, Paul Mortimer, and Michael Bennett who was godfather to their son.

'I won't tell him that!' she roared, after I referred to her husband Carl as a Charlton legend. In fact, according to Michael, Leaburn had scored a hat-trick in the first ever Charlton match he'd been to, away against Ipswich Town.

'Not when I'm asking him to cook dinner!'

Tracey had been working with players already, helping to source accommodation for them, when there was an opening for player liaison officer at the club. Because of her experience, someone recommended her and the rest was history.

Tracey is based at the Sparrows Lane training ground, primarily charged with looking after the first team and the club's management, but every day, she told me, could be different. It could be finding accommodation for new players, or helping foreign players settle, by sourcing bank accounts for them or getting them a mobile phone – things that perhaps wouldn't even occur to most of us, that footballers arriving from a new country might need.

At the time I spoke to Tracey, we were heading into the second lockdown of my baby's then five-month life. With her family in the New Forest, Tracey could relate to the sense of isolation I'd described to her, bringing up a small child under those circumstances.

'I had a great life in London,' she told me, describing her own experience. 'Suddenly you're pregnant, you have a baby, and your life is not your own.'

With Carl away a lot during his playing career while their children were small, Tracey spent a lot of time on her own with them.

'I know how it feels to have no family here – it's tough,' she said, explaining that this gave her something of an insight into the lives of the players she was now charged with helping.

'One of the things people don't think about is that *some* of the players we have on loan, some of them are like nineteen, twenty – and they've never lived on their own before,' she explained to me.

It was obvious to me, just from what I'd already seen of Tracey interacting with the players in videos on social media, that she'd taken on something of a maternal role with some of them.

'I think being a mum makes me worry about them, because I go on a lot of courses, and I know about players who've gone on loan. They're lonely, they're bored, they have no family, they start gambling. That's why I go above and beyond, they say,' she said.

Tracey was one of the few female player liaison officers, she told me, and one of the first. It sort of surprised me, given the almost maternal role she described to me. In fact, some of the players even called her 'mum', and though she laughed about it as she told me, I could tell she felt a sense of pride in it.

For the players' part, I could totally understand it. Tracey was funny and warm, and howled with laughter as she described an incident when she'd frogmarched Jonathan Leko – then a new loanee – round to the local Sainsbury's after discovering he had no food in his flat.

'I was like, right, you've got nothing in your flat, we need to go shopping to buy you plates – and he was like "What?" – cos he'd never lived somewhere on his own before. So we're going round Sainsbury's and I didn't realise he'd videoed it, and I'm there going "Right, you need some Fairy Liquid, and this and that!"' She laughed, raising the pitch and the volume of her voice to a caricature nagging 'mum' voice.

As well as teaching the players how to cook when it's been required of her, a lot of the players had been in and out of the Leaburns' family home for dinners and barbecues as well as the odd football match as spectators, with Carl. At the time of speaking to Tracey they even had four members of the under-18s squad living with them, as well as their own son.

'What, in your *home*?' I shrieked, my hands over my mouth.

'Yeah, in my house!' Tracey roared with laughter, again.

'It's something I just started doing, and I think it's really good because they get the benefit of living with Carl as well, and obviously we have a lot of people from football who come round as well, so they get some experience.'

'Your food bill must be astronomical,' I whispered, still in a state of shock.

'It's *MASSIVE*!'

I was disappointed that Tracey had never watched *Home and Away*, to understand the comparison I went on to make between her and central character, foster mum Pippa Fletcher.

Tracey was keen to point out that not all footballers – or at least not the ones on her watch – were the pampered pooches so often written about by the press.

'People have this image everything is done for them, but I ensure it's not. I show them how to open up their utility accounts, we do inventories on properties – this can take two hours – I make them do them with me. I won't help them if I do it for them, because the next property they go to, they'll get ripped off.'

She was right, I thought, and it seemed to me that in any walk of life, a lot of young men ended up leaving home not really knowing how to look after themselves.

'I didn't cook until I was 24, 25 – I did the Delia Smith book,' she laughed. 'Simple things like that, if you've never done it at home, you're not going to know.'

In her day-to-day job, Tracey also managed players' appearances, which she told me she put a lot of effort into, making sure the causes they were affiliated with suited their personality and the issues they felt strongly about. This was the best way to ensure everyone got something out of them, she thought.

There was a lazy rhetoric around footballers, I thought, perpetuated by the press and particularly regarding players they seemed to have an axe to grind with. They were often portrayed as lazy or greedy, but footballers did a lot of work within their communities, often with little fanfare – they couldn't *all* spearhead a national campaign forcing multiple government policy U-turns as Marcus Rashford had that year, for example. I wondered if the players Tracey dealt with minded doing this kind of work.

'It is part of their job and that's why I think it's vital that they enjoy what they do,' she told me. 'I'm so lucky, I get to see so much of what the Community Trust does, and the players realise how valuable their time is to these projects.'

It wasn't as easy a life for footballers as the papers made out, I reckoned. I wondered what kind of pressures these young men were dealing with and whether or not they were specific to football.

'I think they're specific to football,' she said.

She had personally spent a lot of time talking to players who were having a tough time.

'Mentally it's hard. If you're not in favour with a manager, for example, you can be totally thrown out of the team. There's been stories of players who've played at other clubs, they have to train on their own, or they've trained at night and the lights have been turned off.'

'There's a lot of things people don't know about the pressures a player is under. The loneliness, the boredom, being away from your family. I know lots of people say, "Footballers earn a lot of money," but they're actually human beings.

'I treat them like they're my sons, cos I always think, if that's my son who's moved up to Rangers, for example, I only hope he has someone like me who's going to look after him and really care for him and have his back. A lot of them have been tried to take advantage of, money-wise. And the reason I'm here is to advise them and help them and make them understand the importance of certain things that they need to do to protect themselves.'

I'd never really thought about it before – the intensity of the boredom and the loneliness that a young player must feel, suddenly finding themselves in a brand new area with no family or friends. It would be hard for most people, but players weren't even really in a position to go out and *make* friends, outside of their immediate colleagues, with whom – given the competitive nature of their work – you wondered if their relationships could ever really be completely straightforward. It was not that surprising – given the money they earned – that stories of misadventure made it into the papers so frequently, I thought.

I wondered if Tracey ever worried about the impact of the football world on Miles.

'One hundred per cent,' she told me. 'Obviously he's my son and I love him to bits and I have to try so hard not to get involved. But yeah, absolutely I'm worried for him. It's a really tough industry and you have to *be* tough.

'I've always said to him, you need to make sure that this is what you want – because it's not up to me or your dad. If you want to give up football tomorrow, and do different things, that's no problem with me; I just want you to be happy. But if our son wants to be a footballer, we have to support him in that as much as we can.'

Again, this was where the Charlton family came in handy. When Miles had been released from Chelsea the season before, the Charlton players were on hand, she said, to lend an ear, over one of their many dinners at the Leaburns' house.

Though everyone in the wider Charlton knew who Tracey was, I suspected it wasn't like this at every club. Speaking to a friend one day, I asked them if they knew the name of their club's player liaison officer.

'No,' they responded, slightly baffled. 'Should I?'

It was obvious to me why Tracey was so popular with fans, and speaking with her she was everything I expected her to be from what I'd seen of her on the club's social media – she was warm, funny and extremely personable. Nonetheless, I wondered how Tracey had come to be so well known by fans in the first place.

'I think a lot of it was to do with prostate cancer,' she began, explaining how both her father and grandfather had suffered from the disease, which had ultimately killed her dad. She'd taken part in a London to Amsterdam charity bike ride, representing the club alongside Jason Morgan from the Community Trust and former Charlton goalkeeper, Bob Bolder. It was a big event called Football to Amsterdam, with many other clubs taking part – but Tracey said she couldn't understand why their team was so small compared to others.

After that she was on a mission, she said, and had a team of 30 all kitted out in Charlton garb the following year. The year after that, and they were up to 42 – the biggest team (of staff as well as fans) – and raised £50,000 for charity. It was this, she said, that really connected her with the fans.

'I'll never forget, I was cycling along and I was chatting to a Charlton fan, and I nearly crashed my bike, because he was like, "Yeah, I was one of the ones who went to Belgium." He'd been over to protest [against Duchatelet]. And I was like, "WHAT?!"

'At the time, the relationship was so bad between the club and fans and staff, that it got everyone together and we realised that no one's a bad person; we're all just people who love Charlton. I learnt a lot from that trip, and I think the fans did as well.'

After that, Tracey came up with the idea of running a screening session at the club for fans to come along and be tested for prostate-specific antigens in their blood, which was co-funded by Burnley Football Club thanks to Tracey sweet-talking the owner. The event was a resounding success and Tracey thinks this is one of the projects she's been involved in that cemented her as a fan favourite.

'Ultimately we saved lives. I've had fans come up to me and say, "I need to give you a hug – you saved my life – the club saved my life." Because of that test – they've never had one before – they've found out early and had treatment and they're surviving.'

It seemed to me that the players weren't the only people connected to the club who Tracey felt protective of. As well as looking after public appearances by players, Tracey was charged with dealing with a lot of the fan requests, too. Some of which had been extremely emotional.

'We've arranged for fans to go on coaches to their last ever game – got them sat with the manager on the coach to travel to their last ever game. I've had players come to me, fans come to me, we've been to visit fans – this is one of the saddest ones,' she began.

Tracey had received a call about a fan who was terminally ill.

'They reckoned he was waiting for his Charlton,' she told me.

'So I went with a player with a shirt, and he was in bed and we laid the shirt on him and he just pushed off the covers, cos of this shirt, and we were talking to him about who was on the shirt. It was very emotional and a few hours later his wife called to say, "I told you he was waiting for his Charlton."'

There's something about Tracey's phrase 'waiting for his Charlton' – like Godot? You could be waiting an awfully long time to get much in the way of good news as a Charlton fan. But you could be fairly confident, I thought on the basis of my own experiences, that the club would look after you when it mattered.

'It's those kind of things that make you realise what an impact the club does have on people's lives, and for me personally I feel that whatever we can do to try to help fans – it's important. That's what this club is about, and as long as I'm here …', she trailed off.

Tracey would only grow in popularity over the 19/20 season after an incident which took place under the club's then new owner Matt Southall.

On 12 March 2020, a video of a stony-faced Matt Southall leaving The Valley and jumping into a now infamous Range Rover – one of six bought in the club's name and from the club's purse under Southall's relatively short time in charge – was posted on Twitter by fan and journalist, Louis Mendez.

'Matt, can you tell us what's happened tonight, please?' asks an off-camera voice, presumably belonging to Mendez.

'Do you have a message for the Charlton fans?'

'What's the future of their club?'

'Are you still part of this club, Matt?'

After climbing into the car, the camera rolls as it takes what seems like a preposterously long 70 seconds for Southall to negotiate his way out of the grounds, after getting stuck between two other vehicles, like a scene from an Austin Powers film. A disembodied chuckle could be heard from behind the camera as the farce played out.

It later transpired that along with head of security, Mick Everett, and content officer Olly Groome, Tracey had been enlisted by the majority shareholder Tahnoon Nimer to physically remove Southall from the boardroom. Word of the events unfolding – and that the three had been sacked by Southall – along with accompanying photographs of the stand-off, soon began to spread across social media, to much protest from the alarmed fan base.

'I'm going to get a bit emotional now,' she sighed deeply, as she reflected on her relationship with the fans, who I told her I believed were uniquely loyal. As she wiped her eyes, I realised she had started crying.

'Oh, Tracey!' I exclaimed, in surprise. 'I've just had a baby. I cry at literally everything – come on!'

'You know what?' she asked, regaining her composure. 'With what's gone on in the last nine months, and some things I got involved in – which I never thought I would do, but had to – the support I've had from the fans has been unreal, if I'm honest.

'When certain things came out on social media, the fans

have been so supportive and amazing,' she said, referring again to that fateful night in the boardroom. 'It's really meant the world to me, because – it was horrible. A horrible time and horrible experience, and ...'

She broke off crying, again, and reached for a tissue.

'The fans are amazing, they really are, and I really appreciate them. And I know how much this club means to them, just like it means to me. When the chips are down and you think, "We're going to lose the club" – which we very nearly did.'

The fact of the matter was, Tracey should never have been put in the bizarre situation which played out that night. It became plainly obvious as I spoke to her how damaging the sorry, undignified episode had been for everyone involved, in what seemed to me like a dick-swinging competition between the directors. Although I was horrified by the extent of the damage, Tracey's genuine affection for the club and its fans was extremely endearing.

I got the feeling that Tracey felt personally wronged, on behalf of the club, and on behalf of the fans, by the saga that had played out.

'I've had the worst eight months with what's gone on, and more than probably most people will realise, how much it's taken out of me,' she continued. 'It was all-encompassing – for about six weeks I was probably only sleeping one hour a night.'

In the interviews I'd see the manager give over the latter part of the season, he would look increasingly haunted. Of course there had been rumours, but fans had perhaps not known the true extent of the problems, and that for a time at least, staff at the club had been genuinely worried it would fall into administration.

I wondered about the extent to which that had impacted on Bowyer's and the players' abilities to do their jobs.

'People don't realise what we knew and what was going on, and for Lee, he should have been concentrating on the football but, it wasn't as easy as that,' she told me.

'All of that fighting and what was going on – I knew a lot of what was going on. I was privy to a lot of information and I was very worried for this club.

'I've not had to stand up with Roland, because I know there were issues with the fans, but for me as a member of staff, we were all paid and our club was safe; it wouldn't have gone into administration. Hence why some of us have stood up,' she said, referring to the boardroom standoff again. 'Because we weren't going to let our club go. I wouldn't have let it go for the players, for our fans, for my son – I wasn't going to allow that to happen.'

For all the difficulties of the last season, Tracey didn't have a bad word to say about her place of work.

'I love coming into work,' she told me. 'I love my job.'

I couldn't get Tracey to tell me who her favourite player was, because it would be like choosing your favourite kid, she said, revealing that this was a question the players often asked her. And like Pippa from *Home and Away*, more often than not, she had to eventually let her children go.

'When I first started this job and players were leaving, I was crying my eyes out left, right and centre, and you know … I got better at it, but ones like Naby – I've known him five years. I've seen Naby from coming here as a single man, then getting married. Patrick was the same, having a baby. You can't help but miss them, but they still message me now. You do miss them all, but then you get a card or a bunch of flowers and you're like …' She was beaming.

It seemed to me that Tracey was pretty much living and breathing her Charlton family.

'I've worked here five years, but I was never really into football,' she admitted. 'And now even if I'm not at a game for a day … I went to a spa for the weekend and I was checking the scores constantly. It's really made me realise, it ruins your night if you lose.'

It reminded me of my own mum, someone with absolutely no interest in football, who would check the scores to gauge what the moods in the house might be like later on.

'It's all-consuming,' she told me. 'It's not a job you leave when you go home.'

Especially if half the team lived with you, I supposed. Not much getting away from that.

November:
Charlton Athletic v Preston North End

The next couple of weeks were very much a game of two halves, with a 2-1 loss at Bristol City, a team just below us in the league, followed by a 2-2 draw at West Brom, who were at the top of the table. By this point there was everything to win – and to lose. If I knew anything about supporting Charlton it was not to be complacent, but why was that so very hard when it came to football? It was the same with *every single* World Cup or Euros. You'd go into it assuming England would choke, but *every single time* as the tournament hype gathered momentum, you couldn't help but get carried along with it. There was absolutely no reason to be particularly hopeful about this season for Charlton, but I still couldn't stop myself.

This was, however, the first match that had felt like an *effort*, and I was sure it was no coincidence that this was my first match riding solo. Preston North End were second in the league, and Sky Sports were messing with the fixtures in order to televise this match. Michael had again fallen foul of the rubbish public transport betwixt London and Harwich, and would have had to have left Essex on the twelfth of never to make it for an early Sunday kick-off on the rail replacement bus service. This week, I literally could not give my spare ticket away. I would go on my own, I decided, now a couple of months pregnant and quite deep in my own head anyway.

I was generally pretty comfortable with solo pursuits, and The Valley never felt like an intimidating place, so it didn't strike me in any way that it would be strange to attend a match on my own. After all, Peggy seemed to be there on her own most weeks anyway, though she had obviously struck up some kind of friendship with the season ticket holders around her. I was a little jealous of her easy conversation with the young guys next to her and looked forward to the day I could feel like I was truly part of the club. I wanted to know her story – had she always been to matches on her own, or was it something she had once done with someone else?

As I made my way to Charlton in a haze of tiredness and nausea, but determined to do my bit, I realised I had cocked up the timings and would arrive well into the first half. The passive-aggressive man on the end of the aisle made a big deal of letting me pass again, and this time I actually resented it a bit.

More than this I resented that I had struggled to be here, to watch an absolutely dire performance. The only goal of the match came for Preston after they were awarded a penalty in the 58th minute, which Paul Gallagher managed to convert.

The only entertainment of the day came from a new voice behind me, as this week the man with the young child had brought who I assumed to be his wife with him. She appeared to be slightly more interested than the little girl, and was certainly inquisitive.

'Where's that line gone?' she asked after a line marked out by the ref for a free kick disappeared into the turf.

When the diminutive Erhun Oztumer, a nippy Turkish midfielder, admittedly heads and indeed shoulders below the rest of the players, was substituted in, she exclaimed, to my delight, 'He's a *boy!*'

Something about the atmosphere today felt different. Perhaps it was that I was on my own, perhaps it was because I was pregnant, but all the people jostling and the noise actually made me feel vulnerable, and I had on this occasion wondered if this was partly why football felt less welcoming to so many people out of its target demographic.

November:
Charlton Athletic v Cardiff City

Since the last match, we had lost to local rivals Millwall. It was another rivalry I had little time for – again, having flip-flopped around the leagues for the last decade, we had actually played them so few times that it didn't really seem worth expending any energy on. Not least because Millwall fans were, generally speaking, a terrifying bunch. The loss meant we had slid further away from the hallowed top six spots, but there were so many fixtures in the leagues below the top flight, pretty much any team could go on a rampage after Christmas and still make the play-offs. There was still much to be hopeful about.

This week the schedule had *again* been messed around with by the broadcast schedule. Michael was once again watching from home, and I invited Conman to return to The Valley with me.

Conman had his own football woes to contend with as the world's loveliest manager, Mauricio Pochettino, had been sacked by Spurs and replaced by Jose 'two seasons is all I've got for you' Mourinho. At the time, Mourinho was probably my most disliked manager. The king of deflection, Mourinho seemed to have no problem with singling out and naming specific players in a post-match interview if the questions got tough. Although some time later, I had enjoyed watching the eccentricities of his character play out on his social media accounts.

●

Luckily the 12.30 kick-off gave me a semi-believable excuse to swerve the match-day pint and instead we opted for hot chocolates.

'I like my club a little bit less with him in charge,' Conman said glumly, staring at the cup of boiling murky brown water in his hands. The further in we got, the more it actually tasted of hot chocolate, reaching a sort of tepid, sweet crescendo in the final dregs.

'You know how long *The Irishman* is?' He asked me, referring to the recently released Martin Scorsese film. 'When I went in Poch was the manager, and when I came out it was Armani Sean Dyche.'

I felt Conman could benefit from the *Schadenfreude* a Charlton match was likely to provide, especially at this stage of the season with a number of crucial injuries.

But we played well. Probably the best I'd ever seen us play. Conor Gallagher scored within the first fifteen minutes, and Jonathan Leko again before the end of the first half – we were 2-0 up against a team who had only just been relegated from the Premier League.

The visitors came back in the second half, scoring twice. It was never massively easy to see what was happening at the other end of the pitch from our cheap seats, but it looked like both were as a result of our errors. All in all, Conman and I both agreed we'd outplayed Cardiff despite the draw. I was disappointed not to take all the points, but I couldn't say the match hadn't been entertaining to watch.

Like clockwork, my phone pinged in my coat pocket.

'Bloody hell!' said Michael, who was a little less happy with the result than me, pointing out later in the day that our eleventh senior player was now out with a potentially long-term injury.

Despite the point we had taken from the draw, further south we headed still, to thirteenth – now well and truly into mid-table obscurity.

'You're treated like a man as soon as you enter the system' – Marvin and mental health in men's football

Marvin Sordell seemed a little nervous, I thought, as I reeled through my not quite honed elevator pitch for this book, via Zoom. I could tell he was used to giving interviews, or at the very least taking part in Zoom meetings, because he was wearing good quality headphones. After the best part of a year of communicating in this way, I had learnt to spot a pro.

It might not have helped, as I introduced myself and the concept of the book, that I blustered my way through an explanation that I had lost my eldest brother to suicide. I did the same awkward dance I had taken to in recent years – reassuring the person I was speaking to that it was a long time ago, so, you know, totally fine. Well, not fine, but you know, not *raw*. It was a delicate balance, I felt, to try to articulate that you weren't going to *cry* on them, or anything, but that you weren't made of stone, or oblivious to the fact that this might be quite shocking news to the recipient.

I continued to tell him that whilst I had written about Stephen, and about mental health quite a bit, I'd never actually *interviewed* someone about a suicide attempt before. Not that we were going to go into *details*, I quickly added – because that wouldn't be appropriate or responsible. Just, you know, I wanted to give him a heads-up.

Marvin nodded and made appropriate 'mm-hmms' and

'yeps' throughout. He'd spoken about these issues a lot, he said, and he was very comfortable and open about the subject.

Suicide is – and has been for many years – the single biggest killer of men under the age of 45 in the UK, although men aged between 45 and 49 had the highest age-specific suicide rate in England and Wales in 2019, according to official government statistics. In the same year, men accounted for a massive 75 per cent of all suicides.*

My brother had been one of these tragic statistics, but at the time, in 2004, it was something that was spoken of far less than it is today. In the years that had followed, I'd come to learn that suicide was, in fact, far more common than I had ever known.

As well as the obvious devastation I had felt about my brother's death, at the time it had also felt almost shameful – that me and my family were somehow tarnished. As if we too might have mental health problems – because everyone knew these things ran in families, right? But also that perhaps we had been a bit, well, crap. Why hadn't we noticed he was struggling? How had we *allowed* it to happen? These were thoughts that, on my darker days, I still struggled with, but the conversation was changing and there was a much greater awareness of mental health problems and, specifically, male suicide in 2021 than there had been in 2004.

Indeed, I had come to learn of Marvin's story through the work he was now doing as a public speaker and mental health advocate. He was young for a retired footballer, but he'd called time on his professional career in 2019, then aged 28, citing

* https://www.ons.gov.uk/peoplepopulationandcommunity/births deathsandmarriages/deaths/bulletins/suicidesintheunitedkingdom/2019 registrations

mental health as the primary reason. By that point, he had already spoken publicly about an attempt he had made to take his own life in 2013, while on loan to Charlton Athletic.

On paper, at least, Marvin's career – by professional footballing standards – had been good. He'd played predominantly in the Championship, but also briefly in the Premier League. Additionally, he was part of the 2012 GB football team – the only time in my lifetime that Great Britain had entered a men's football team at a Summer Olympics, and it was a big deal to have been selected.

His career had started at the age of fourteen at Fulham. All he wanted to do, he told me, was to play football – and that was all he *did*. He was completely focused on the task at hand, of becoming a professional footballer. So it was a shock to find that when he got there, it was not all he had thought it might be.

'When I first went to Fulham,' he began, 'getting into that dressing room environment, being exposed for the first time, I found … uncomfortable,' he offered, after a long pause.

In fact, he told me, though he became more accustomed to it, he never particularly enjoyed the dressing room environment.

'It's a very testosterone-heavy and very masculine environment,' he explained. 'And I realised from a very young age, I was very different from a lot of people. I was quite sensitive, quite introverted, and I thought about things in probably a very different way to most teenagers.'

It was easy, I thought, to forget how young professional athletes usually are when they are starting out in their chosen sports. The older I got, the more I thought about this when I saw a tabloid article about a footballer's misadventure, or some abuse directed at a footballer online.

'I questioned many times, particularly in my teenage years

between fourteen and seventeen, whether I wanted to be a professional football player,' he told me. 'If this is what it was going to be like, you know, the environment in the changing room and the interaction between people and coaches as well, in particular.'

He was ultimately able to convince himself that it might not be like this at *all* clubs, and that perhaps this was just what he had to accept – the necessary price of fulfilling his childhood dream, which he was within spitting distance of reaching.

Not only did Marvin find that the 'ladz ladz ladz' culture of the dressing room was not something he enjoyed, the interaction he had with coaches was something he found very difficult. It was not an easy relationship to navigate at any age, but particularly as a teenager, he said.

'When you're young, you're not exposed to that, particularly at school or in any other walk of life. You're treated like a man as soon as you enter the system,' he explained.

'At fourteen you get spoken to – shouted at – the same way I would have done when I was 27, 28. And I couldn't understand why somebody would speak to somebody in that way, particularly a child.'

It was weird, I thought. When we thought about the word 'coaching' it kind of conjured warm and fuzzy images of getting the best out of people, helping them to reach their potential. But in football this was almost seen as a failure. One of the criticisms of former Arsenal manager Arsène Wenger, which I had heard repeated by football fans many times, was that his players were 'spoiled' – they *liked* playing for him. That they were mollycoddled because he was thought to have favoured the carrot over the stick. The best coaches, Marvin said, were able to individualise their approaches to suit specific players.

Marvin did not sound like someone who necessarily took to 'taking orders' perhaps, as well as coaches might have liked – might have thought necessary, even.

'I'm a person and have always been a person that believes in specific things and standing up for them. If you don't think it's right, you know, you challenge it. If you think something is wrong, you question it,' he told me.

'That's something that is not very welcome in the football industry – football, as an industry, very much has a hierarchy, and players are at the bottom of that,' he added.

My brain took me to that oft-peddled rhetoric around footballers – they were lazy, spoilt, greedy and selfish. They could say they were injured and get out of playing if they didn't want to. They could hold their clubs to ransom if they decided they wanted to break their contracts and head to pastures new. They would, essentially, do whatever they wanted to please themselves.

'I would say it's not definitely *not* the case,' Marvin told me.

'There are isolated incidents,' he conceded. 'On the whole, in football players don't have power, or they don't understand or utilise their power.

'They're told what to do and what you may see outwardly is a projection of their fears and the insecurities in which I was very much the same. And you let your ego do the talking for you. You let your ego act for you,' he went on.

But that was not the way Marvin wanted to live his life. Questioning that, and who or what his purpose was, he said, was a major contributory factor to the poor state of his mental health.

'I didn't like myself and I didn't like the situation I was in. I didn't like having to conform to a stereotype,' he said.

And Marvin would not have been alone in this. In a 2021 survey conducted by suicide prevention charity, CALM, 64 per cent of those questioned said that they thought that male stereotypes did real psychological harm.*

It would have been extremely hard, I thought, to accept that, after chasing this dream for his entire childhood and teenage years, perhaps it was not one he actually wanted, though it took him a long time to get to this point of realisation, he said. In fact it wasn't until he'd made the move after a three-year stint, from Watford to Bolton, in 2012, that things started to really deteriorate.

'Watford were a small club – a family club – and had a lot of academy players,' he told me, explaining how different the environment had been to where he ended up, at Bolton.

'When I was playing in the first team I bought my first place round the corner from the stadium. I grew up twenty minutes away, so I had my family, my friends, all the players I had come through the academy with were playing in the first team with me. The fans were like friends, family – it was very close-knit.

'When I moved to Bolton, where everything was different – the expectation, the pressure, the size of the club, the fan base, my personal situation with family and friends not being around – I started to realise that the dream and the job were not synonymous, even though I was desperately searching for it and desperately wanting it to be so.'

For Bolton, Marvin played in the Premier League a few times before the club was relegated to the Championship. By this point, it was hard to remember that Bolton had, like

---

* https://www.thecalmzone.net/2021/04/what-it-means-to-be-a-man-today/

Charlton, once been an established Premier League side, such had been the rapid fall from grace. Nonetheless, this should have been the dream – reaching the dizzy heights of the Premier League. But for Marvin, reaching that level actually made him realise he didn't want to be there, he said.

'The expectations – how different life would be,' he explained. 'I like to do a lot of different things, and I like to live my life the way I want to live my life, and not by somebody else's expectations or rules.

'Being a professional football player at that level, you're always living by somebody else's expectation. I didn't enjoy people telling me I shouldn't be watching a film or going to the cinema or going for a meal.

'Everything was always "concentrate on football!" I have always had a lot of interests other than football. And that was another one, you know, people saying I shouldn't be playing the piano, I shouldn't be learning to fly or I shouldn't be writing and I shouldn't be doing all these things.'

These limitations seemed to Marvin, he said, like the opposite of success.

It was hard to understand, as an outsider, what was actually expected of a professional footballer. I couldn't understand how it was viewed that going out for dinner or playing the piano somehow weren't compatible with professional ambition in the game. Of course if he'd spent more of his time playing piano than playing football, it would be easier to understand, but the expectation he described to me felt completely unachievable. Perhaps that's why I wasn't a professional footballer.

What did it actually mean, though? Was a professional footballer supposed to spend the rest of the day kicking a football around their garden when they weren't training at their clubs?

'I honestly don't know,' he told me. 'Because I train hard, I do my extras. And when I go home – I'm home by two or three o'clock, because that's the day of a football player – and then why should I not be able to do something else?'

It was another thing I'd not really spent much time thinking about, especially in the context of how young footballers were, until my conversations with Tracey and with Marvin. The idea of suddenly being uprooted, moved away from family with a shedload of cash in the bank but nothing to do once you got home. The picture Marvin was painting seemed to me to be an extremely lonely existence.

By the time he was sent on loan to Charlton in 2013, I wondered what kind of frame of mind he was in.

'I very much felt unwanted; that's probably the biggest thing,' he told me. 'I felt confused and I felt extremely vulnerable.

'I felt like I was being attacked and broken down on a regular basis. [By] football fans, media and probably even, you know, friends and family, without knowing.'

By that point, even the questions of well-meaning friends and family wanting to know why he wasn't playing, when might he be playing, was he not working hard enough, etc. All of it built a level of expectation Marvin felt he simply couldn't live up to.

'My self-worth was pretty much negative,' he admitted. 'I found it very tough getting up and going out there to face the world, ready to go to training every day and not feel accepted, wanted or appreciated in any way, and that was difficult.'

The feeling of rejection was heightened by the fact that Marvin was told he had to go on loan to Charlton – it was not a choice he had made for himself. He was told, he said, through an exchange between the club and his agent, relayed to him, that if he did not go to Charlton, his life at the club would be made 'a living hell'.

It sounded to me, from what Marvin had said, that perhaps his personality didn't suit the professional football environment. That said, I felt that a lot of people wouldn't have suited the environment he had described to me. I wondered if poor mental health was rife within the game; if there were many others feeling as he had?

'Yeah, it's extremely common,' he told me, explaining that he had both witnessed it, *and* been contacted by a number of players since his retirement.

In Marvin's view, football was an oppressive environment, because you weren't able to think for yourself, or allowed to challenge or question the authority of the hierarchy and its decisions.

'You don't have that freedom of action, which is a massive thing,' he told me. 'It's going to add to the environment where you may not be happy in any way, but there is no way of you showing it to those people.'

It came back to that word he had used a lot in our conversation – expectation. People *expected* because you were a footballer, and because you were earning good money, that you would be happy with your lot. To add to that, I thought that footballers were also expected, because of that wealth and perhaps the feeling that they were living the life of Riley, to just take any amount of abuse that fans or other spectators wanted to hurl at them.

Football was strange, in so many ways, I thought, but there was something of a paradox that in this uber-macho culture and environment, it was perhaps one of the few places in which men were almost *expected* to show their emotions, rather than suppress them. In the same stadium where grown men were shouting obscenities at – sometimes – children, they were crying into their England flags. While it was not OK, Marvin had felt, to tell his superiors how unhappy he was, all of this emotion in the spectators was perfectly acceptable. This, Marvin thought, was because we could call it *passion*, which seemed a more masculine trait.

'We've seen hundreds, thousands of men cry. Of joy, of sadness, when a team wins a trophy, or gets relegated and that's completely fine because they're showing passion – players included,' he said. 'But you take that outside the environment and it's just not accepted. It doesn't make any sense to me.'

Sports journalist John Brewin had attended football matches regularly as a fan, he told me, until his late twenties. His team had originally been Manchester United, though Macclesfield were his local team.

It was more accepted now, he said, but it wasn't really the done thing in the nineties, for example, to hug your mates. He said there was a time when his friends would go to shake his hand when they met up.

'And you're like, "What do you want to shake my hand for? We've met before,"' he said, laughing.

But he remembered a match he'd been to in Barcelona in 1999 – not just any match, to be fair, but in fact the Champions League final in which Ole Gunnar Solskjær had scored an injury-time winner for United.

'I was with my best friend, and we got into the Bayern Munich end through a very convoluted story about touts and all the rest of it, and there was a guy there who'd also got in through the same routes,' he told me.

'When we won the game, there was this crushing manly embrace between the three of us and the excitement, you know, I'll never see that guy again, and we shared that moment.'

He stopped enjoying football as a fan when he became, he said, a 'proper writer', though he still enjoyed watching United's rivals lose, he told me. However, he rejected the notion I put to him that he was a hater rather than a lover.

'Well, no. I mean, I definitely *was* a lover of it,' he responded to my accusation. 'I was lucky to support United at a very good time. And there were times when I would leave the ground in this sort of ecstatic state really, where, you know, they'd scored a last-minute winner against Liverpool or something, and you feel like your feet aren't touching the ground.

'When I used to go to Old Trafford, there's a guy in front of us that – and just remember Manchester United, we were the best team for twenty years – this guy was just catastrophising his way through. Every game, "Oh no! Oh fucking hell! Bloody hell!" Just completely and utterly losing himself.

'I often used to think about this guy and the guy he sat next to, obviously his mate, and I wondered what they were like at home with their wives, you know, you see a wedding ring on and all that. But you wondered what their lives were like beyond football, because it was like it was an outlet for them.'

Another outlet football gave fans was a sense of status, he argued.

'If your life is not, you know, you're not a captain of industry, you're not successful in your job or whatever, attaching yourself to a football club that's successful gains you a bit of status as well – they make you flush with that status.

'I used to see a lot of that with United. You would see that where they would come to, say, QPR or something – QPR is a much smaller club – and you would see them strutting around with this idea of being "I'm better than you because I support this club" and all that type of thing.

'That's a very male behaviour,' he said. 'There's a lot of toxic masculinity involved there, you'd have to say.'

The friend John had been at the Champions League final with in 1999 was his best friend from school, Neil, who died in a motorbike accident at the age of 28. Neil was someone he was especially close to, he said, and someone with whom he shared football.

'The funny thing is,' he said, 'if I watch the Ole Gunnar Solskjær goal, I think of him and I find it very hard to watch now. And the FA Cup Final, which is where I was on the day he died. I've never watched that again, because I just don't want to think about that.'

Although we had supported different teams, I felt a similar kind of sentimentality about football regarding Stephen, because it was something we'd shared, as with Michael.

'There was a point where supporting United became very, very emotional because of that reason for me – because of loss. And I still speak to his mum, you know, we text each other, and I haven't really been able to admit to her that I don't even really care about United any more,' he said.

Football had changed a bit, in recent years – in fact the rhetoric around men's mental health had changed a bit, full stop. This was in part thanks to the work done by people such as Marvin, and campaigns such as Heads Up, a joint initiative by the FA and mental health charity Heads Together, not to mention important work being done in the wider suicide prevention space by charities such as CALM and Samaritans.

Guardian sports writer, and host of the *Fans* podcast, Sachin

Nakrani, agreed with John that the idea that men were only allowed to experience emotion in relation to sport was somewhat outdated now.

'Male football fans traditionally, for a long time, the one thing that they felt absolutely OK saying is exactly what you're saying,' he told me, adding, 'and almost like a badge of honour to say how emotional they get about their team.

'"Oh God, yeah,"' he mimicked. '"When that goal went in, I burst into tears," whereas they wouldn't say that probably about their own child being born, for many, many generations. "Oh yeah, my daughter being born – I wasn't even in the room at the time. But that goal that my team conceded in the FA Cup final in 1974, oh my God, I couldn't stop crying for four days!"

'I think there is that sort of thing, almost a badge of honour,' he repeated. 'To say the more upset you got by something obviously means the more you love your club, so yeah, you just take it to the nth degree.

'I think maybe it's changed now a little bit, and yeah, as you see on Twitter, people get incredibly passionate about their favourite TV programme or their favourite box set, or their favourite band – or being fathers, for instance!' he quickly added.

'You see so many people now just taking great pride – men taking pride – in being dads and stuff in a way perhaps you didn't see a generation before. So that sort of thing where football was the only place men would get emotional, I think probably doesn't feel like the case any more.

'I think we all – whoever you are, if you're the most kind of stoic, stiff upper lip man, even – we all want to feel things in life, and I think that's why football is so important to not just men, to women, to anyone,' he continued.

The same 2021 CALM survey found that 56 per cent of younger men said that the best way to promote positive perceptions of masculinity was to normalise getting help for mental health problems.* In fact, one thing Marvin had publicly called for in the past was trained counsellors at every football club, which didn't sound like a huge ask. I wondered how much help was currently available at football clubs. As ever, when it came to facilities available at football clubs, it was a mixed bag, he said.

'It varies from club to club,' Marvin told me. 'Some clubs are amazing at it, some clubs don't do anything.

'The PFA [Professional Footballers Association] come in once a year and they leave the cards and they speak about what the PFA does and about Sporting Chance for two minutes and leave the cards there and nobody even looks at them and that'd be it,' he told me, referring to the charity and its recovery facility for athletes with addiction problems, set up by former Arsenal and England captain Tony Adams.

'If they're struggling they just have to hope that they've got someone around them who can notice it and support them and can lead them in the right direction. Because if they don't, who knows?'

It was a pretty bleak outlook, I thought, but there had to be some light somewhere in all this, just in the fact that the conversations were at least now taking place. I wondered what role Marvin thought football had in highlighting issues around mental health.

'Just by having the conversation, football has already

....

* https://www.thecalmzone.net/2021/04/what-it-means-to-be-a-man-today/

played a big role. Increasing visibility increases the conversation because football is the centre of our society, whether we like it or not,' he said.

For Sachin, the camaraderie of football was an important factor too, and I could totally see the importance of that, in terms of mental health.

'I love football, I love the sport, I love watching football,' he said. 'But increasingly as I get older, for me the most important aspect of football is not the eleven men playing.

'It's how football can make people feel, which I think is the most important and powerful thing. About how we bring people together – how we can make people who maybe feel kind of excluded in other parts of life feel included.'

In non-Covid times, Sachin took the coach with 30 other people to Anfield on a regular basis, and one of his 'best coach pals' was a 60-year-old retired schoolteacher, with whom he'd forged a bond and ended up having deep and meaningful conversations about his family on their football outings.

'That's come through football – that's the power of football,' he enthused. 'People who didn't know each other, getting to know each other through football, and then talking and sharing – and it is a great environment for men, *also* for women, just to express themselves, and to *feel* something.

'Feeling something is absolutely lovely,' he added. 'And that's what football gives you.'

As well as the reach that Marvin had spoken of, and the camaraderie that Sachin had enthusiastically described, I thought there was something in the message to men, specifically, that mental health problems did not discriminate. That even footballers, with all their money and status, could experience hard times, too.

November:
Charlton Athletic v Sheffield Wednesday

There was a joke about Charlton, from their Premier League days, that they came down faster than the decorations after Christmas. It was almost as if once they knew they'd secured enough points to avoid relegation, there wasn't much point keeping their feet on the gas. Rather than write off the beginning of the season as a fluke, which perhaps would have been sensible at this point, I found myself wondering if Christmas had come early this year.

Another loss had been endured, which this time I'd watched on The Valley Pass, Charlton's online games coverage platform, with Michael and Kerry while at home for a family visit. Everything about our 2-1 defeat at Luton, who were third from bottom, was amateurish and genuinely painful to watch, not least because of the metal pole we were told was obscuring the commentary team's view. I almost wished for one myself.

I had started to feel a little despondent about our recent performances after the initial giddiness, when one morning I found myself freelancing at my usual Eurosport gig.

'Charlton have been sold,' my editor commented in a casual fashion from the other end of our bank of desks.

'What?' I asked.

'They've been sold,' he repeated. 'Charlton have been bought by someone.'

'SHUT UP!' I shouted, frantically typing into the Google search bar.

In the excitement of the season, I had almost forgotten we were even up for sale. Roland Duchatelet had made a vaguely sensible decision in refusing to sell Lyle Taylor and I'd thought little more about our owner after the transfer window had closed.

The club statement confirmed that the new owners, East Street Investments (ESI), were both 'proud' and 'delighted' to have agreed the purchase.

Though the deal was still subject to approval by the EFL, the statement said: 'While we may be the club owners, truly we are only the custodians. The true spirit of this football club rests with the fans, it is nothing without them.'

So far, so good, I thought.

The new club chairman was a man named Matt Southall, along with directors Jonathan Heller and His Excellency Tahnoon Nimer, chairman of Abu Dhabi Business Development, the private office of Sheikh Saeed Bin Tahnoon Al Nahyan.

'WE'VE BEEN BOUGHT BY A WEALTHY ARAB CONGLOMERATE!' I shrieked, simultaneously punching 'CHARLTON HAVE BEEN SOLD!' into a text message to my brother.

'We've *basically* been bought by the royal family of Abu Dhabi,' I said. 'What I'm saying is, we're the new Man City!'

'And do you think that's a good thing?' one of my colleagues piped up.

'Look, if we win the Premier League in a couple of seasons' time, I'll find a way to square that moral conundrum – I'm fine with it,' I said. And I was. I was delighted.

'Investment company,' Michael replied. 'Slightly worrying. Still, anything's better.'

'If you have a boy, you should call him East Street Investments,' he added. 'Just a thought.'

•

The next day, Charlton played Sheffield Wednesday at The Valley, where Matt Southall was on a charm offensive and the fans – myself included – were lapping it up.

Both Michael and I missed the game because of Christmas-related commitments, and both lamented having missed seeing the new management in action, schmoozing fans in Crossbars – the club's bar.

I had, pretty much immediately after speaking to Michael about the sale, consulted my new Charlton Athletic guru, Alan, who I had met at the museum.

I received a reply from Alan ahead of the match, looking forward to what could be a 'special' day, he said. He was cautiously optimistic about the sale, but most definitely glad to see the back of Duchatelet, by whom he said he felt 'betrayed'.

'A degree of scepticism, or at least caution, would be wise,' he warned. 'The word-perfect (new) Chairman's statement is almost too good to be true.'

I wanted everyone to be as excited as I was about what was surely going to be the best thing that had ever happened to Charlton, though I hadn't really appreciated at the time that fans, the proper diehard ones who had continued to attend dire League One matches despite the ongoing beef with Duchatelet, as well as the ones who had refused to attend in protest, had been burnt before.

I had once overheard a conversation between two men in my local gym talking about how they were not going to attend a Champions League match at the Emirates Stadium because they had seen whichever European team Arsenal were playing before, and they did not want to support the continued management by Arsène Wenger.

'Did you see what the Charlton fans did?' one of the men asked the other. 'They went over to *Belgium*!' he added, referring to the protest against Duchatelet in his home country.

'*That's* how you do a protest!' he exclaimed as he excitedly clicked his fingers.

It seemed to me that Charlton fans had a reputation, and quite rightly so with our history of protest, and it must be pretty obvious by now that we weren't to be messed with. We did not seem to me to be the obvious club for someone with dishonourable intentions.

Nonetheless, the change in ownership did little to inspire events on the pitch, as Charlton lost 3-1 at home and slipped to seventeenth.

'We didn't do nothing' – Richard, Alan and the proud Charlton tradition of fighting back

Retired housing charity executive turned occasional funeral celebrant, Richard Wiseman was also the vice-chair of the Charlton Athletic Supporters' Trust (CAST). He lived locally to the club, and went to his first Charlton match in the 1960/61 season when he was ten years old.

The Trust was launched on 5 December 2012. With the first supporters' trust in English football established in 1992 at Northampton Town, Charlton were relatively late to the game, he told me. The reason for this, he thought, was the perception that Charlton didn't *need* a supporters' trust. In the elected supporter role on the club's board, awarded to fans after their efforts in bringing about the return to The Valley, and for which anyone with a season ticket could nominate themselves, the club had a fan on the board from the mid-90s to 2008, making it – in Richard's opinion – the model club, in terms of fan engagement.

There had been a few vague efforts to get a supporters' trust off the ground previously but a growing sense that fans had lost control of the club and, he said, the benevolence of the owners – then Michael Slater and Tony Jimenez – was eventually the impetus to establish CAST.

According to Richard, though the trust had relatively good communication with the owners, there was a general feeling of distrust. When Roland Duchatelet bought the club in 2014, it was welcomed, because Duchatelet had seemed a decent and honest man, Richard told me.

Indeed, although this was during my wilderness years as a Charlton supporter, I could remember Michael being most excited by the development. Duchatelet had the double appeal, to us at least, of being a left-leaning man in his politics, and one with an absolute shitload of cash. In fairness to Michael, who is far more principled than me, and such was my engagement with the club at this time, the latter was probably more appealing to me than it was to him. However, I doubt many football fans would object to having an owner who could afford to part with a few quid during the transfer window.

CAST had a meeting with Duchatelet's right-hand woman, Katrien Meire, early on after his purchase of the club, which Richard described as 'positive', though her line was that she wanted to deal with supporters rather than a specific organisation. How she had planned to do this, if not through a supporters' organisation, was anyone's guess.

At any rate, Meire had been – as was Duchatelet – hugely unpopular with fans, not least when the club began referring to them as 'customers' in official statements. It reminded me of the time when I had worked with Steve at Defra's Customer Contact Unit.

'I'm not a customer, I'm a *taxpayer*!' came the inevitable – and understandable – enraged responses.

Football clubs and fans had the same sort of chicken and egg situation, I thought – you couldn't have one without the other, and much like politicians, clubs often forgot that really, they worked for the fans, not the other way round. Fans, much like the electorate, were more fundamentally important than the title 'customer' seemed to imply. Even if we were only 'customers', this was, frankly, appallingly bad service. You couldn't blame them, then, if they wanted their money back.

Meire wanted fans to understand that Duchatelet did things his own way, and that was his right, as the owner. But fans had gone from some sort of democratic utopia, through a period of centrist disillusionment, and landed in some kind of bizarre dictatorship. The fans, thought Richard, had simply not been given the consultation they felt they deserved.

At that point in time, the club wasn't struggling in the league, and it had no financial problems – at face value, there wasn't really a problem, but nonetheless it became obvious there was dissent in the ranks. CAST arranged a meeting of supporters on the freezing cold night of 15 February 2015 using, Richard said, 'some pretty neutral language', to discuss the current position of the club.

They had no idea how many people to expect at the old picture house on Wellington Street in nearby Woolwich, then empty awaiting redevelopment into a block of luxury apartments, as it stands today. Nonetheless, spurred on by the sense that 'what it meant to be Charlton' had gone, Richard thought, around 400 turned up.

Recalling the night in question, Richard told me, what struck him the most was that this wasn't a club in crisis – nowhere near the crisis that would befall us in 2020 – but a club whose sense of identity was being eroded.

'The fact that 400 people came on a freezing cold night in February was quite extraordinary,' he said. 'There were various speakers – the usual culprits – but the overall message was, we want you, the Supporters' Trust, to continue to try and get dialogue with Duchatelet and Katrien Meire. We don't want to boycott.'

It wasn't a combative vibe, Richard thought, but a constructive way forward. And so the Supporters' Trust spent another twelve months unsuccessfully trying to work with Duchatelet, only to be consistently referred back to Meire, acting on his behalf. There was talk of a strategic group of supporters and sponsors to look at high-level, broader issues – Meire even told the then chair of the trust to put a date in his diary – but nothing further was heard, and the meeting never transpired.

'It was poor customer service, if you like,' Richard quipped.

Not long after, the Coalition Against Roland Duchatelet, or CARD, was formed, kicking off proceedings with a meeting in the Bugle pub in Charlton Village. It was presented, Richard said, as a coalition of supporter groups, but in fact it was more like a group of individuals – some of whom went back as far as The Valley Party days – and the Supporters' Trust, and it was agreed that active CARD members wouldn't 'out' fellow members.

Despite the growing sense of concern among fans, CARD wasn't for everyone.

'We lost members of the Trust,' Richard told me. 'There was that whole group of people who thought they were a bunch of troublemaking lefties, or didn't want to rock the boat, or – and this is one of my big things – you know, be careful what you wish for. We also lost members because we weren't militant enough.'

Indeed, I had come to think of the Trust as the suffragists to CARD's suffragettes, and had wondered if there was much love lost between the two organisations, if you could call CARD that.

'There was a certain element of bullet and ballot box, which was the image that we used, you know, that CARD could be more militant,' Richard chuckled at my comparison. 'Although, you know, we're talking throwing pigs on the pitch,' he said, referring to one of CARD's organised activities, 'not setting fire to the boardroom.

'But actually, no, I think it is one of the great successes, that it was a coalition.'

There were incredibly talented and imaginative people involved in CARD, Richard thought, though he did not count himself as one of those people. He was certainly committed to his club, however, having been one of the fans who rode in the now famous taxi to Brussels in protest against Duchatelet.

'It's a long way and it's not comfortable,' he told me, but he was impressed by the idea, which made a big impact.

He was also a pivotal part of one of the first big demonstrations – a mock funeral – leading the procession.

'Whether of course CARD and the existence of it had any effect whatsoever on Duchatelet deciding to sell the club, we'll never know,' he said, philosophical about the ultimate impact of CARD, but seeing the benefit of it regardless of tangible results.

'My line on that has always been, OK, maybe it did – we don't know. But if it didn't, it gave us all a sense of self-respect. I think the activism of CARD enabled Charlton supporters to feel, "OK, this happened to our club, we were beginning to become a laughing stock, we'd lost any sense of identity but we didn't do nothing."'

Charlton's identity had become something of a crucial element for me, throughout my time as a fan, and it seemed pretty obvious that it was to many other fans. You didn't love a team like Charlton for its results.

In fact I had recently had a conversation with a friend about what made us both happy.

'Football,' had been one of their responses. I wasn't sure Arsenal could have given them *much* to feel happy about in recent times, but even so.

'No,' I'd responded, quite seriously. 'You're doing football wrong – it's not *supposed* to make you *happy*.'

As an English Charlton Athletic supporter, I so seldom had anything to be happy about when it came to football, so why on earth did we persist in such repetitive, consistent self-flagellation?

'You can come up with clichés like, "Oh, it's a club rooted in its community,"' Richard told me, alluding to the fact that he thought it was more than just that. 'I suppose you could then say, well, show me a club that isn't.'

'I think that the identity was forged in the whole "Back to The Valley" thing. So what it was before that, I mean, I don't know,' he pondered. 'I was a supporter, but I don't remember even thinking about the identity of the club.

'I went along to watch the team play, and I suppose it's because there wasn't the social media, there wasn't the contact. And I always used to view going to football as quite a solitary thing. I get so engrossed in the game that I didn't need to be part of any group. So I don't think I really became aware of there being a community and that you could have some influence.

'I wasn't particularly active in the Back to The Valley campaign, but I think an identity was forged there.'

What came out of the Back to The Valley campaign, Richard said, was a real sense of joint enterprise between supporters and directors. The Valley Investment Plan – abbreviated to VIP – gave supporters the opportunity to pay into a fund, buying them anything from money off merchandise and club purchases, to buying a ten-year season ticket up front, in order to boost the club's short-term finances. Effectively the club ended up mortgaging its future, but it worked at the time, raising what would have seemed like a staggering amount back then, of £1 million. VIP members were given the added incentive of electing the supporter to the club's board.

'So there was,' Richard told me, 'out of adversity, this real sense of, we're a club, where the supporters are at the heart of it. So I guess that's what was lost. And particularly under Duchatelet, because he wasn't a crook. He wasn't a nasty piece of work. You know, we've seen plenty of those, but Duchatelet was just distant – absent.

'When you've got an owner who's absent and only comes to three games in five years, comes out with nonsense that alienates people, and the club is basically going downhill, then you're going to feel a loss of identity.'

I personally thought Richard hadn't given CARD the credit it deserved. Duchatelet had put the club on the market in 2017, apparently having decided it wasn't worth the trouble to him, and it would be fair to say that CARD had made the strength of fans' feelings clear. However, for all of his flaws, looking back on the last few years with the wisdom of hindsight, it now seemed to be very much a case of better the devil you know, with Duchatelet.

I was speaking to Richard after the tumult of the 19/20 season had played out, and when the future of the club looked more precarious than ever. Richard, like me, had initially been 'thrilled' he said to learn of the sale of the club to ESI.

'I went to a meeting of supporters and Matthew Southall spoke quite well at that meeting,' he recalled.

The Trust had interviewed him for its website and was, said Richard, complimentary.

'Why wouldn't it be? We had one or two question marks as the transfer window came to an end in January, that nothing much had happened, but I don't think that the scales dropped from my eyes particularly until Nimer's outburst.

'The only thing was that when we interviewed Southall, that was the first time he said that they hadn't bought the club lock, stock and barrel. But what he said was we've got an agreement to buy the freeholds within six months. And the reason we haven't done that at the start is because that was going to be complicated. And we wanted to get on and improve the team during the January window. So that was the first discrepancy, because we'd been told it had.

'And then the six months thing became clear that actually I think what it might have been was an agreement that anytime from six months to five years, there was an option to buy the freeholds and then whether that was an option or an obligation was another issue, but on the whole it wasn't really until Nimer's outburst.'

The Trust had asked for a meeting with Southall, which they got, and ended up asking for his resignation. At which point things started to get a bit nasty from Southall in response, on Twitter.

'I guess that sort of leads us to come full circle,' Richard said. 'To the question of, be careful what you wish for. And the Trust sort of became even more important in the last season, because obviously the situation got really quite dire.

'No one liked Roland, but we weren't in trouble then. And we really were in trouble last season.'

I wondered the extent to which Richard really believed the club might cease to exist? I never really believed it would happen, but perhaps I should have been more concerned because it had happened and it was happening at an increasing number of clubs.

'I woke up one morning and worked out that there were 43 days till the first game of the 2020/21 season. So probably it was around when they published the fixtures and when we knew 12 September was going to be the start of the new season. So sometime in July,' he pondered.

'I thought, "OK. We haven't got an owner – whether it be Nimer or Elliott or anybody else – who is able to prove sufficiency of funds to the EFL. And we aren't going to be allowed to kick off the season unless we can do that." And that's when we [the Trust] went into real activity mode.'

The Trust busied themselves on a supporter drive, wanting to be ready to come up with some sort of supporter bid to buy the club or at the very least involvement, if it was needed. The fans had, after all, stepped up with the supporters' fund for CARD, in the past.

It seemed to me that Charlton was a sort of perennial under dog. More than once we had been under threat, but every time we had stood our ground, even with the odds massively against us. I wondered if that was part of our identity?

'Charlton has a record of punching above its weight, or it certainly had a record of punching above its weight in the first decade from 1997/98 onwards. A club that has never had millions to throw at success, but has achieved it anyway, for that period of time.'

It was my belief that Charlton Athletic's spiritual home was 15th in the Premier League – there was always an element of danger, but we just about managed to scrape by. Richard's vision of Charlton was perhaps a bit more realistic than my own, and he saw the Premier League years as 'a nice little bonus' rather than where we ought really to be. It was different for me as Charlton had played in the Premier League for the best part of a decade of the 24 years I'd been a fan, but he'd been in it for the long haul.

'Sometime last year, I must have been quite bored, but I went through the finishing position of Charlton every single year since I first went in 1961, and it came out at twelfth in the Championship was the average position over those years. And I guess probably that's why I see the years in the Premier League as a little bonus.

'If Charlton were a Championship club for the rest of my supporting life, and sometimes they're in the top six and promotion is possible, I'm not going to feel upset and disappointed by that.'

Sports coverage in England was so ridiculously saturated by the Premier League that you could almost forget there was any other sport, or any other competition. But as someone who didn't support a Premier League side, I'd actually started to enjoy the top tier more, treating it like the trash it was, really. I'd been able to watch it like a soap opera in recent years, just following the story arcs, like the predictable bi-seasonal demise of Jose Mourinho, or disappointment at whoever the current post-Fergie Manchester United manager was, or the excitement of the very occasional dark horse in the top four race. But that last season, I had pretty much forgotten to even care about that.

'If we're in the Premier League, you're going to pay 50 quid for an away ticket. In the Premier League, how many youth players are going to come through into our first team? Probably none,' Richard speculated.

'I'd rather be supporting a club that I really believe in and feel part of, not priced out of, that I can see players come through. And if that's in the Championship, I'd rather that than a soulless existence in the Premier League.'

By this point, I'd had the argument with my baby's father more than once now, about who they would support. For the most part I felt he humoured me and thought that they would ultimately *want* to support Arsenal. For a start, I told him, we couldn't afford Arsenal, reiterating what I'd said to Michael.

I felt that, in the same way that Charlton weren't currently a Premier League club, at that point in time Arsenal weren't a top four club, either – they'd had a good run, but at least for the time being, the jig was up. I *hated* the way the fan base had turned on Arsène Wenger. It left a nasty taste in the mouth, and to my mind, the whole sorry business told me that this was a club that lacked *heart*.

Charlton was a club *with* heart – that's what I thought being a Charlton fan meant, and here was a man, driving around Europe in a black cab, leading funeral processions and giving up time to organise this ragtag group of protesters. So what did being a Charlton fan mean to him?

'It was the week before Wembley in '98. I was waking up at five o'clock every morning. And, you know, clearly it was excitement building up. And I remember saying to my wife, who's not interested in football at all, as I get older I won't be so excited about all this. And it's the opposite. I'm beginning to think how many more years have I got being able to go and have this communal experience and watch this team?

'So it matters as much to me if not more than it always did. Don't ask me why, I can't explain it. I can talk about a human need to be part of something that's bigger than yourself. I've never been interested in religion, but I can see that need, I can see that wonderful sense of community. Why, for me, that comes through Charlton Athletic … Just, you know, I was taken along there when I was ten. I thought, "Wow, this is awesome!" And it's just stayed with me.'

•

When the sale of the club to ESI was announced, Richard's fellow CARD activist Alan Davies was also excited – or at least *mostly* excited.

'I was 70 per cent "Wow, this is fantastic," – and that 70 per cent drove me to get season tickets for me and my son,' he told me.

But as with other fans, there was still a niggling voice at the back of his mind that it might be too good to be true, and indeed, he was warned by a friend, who he claimed was well connected within the football world, that Southall had been linked to other takeover bids in the past.

'I was nervous because of that,' he said. 'But I said, "Let's give him a chance you know. We've fought for years, let's try and enjoy it," and then the transfer window happened, or didn't happen, and it became clear this was BS.'

Some of the names associated with Charlton during that strange wilderness period of the latter part of the 2019/20 season had been associated with any number of other struggling clubs, such as Bolton and Bury. It shouldn't have been possible for us to get into the situation we were in, I told Alan.

'The problem is the EFL is run by the clubs, they exist to run the fixtures, they are the secretaries of the people who run the league, if they try to effect change and bring in rules that go against the interests of the clubs, they'd simply get voted down,' he remarked.

'If you own the company you want the maximum freedom to do what's right for your business, and that's the dilemma, because what's right for a company from a business point of view is not necessarily the right thing for the club, and the future of football, fans etc. So I feel a degree of sympathy – but not a lot.'

Born in Woolwich in 1955, Alan Davies lived in Charlton with his parents and brother from 1958, before moving out to nearby Eltham, by that point joined by a younger sister, in 1966. His entire family supported Charlton Athletic, and in fact his paternal grandfather's address when he returned from the First World War in 1919 was Floyd Road. He would actually have seen – and possibly helped with – The Valley being built. Alan's father lived on Floyd Road from birth and so, he says, it was hardly surprising that he became a lifelong fan himself.

'My dad took me to my first game, and I don't remember who it was against. But I remember the experience of the stadium more than anything else. It was the 1960/61 season when I was five years old ... I still remember where we stood in those days,' he told me.

In fact, Alan and his family stood in the main stand, on the side of the pitch between there and what is now the Jimmy Seed Stand, in The Paddock, as it was known.

'We used to walk in The Valley Grove entrance across that kind of big mound of earth and grass that was there then, where they used to have a goal and practise shooting,' he reminisced.

There still is a big mound of earth and grass down in that bottom right-hand corner, as you looked at it from our seats in the Covered End. Though apparently back then it was much bigger, and eventually sold off for development of the tower block that now looms over The Valley.

Alan continued to watch matches at The Valley, supporting Charlton, into his teens. He was quite serious about it, sitting in the Covered End by then, and going to away games with friends. By the mid 1980s, however, he was raising a young family and embroiled in the kind of pursuits that go with this, spending his weekends DIY-ing their home, and concentrating on rising up the ranks at work.

He went to a few games a season, including at Selhurst Park and Upton Park, while the club was away from The Valley for that period, with his dad or sons. Though his eldest had little interest, his younger son became the fourth generation of Addick in his family. Alan and his son had season tickets from the 1994/95 season right through to the Duchatelet reign.

'I've always been someone who went to football with family, with friends and didn't get involved in football supporter politics, supporters' clubs or groups or anything like that. And so I wasn't an obvious candidate to get involved in these things really,' he admitted.

Like many others, he was initially pleased when Duchatelet took over, thanks to his healthy bank balance. He was also impressed when Katrien Meire was appointed. Having been 'on the front foot' in the fight against racism, Alan was pleased to see Charlton also playing a key role in introducing greater gender diversity in football clubs. But his initial enthusiasm about both the new owner *and* the new CEO waned pretty quickly.

'The concept of customers didn't offend me over much,' he told me, referring to the same infamous club statement I'd discussed with Richard. 'But saying she thought it was weird that fans thought they had a stake in the club, for example, showed a complete lack of understanding of how football fans feel.'

Alan began to feel increasingly helpless and angry about

what was happening to the club, and he started to get more active online, making his voice known on the Charlton Life fan forum. The removal of Chris Powell from his position of manager was one of the last straws, as he saw it.

'All of the things that my family had seen and done with Charlton in the past. In *my* past, I'd been at The Valley, clearing up the terraces on that wet, cold day where we were trying to get The Valley back,' he said, referring to the mass clean-up of the dilapidated stadium by fans in 1989, in preparation for the move back from Selhurst Park, which then didn't eventually happen for another three years.

'I went there as an individual fan,' he explained.

'Although it sounds, you know, a bit mawkish,' he said, 'I thought of my dad and my granddad and all of the years that they'd had at the club – my uncle even played for Charlton reserves a couple of times.

'So I felt it was like an attack on my family in some ways, what Duchatelet was doing – it just felt like this was doing irreparable damage to something I love.'

And so it was because of this that Alan decided to drive over by himself from his home, which was by then in Berkshire, to the meeting in Woolwich that Richard had also spoken of. Alan also described it as 'freezing'.

The way it was described to me by both men conjured the image of an incredibly banal sort of *Fight Club*, almost. Where these kind of radicalised fans came together to plot the downfall of The Man – but with much less extreme tactics, as Richard had pointed out.

CARD itself was an informal organisation, and Alan told me, chuckling, on hearing my suffragette/suffragist analogy, they thought of themselves more as the 'provisional wing'. There was no hierarchy or leader, just a group of people who came together out of their love of Charlton and operated on the basis that whoever was best placed to take the lead on something generally did so.

Alan had been supportive of the growing voice of discontent, suggesting that something should be done about the situation the club found itself in. Having put some money himself into the so-called 'black and white' campaign – a campaign asking the board to spell out its intentions for the club in black and white – he thought perhaps other fans might, too.

With the help of the Charlton Life forum and other prominent fans, Alan launched the protest fund in the January of 2016. Initially, he'd hoped to raise £5,000, in order to fund some different schemes designed to raise the profile of the fans' grievances. They met their target within three days.

Alan was then invited to attend the same meeting at the Bugle pub as Richard, which he drove to again from Berkshire, having no idea who else would be in attendance or what to expect. He'd not thought he would necessarily contribute much, other than to help fundraise, but he ended up being more vocal than he'd anticipated. He was a retired human resources director and it just happened to suit the work he ended up getting involved in with CARD.

By the end of the meeting, they'd agreed a set of actions, and to meet again, as well as drawing up a criteria any planned protests had to meet.

'We didn't want to do anything that was illegal,' he said. 'We wanted to have the widest possible acceptance amongst Charlton fans – that's one reason why we never ever interrupted a game in progress, or tried to get a match called off, because a lot of fans would turn against us.'

They did, however, delay the start of a number of matches.

'We did beach balls and balloons and we ordered all this stuff, and we said on Charlton Life, can you come and help distribute, and we had no idea how many people would turn up, but we had a small army of volunteers who turned up, took these things, handed them out with instructions to pass on, about what we were going to do with these things and when,' he recalled.

'I was sitting with one of the other organisers in the East Stand, heart in mouth, thinking, "Is this going to fall flat?" Because things sometimes do – nobody will do it – and just as we were approaching the referee's whistle, the first person threw their beach ball down, followed by an absolute cascade – an avalanche of black-and-white balloons that were all over the pitch and they had to try and clear it.'

The match was delayed by seven minutes, and Alan described a feeling of euphoria that their protest had worked, after his initial nerves.

Of course, not all of the fans were supportive of CARD. There were some who objected to the disruption and thought it was damaging to the club. The best way, they thought, was to get behind the club. Others thought some of the more prominent members were effectively attention-seeking, or touting for work at the club – a strange tactic, had that been the case, I thought.

'I've personally been approached by groups of people outside the stadium while we were getting things distributed, and been told – quite forcefully,' he said, 'that I was hurting the club and I wasn't a proper Charlton fan. I was invited to put certain things where the sun doesn't shine, and so on and so forth.'

As well as being legal and acceptable, in order to successfully 'bid' as it were, for backing from the central fund, a protest had to be doable, and have a big impact for the money being spent – it had to deliver good value for money, basically.

The protest fund eventually made around £60,000, thanks to the donations of fans.

'Charlton have got some fairly wealthy fans, and there are three – I will not name them for obvious reasons – who made quite significant personal contributions,' he told me, leaving my mind racing through the club's Twitter account list of famous Charlton fans, wondering *just how much* Lee from Blue really did support Charlton Athletic.

'When we had the banner towed over the stadium at Gillingham, it was 'Duchatelet and Meire out' being towed behind an aircraft. A particular fan paid for that.'

The protest fund even received donations from Coventry fans, from Brighton fans – it was a cause that football fans of all colours could relate to, such was the frequency of disputes between fans and owners, in the modern game.

The campaigns funded by the donations were pretty good, to my mind, ranging from delaying matches with beach balls and plastic pigs, to parking advertising vans in Sparrows Lane announcing 'The only score they care about' alongside the picture of a twenty-pound note, and, of course, the trip to Belgium in the taxi.

The trip to Belgium garnered a lot of media attention and though it cost them £2,000, it had apparently generated hundreds of thousands of pounds' worth of coverage, with the added bonus of embarrassing Duchatelet in his own backyard.

CARD's objective, said Alan, obviously was to make Duchatelet abandon Charlton and sell up, like the fabled ghosts who wanted their house back. The way they went about it was a campaign of ultimately quite benign reputational damage, aimed at embarrassing him into leaving.

Such as the road trip to Belgium, there were big gestures, like turning up at the EFL headquarters to make their case, alongside Blackpool fans who were also demonstrating against ownership of their club. They went to the Belgian Embassy in London to protest against Duchatelet and were even invited in to explain what they were protesting over. But most of their campaign had been at The Valley itself.

'We bought hampers for all of the Charlton staff,' he told me. 'Because they were getting nothing. This is the admin and ticket office staff, and people like that. It wasn't big stuff. It wasn't expensive, but it was some chocolates and things like that – a little gift package.'

The message was that the fans would look after them, he said – their quarrel was not with the staff.

'We had Christmas cards made up that year of the famous pig,' he said, referring to the protest in October the same year. 'And we had an image of one of those pigs in a snowy scene, sent to all of the 92 Football League clubs, from CARD Charlton fans with a message about Duchatelet and the damage he was doing to our club.'

In the end, he thought perhaps it had destabilised Meire more than it had Duchatelet, though perhaps that her departure to Sheffield Wednesday was the catalyst for Duchatelet admitting defeat.

'I don't think anything really got to Duchatelet so much that it was the trigger point. There wasn't a knockout blow,' he said. 'But there was quite a lot of pummelling. And I think ultimately he just got fed up with it.'

As Richard had said, it was, as ever, a case of 'be careful

what you wish for'. For now, at least, the club that he and Alan
– and Michael and I – both loved, and I hoped one day my
child would love too, had averted disaster. Life as a Charlton
fan could be pretty miserable sometimes, but we always seemed
to come through when it mattered, and on this occasion – like
the play-off final the year before – we had somehow snatched
victory from the jaws of defeat, rather than vice versa.

I wondered what being a Charlton fan meant to Alan, this
practical-seeming, professional man, and unlikely participant in
the *coup d'état* against Roland Duchatelet.

'If you think of your life as a tapestry, it's the threads running right the way through from start to finish,' he told me,
explaining his two-year-old granddaughter's indoctrination into
the club, already in a Charlton kit.

'I'm hoping many years after I'm not around to worry about
it any more, there'll still be a Charlton, there'll still be a Davies,
and they'll still be down at The Valley.'

In terms of the club's future success, Alan was measured.
He'd love to see the club back in the Premier League one day,
he told me, but he'd take being reasonably competitive in the
Championship.

'I don't think there's a hope in hell that we're going to be
playing European football in eight years,' he told me, explaining
his real ambition for the club.

'I want my club to be something bright in the lives of the
people that know and love it – that's all. I want to get wholeheartedly behind my team, and if that involves moaning about
them, that's OK – that's what football fans do.'

December:
Charlton Athletic v Huddersfield Town

After another defeat, this time by Middlesbrough, we remained in seventeenth place going into our midweek clash against Huddersfield. Huddersfield were, at least, a couple of places below us in the league and so, I thought, we had a decent chance of picking up some points tonight, even if it was a little miserable, weather-wise.

On this occasion I took my friend Bayo with me. Bayo, like Conman a Spurs fan and a native South Londoner, actually genuinely knew a bit about football, running his own five-a-side league in South London and playing regularly in a couple of teams. I was interested in hearing his take on the footballing antics in SE7.

'I don't know much about Charlton,' he told me on the way to the match on the train. 'I tuned out at Kevin Lisbie.'

'Kevin Lisbie?' I asked. 'That's a blast from the past.'

'He had something of the Berahino about him,' Bayo added.

Kevin Lisbie was a striker signed to Charlton between 1996 and 2007, spending much of his time away on loan. According to Wikipedia, he had scored sixteen goals in 155 appearances. I didn't ask Bayo to elaborate.

Michael and I had predicted that our pitchside seats, which were not particularly sheltered, would be markedly less fun when the weather turned, and this looked to be the first time I would fully experience this. The weather deteriorated during the first half, and before long Bayo and I were looking for an alternative. Eventually we found two seats together some way back, but we were already soaked.

I felt bad to have abandoned our seats, like season-ticket lightweights, but I did at least see Peggy in the toilets at half-time, who gave me a smile, cementing my place as an established fan. I was delighted.

It was a fairly uninspiring match, and though Bayo said it was better than he had expected, he didn't think they looked as if they were playing 'freely', he told me.

'They're doing an excellent job of bypassing their entire midfield,' he remarked.

'But why would they do that?' I asked.

He gave me a knowing look and shrugged.

•

Lyle Taylor, who had returned to action for the first time since September during our last match against Middlesbrough, was warming up on the sidelines. Lee Bowyer had already said Taylor's playing time would have to be carefully managed after his recent injury but I was hoping an appearance now might break this tedious deadlock.

Though however much I may have wanted Taylor to get on the pitch and make an impact, I could not deny he was waning in my affections after some particularly ill-advised social media commentary on the upcoming general election, which was happening later that week.

Most footballers – I presumed on the advice of their management – kept their social media posts pretty light, but Lyle Taylor had a lot to say for himself, politically speaking, and it was hard to know what he was about. On the one hand, he was extremely vocal about racism in football, and a recent appearance in a video for the Children's BBC programme *Newsround* with a young Sikh boy was enough to warm the chilliest of hearts, I thought. On the other, he seemed to be pretty disparaging about the rights of other minority groups, and those concerned in the preservation of them were routinely dismissed as snowflakes, or similar. I wasn't sure if he was as right-wing as he often presented, or just a standard contrarian Twitter attention-seeker.

Earlier on in November, he had spoken out on Twitter about then leader of the Labour Party Jeremy Corbyn's thoughts on a fair society.

Corbyn had tweeted: 'There are 150 billionaires in the UK while 14 million people live in poverty. In a fair society there would be no billionaires and no one would live in poverty.'

I considered myself to be pretty left-leaning but thought we could probably all agree that living in poverty was fundamentally Not Good. But then that probably depended on whether or not you thought the system rewarded everyone equally.

Taylor apparently had views, responding: 'Because those 150 billionaires definitely sat on their backsides and were just handed this money right?! So now we live in a world where you work hard and reward those who don't want to work? Swear down, Jezza. Fool.'*

It would be fair to say that Taylor's tweet provoked a mixed response from those who agreed and those who did not – perhaps unsurprising when you looked at the state of the world, and indeed the state of social media. Answering his critics,

---

* https://twitter.com/lyletaylor90/status/1190397784429600768?s=20

Taylor said he wouldn't vote 'for someone to take more of the money I work for away from me'.*

It was an odd stance, I thought, to believe that somehow you worked harder by kicking a ball around and were more deserving of wealth than, for example, someone who worked three jobs at minimum wage in order to feed their family, who didn't happen by chance to be good at football.

Michael had messaged me earlier in the day telling me he would have to stop following Taylor on Twitter in order to continue to enjoy watching him play for Charlton, and it seemed to me he wasn't on his own. I was happy enough to ignore his political tweets, but as he kept doubling down on his stance, I began to feel increasingly irritated, like the snowflake I was.

'Amazing how people expect me to be happy about paying more tax ... I'm not a millionaire. I don't come from money. I have gone out and made mine in this world. Why on earth would I WANT to pay more tax to entities who piss it down the drain?'† he continued.

I don't know, I thought to myself, because you happen to have been born with an ability which this society values monetarily more than, for example, teachers or doctors and certainly more than shelf stackers or manual labourers.

As Taylor eventually came on to the pitch in the 69th minute on that miserable evening, I pointed him out to Bayo and gave him a potted history of events.

Bayo noted that he was wearing long sleeves and gloves.

....

* https://twitter.com/lyletaylor90/status/1190409576878882823?s=20

† https://twitter.com/lyletaylor90/status/1190608788031705089?s=20

'It tells me how much running a player is going to be doing if he's in long sleeves and gloves,' he explained.

Bayo and I left before the end of the miserable match, eager to beat the rush to the station, and just in time to miss Huddersfield's 92nd minute goal to win the match 1-0.

December:
Charlton Athletic v Hull City

Just three days later I was back at The Valley again for what would be my last match of the year, another week-night match set to take place in bleak weather conditions. I had arranged to meet a journalist friend, Sean, who I had met through other friends and had bonded with over our mutual support for Charlton. Sean lived in Berlin but was home in South East London with family for Christmas.

The good news about *another* rearranged match was that I could go home early for Christmas to be pampered by my mum. I had recently had my twelve-week scan which had returned some potentially concerning results, neces-sitating another scan, this time one I would have to pay for privately. With this fancy private technology, I could find out the sex of my baby several weeks early. Having always thought I wouldn't want to do this, if I ever had a baby myself, I had by this stage of my pregnancy invested quite heavily in the particulars of the relationship I was going to have with my assumed son and I decided I was absolutely not up for a surprise come June.

●

After running around London to arrange said scan, I met Sean outside the shop at The Valley. I had just bought Michael a photo of Chuks Aneke for a Christmas joke. Michael had been, suffice to say, a little disappointed by Aneke's perform-ance thus far that season, and with reasonable cause, to be fair.

Many a conversation between Michael and I had focused on whether or not there was some sort of *problem* with Chuks.

'I just think things go *against* him *all the time*,' I had often said.

'You just *want* to believe that because you *fancy* him!' he would usually retort.

As Sean and I settled into our seats, I noticed out of the corner of my eye someone dressed as Mr Blobby in a half-empty block in the corner of the West Stand, to our right. It was the kind of vision of dystopian nightmare that an occasion such as this deserved.

'What?' I asked pointing at Mr Blobby. 'Anyone under the age of 30 surely won't understand who that is, and anyone over ...?'

'Well, at least he's dry,' Sean offered, as we huddled in the freezing cold rain, which was for me, the second time in less than a week.

•

It was a good start by Charlton as so often it had been, with Darren Pratley scoring in the 34th minute. Darren Pratley was one of Michael's favourites on account of the fact that he 'didn't do much wrong', he had previously told me.

We held on to the lead until the start of the second half when the league's player of the month, Jarrod Bowen, equalised. But just minutes later Naby Sarr put us ahead again. Naby Sarr scored a surprising number of goals for a defender.

'I'm not sure he knows he's a defender,' I had previously said to Michael.

'I think Bowyer has obviously told him to come up and have

a crack from time to time if he thinks he can do something,' Michael had replied, adding, 'I like Naby Sarr a lot.'

'He does some really *random* things,' I said.

There's a sweet spot when you're playing pool in the pub. When you start, stone-cold sober, you can see immediately in your mind's eye what you need to do, exactly where you need to hit the ball in order to pot it, but you overthink it. Two pints in and you're at your best – you've just enough confidence to play the shot without too much hesitation. Three pints and you've tipped the balance – some of your shots will be absolutely genius, but a lot of them just ... won't work.

This was a rule you could apply to most things in life, I thought. Two pints drunk and you're living your best life, but everything thereafter was a steady decline. To me, Naby Sarr's approach to football was a bit like this, but tonight he had pulled it off, and I appreciated the maverick in him, right now.

Thank God, I thought as we headed into the final minutes of the game; at last we were going to get three points and put a bit of distance between us and the relegation zone.

I was always a little nervous when the ref added more than two minutes of injury time, and experience showed me I was right to be nervous. Tonight was no exception after Keane Lewis-Potter's deflection came off Dillon Phillips to go down as an own goal – in the 96th minute of the match.

The midweek matches were hard at the best of times, hurrying off from work at the end of the day to travel an hour for a match with a late night at the end of it, let alone the three-months-pregnant times. Let alone the miserable weather times, sitting in a pair of jeans with tights underneath, clinging with damp to your legs, your coat heavy with rain and your soggy hands frozen. It was one thing not to have taken a win in either of this week's matches (or indeed, the last ten) but to have shat the bed in the final touches of both games just felt cruel.

I left The Valley that night feeling relieved that I wouldn't be returning for a month and prayed for a decent transfer window.

•

Christmas had been a nice relaxing time, after the excitement/misery of the last two games at The Valley. Having had my additional scan, the results came back clear, and the sex was at last revealed, though unceremoniously in an email, rather than a cannon of gendered glitter or similar.

I personally couldn't have cared less what the sex of the baby was, but I had started to think about it quite specifically as a boy. I was convinced of it and had started telling friends as much. I was looking forward to raising a little feminist and 'watching football and having bantz together'.

My day job was producing and presenting a feminist podcast. I did not believe that these things would not be possible with a girl, but it just didn't occur to me to think about those things in relation to one. The social conditioning around gender norms was surprisingly ingrained, it seemed, even to me as someone who spent much of their professional life talking about them.

In my mind little Squidge Offord was going to be tall and athletic, to love his mum, and to have weekly outings to The Valley with her. I would not be *disappointed* if Squidge turned out to be a girl, but I would be *surprised* at this stage, and I didn't want to misinterpret that emotion when the time came, so best to find out right now, I thought. And quite right I had been, too, as it transpired that little Squidge Offord was, in fact, a girl.

January:
Charlton Athletic v West Bromwich Albion

Matt Southall had been parading his very cute daughter around at matches, and I began looking forward to taking my own at some point in the future – since the baby was a girl, I thought her dad might care rather less about whether or not she supported Arsenal (reader, I was wrong). Still, not even the new management's grandiose gestures were enough to stop the inevitable.

It had been a mixed bag for the Addicks over the festive season, taking a draw against QPR, a win against Bristol City, and ending the year with a loss at Derby. We saw in the new year with a defeat at Swansea, leaving us in nineteenth place, with now just five points between us and the relegation zone.

How had we managed to do so badly since all our prayers had been answered by East Street Investments, who were *bound* to pour all their Abu Dhabi wealth into the club and make us the next Man City? It was baffling.

It was around this time that I had a dream that I'd infiltrated a Charlton Athletic staff away day, by pretending to be a cleaner. In my dream, I'd been discovered by Matt Southall, and I'd *wished* afterwards I could remember exactly what had happened, that led to my eventual distrust, but I knew it had been sinister and could not shake off the feeling. Southall seemed pleasant enough, he *obviously* cared about Charlton as he was certainly making all the right noises about signing some players in the January transfer window, but it was a bit like the time I dreamt Idris Elba was a vampire angling for an invite into my home and lurking menacingly after it wasn't forthcoming – things were just never the same between us afterwards.

Still, I knew that these dreams were neither a sensible nor reasonable basis for distrust, even if I *had* subsequently gone on to discover Idris Elba's *Private Garden* music video. I was refreshed after my Charlton time-out, and ready to return, not least because on this occasion, so too was my brother. If I was honest, getting to hang out with Michael was the best thing about going to Charlton.

•

Since the new management had taken control of Charlton, they had focused attention on getting bums on seats at The Valley – a sensible course of action in terms of the sustainability of the club. The hype had worked and today's match against West Brom was a sell-out. As I met Michael outside the busy stadium, as ever, he went to collect his programme.

'Do you want one?' he asked, knowing I wouldn't have thought to bring any cash with me.

'No,' I said, turning and pointing, 'but I do want one of those.'

I had spotted, on the corner of Floyd Road opposite the main gates into the West Stand, a man selling copies of *Voice of The Valley: An Independent Charlton Fanzine*.

Voice of The Valley was a pound cheaper than the match-day programme, but, more importantly, it was edited by a man named Rick Everitt, who was something of a Charlton legend.

'Are you sure, sis?' Michael asked, looking slightly bemused, but I was off.

Everitt was a former Charlton reporter, communications manager at the club, and the author of one of the books handed over to me by the guys at the museum. He was also one of the organisers of The Valley Party's 1990 election campaign and a prominent member of Coalition Against Roland Duchatelet.

The front of the January edition was headlined 'It's the end of an error!' with a photo of the club's statue of Jimmy Seed, saying, 'Waiting for the EFL is worse than waiting for VAR!', referring to the owners' and directors' test, which was yet to be officially met by the new administration.

●

Michael was pleased to be back at The Valley and told me of a rumour he had heard on some Charlton fan forum.

'Apparently they're going to play *Mull of Kintyre* before kick-off today,' he said.

Mull of Kintyre, the famously untrendy song by Paul McCartney and Wings, was the tune to which 'Valley Floyd Road', the club's song, was sung. For many, many years, I had thought the words were 'The mist rolling in from the seats'. Alas, it was – quite rightly – the Thames. Misty seats were not a particularly appealing prospect.

The tempo of the Charlton reworking of the song was always a little haphazard. Michael said the reason *Mull of Kintyre* was to be played was to give the crowd's rendition a little *je ne sais quoi*.

'Imagine if it was sung at the same tempo as *Mull of Kintyre* – the tempo it's actually supposed to be sung at?' he asked me. 'I think I'll be quite emotional!'

He wasn't joking, but when the time came not even the clear demonstration by Sir Paul could cajole supporters into the correct rhythm. I think Michael still felt quite emotional, nonetheless.

●

It was a pretty rough match, and there were a lot of yellow cards flying around. At one point, one of the West Brom players appeared to have one of ours in a headlock, but somehow managed to avoid any serious sanction. It had been hard to feel like the referees had been on our side this season.

But if anyone had been on our side, it was the ball boys. A West Brom player stood in front of us by the end of the pitch, between the goal and the near corner, his arms outstretched to receive the ball from the young lad, who, in an absolutely stunning burn, instead threw it at his feet when he approached. It was one of the more entertaining moments of the match, from a Charlton perspective.

Still, a 2-2 draw with the club currently second from top was plenty for me, on this occasion.

February:
Charlton Athletic v Barnsley

I had missed the last home match at Charlton, a 0-0 draw with Fulham. As my pelvis started to literally move apart to accommodate the growing baby, I had been rendered immobile, and slightly terrified for most of that week. I was not sure this was what I had signed up for.

Nor did I think I had signed up for our recent run of results. Prior to the Fulham match, a 2-1 defeat by Preston North End had left us in twentieth place in the league, teetering dangerously on the edge of the relegation zone. By this point, my hopes for the season had been forced to alter dramatically. With seventeen matches left of the season, we were 25 points behind table-toppers, Dirty Leeds.

The January transfer window had been and gone, and despite the promise of signings, little had transpired. Worse still, we'd lost our Chelsea loanee, Conor Gallagher, who in all fairness was way too good to be caught in a relegation dogfight, and his club must have known it. We'd kept hold of Lyle Taylor, though, so it wasn't all bad. The one signing we *had* made – possibly the most important of all – was Lee Bowyer, who having looked like he was leaving at the start of the season, had now committed to the club until 2023. So surely things were moving in the right direction, even if the results didn't show it, yet. There was one thing about the transfer window that had continued to play on my mind, however.

On 30 January, Southall posted a picture on Twitter,

captioned 'Fully stocked ready for a crazy 29 hours [zany face emoji] #DeadlineDay #cafc.'

The picture was of a haul of snacks, presumably intended to see them through a busy day on the phone to other clubs, wheeling and dealing. But the snacks were shit. Mini rolls, Doritos, a multipack of 7Up and other assorted sugar- and salt-laden goodies. It looked like they had just done a smash and grab at Poundland.

'Fucking hell,' I messaged Michael. 'You own a football club – at least go to Waitrose.'

'Yeah, I saw that,' he replied. 'I think he actually put a winky face up saying it's from Waitrose.'

'This is straight from the Sainos on Church Lane. Either that or Lee Bowyer has the diet of an eight-year-old. No one goes to Waitrose to buy this shite.'

'You do when you're playing with Abu Dhabi gold ...'

Michael was obviously seeing the funny side, but I was actually quite serious.

There had been another 'incident' earlier in the season which I had found odd. On Southall's Twitter account, he'd changed his profile picture to one of him at The Valley, but with a Getty Images watermark still adorning it. Surely a man who could afford to buy a football club could afford to pay to actually download the picture? Or, you know, at least the club could?

'Matt Southall does not eat this food,' I replied. 'This man gyms and he eats quinoa and smashed avocado on toast. He is not a pickled onion Monster Munch kind of a guy.'

'I think you're right,' Michael replied. 'Unless they think they can sway players with a few cans of Coke and a bag of Haribo?'

'Gotta sway 'em with something.'

'Genius – and probably why we're not doing very well.'

It was silly, and I was at least half joking, but it did stay with me.

•

It was a big day at The Valley and this week we were there en masse. Continuing their efforts to get people at The Valley to watch the football, the club had given season ticket holders the opportunity to each get a free ticket to bring someone else with them. Michael was bringing Kerry, and I was bringing Conman for his THIRD match as a Charlton fan, of sorts. Michael and Kerry were going to check out another seating area in the West Stand, by the tunnel. I was a bit jealous.

Not only was The Valley rocking again with a packed home crowd, but new majority shareholder, His Excellency Tahnoon Nimer, was also in attendance for his first match.

Conman had been waiting for us to arrive and, not for the first time during these jaunts, he decided to have a little exploration of the local area.

'I'm not even joking – it's about five minutes away from here – I found myself in a *quarry*!' he told me excitedly.

'But then right, there's this thing there which tells you where the bit of the ground is from, because you know, it's really deep, and it mentions *Harwich*, right?!'

'Like, my Harwich?' I asked him. 'H-A-R-W-I-C-H Harwich?'

Conman nodded enthusiastically.

'How weird is that?' he asked.

It was quite weird.

'Could I go there?'

'Maybe not this season,' he said, nodding at my stomach. 'It's quite steep.'

'I'm going to look it up!' I told him.

Gilbert's Pit, it was apparently called, and one user had left a review. Five stars, they said.

'"Good for a stroll. Steep climbs though,"' I read out. Conman nodded, again.

•

As we waited for the match to start, I told Conman about our disappointing transfer business, and more importantly *that* tweet.

The more I talked about it, the loftier I felt Matt Southall's edible ambitions should have been. By this point, he should have been ordering in sushi from Harrods, or *at the very least* one of those mixed sandwich platters from Marks & Spencer – a working lunch *classic*.

'Nah,' Conman agreed. 'The only person eating that is an eight-year-old at a birthday party in Redbridge.'

•

Despite the sense of occasion, it was not a fun game to watch, but Charlton did what they had done for most of the season – let the opposition take the bulk of possession and take the opportunities where they found them. We went a goal up thanks to Lyle Taylor in the ninth minute, with new boy Andre Green – one of the few loanees we'd taken on in January – scoring a second during added time in the first half.

In the 71st minute, Barnsley clawed a goal back, which left us with a tense twenty minutes or so to wait for the inevitable equaliser. But on this occasion, it didn't come. Charlton had been shit, but Barnsley had been shitter, and I would take those three points.

February:
Charlton Athletic v Luton Town

Another three games had passed before I returned to SE7. We were in deep doo-doo after losing 3-1 at Stoke, who were one of five teams below us in the league – it was a bad game to have lost. Surprisingly, Nottingham Forest – a team who were actually doing quite well – seemed to be pretty much the only team incapable of beating Charlton as we took a 1-0 win.

Four days later and I was prevented from attending our home game against Blackburn Rovers thanks to the underwhelmingly-named Storm Dennis, but I was ultimately glad to miss what was a 2-0 defeat in our own backyard.

A week later, we had summoned an entire posse for the next *crucial* match against Luton, who were second from bottom – a six-pointer. I'd met with my best friend Vera who had come to London from Worthing for the occasion. Previously we had been to the North London derby between Arsenal's and Tottenham's women's teams at White Hart Lane, and had watched Spurs spank Stoke City 5-1 at Wembley a few years before, and so, she said, 'You've been to our church – now let us come to yours.'

Vera had not been particularly interested in football, but her boyfriend John, the Spurs fan responsible for these outings, had introduced her to its dubious charm. It was a pretty good example of, I thought, 'If you book them, they will come.'

Vera's dad had not been into football, nor her younger brother, and so she had never been exposed to it when she was a kid – like many young girls of my generation and older, and this was quite possibly still the case. It always struck me as odd that some people seemed to genuinely believe that almost genetically, women could not be interested in football.

As well as Vera, three of Michael's friends from home were joining us. Ben, of his dad held the train up at Liverpool Street fame, and Jamie, who had come to the play-off finals with us, as well as Dave – an Aston Villa fan. Having spent the morning at the Tate, Vera and I met the others outside The Rose of Denmark – one of the local home fans' pubs – where they had suitably lubricated themselves for an afternoon in the eye of the Covered End storm. Or rather, the lairiest part of the home side seating.

That afternoon the distortion on the PA system at The Valley was particularly brutal – the tune to any particular song rendered basically impossible to distinguish.

Vera, having only ever watched football matches at Wembley Stadium or Spurs' new stadium, said to me warmly, 'It's much more what I thought football would be like.'

It was a good day to have brought a posse of honorary Charlton fans with us, it transpired. Lyle Taylor scored first to rapturous applause in the 34th minute, though Luton equalised just two minutes later. A trademark Taylor penalty, taken by casually sauntering up to the ball before blasting it into the back of the net, put us ahead again in the 61st minute, with George Lapslie sealing the deal in the 87th minute.

It wasn't so much that we had played a good game as it was that Luton appeared to have fielded *actual clowns*. They had played farcically badly, and the ball at times was hoofed into parts of the stadium I had not in this season seen it reach. At this stage, I did not care – three points would put some distance between us and the danger zone, at last.

March:
Charlton Athletic v Middlesbrough

February seemed to last forever. After the last match at The Valley there were another two away matches to get through. Charlton again conceded in the last minute of injury time at Sheffield Wednesday to lose 1-0. Another senseless loss of a point.

But it was at least close, unlike the next game against Huddersfield which we lost 4-0.

'I've been pretending to be hopeful but I think we are done for … Back to League One,' Michael messaged me after the match.

'All the teams around us are picking up while we're getting worse. Really looked bad at Sheffield Wednesday, and now this.'

At this point, anxiety was high, but it wasn't just related to the football, now.

A story had been rumbling away in the background for a month or so now of a new killer disease which had originated in a wet market in the Wuhan province of China. Apparently it had been something to do with a bat.

Though it was not as deadly as SARS, it was in the same family of respiratory diseases, and was much more contagious and, having resulted in many deaths in China already, had been spreading across the world, and now Europe. I wasn't particularly worried about it, despite my pregnancy. The last time I had visited, my GP had said that she didn't think it would be any worse than the flu.

Yes, people were dying, I had reasoned with my colleague, Hannah, but that's because they lived in developing countries where their living conditions were poor and they didn't have a National Health Service. We'd be fine, I thought, even though in the last week things in Italy had started looking really quite bad.

Although there were now confirmed cases in England – quite a few, actually – and the first couple of deaths had also been reported, it didn't occur to me not to attend Charlton's match against Middlesbrough. Well, perhaps it did, but not for those reasons.

I was joined again by Conman for another six-pointer. We were in twentieth place in the league table and Middlesbrough were below us in the relegation zone in 22nd place. There was time for us to turn this season around – including today's match there were ten games left to play – but each match felt increasingly crucial. It didn't make any sense that we were performing so badly, that we'd basically brought in no players in the transfer window, and that the new management were messing up Lyle Taylor's contract renegotiations so badly, even if I had said to Michael earlier in the season, 'Fuck him, let him go. We'll be fine – we're the new Manchester City.'

We were not, apparently, the new Manchester City just yet.

Middlesbrough scored in the seventeenth minute and neither team managed to add to the goal tally in the long 73 minutes that followed. Middlesbrough had more shots, to be fair to them, but neither team dazzled or even faintly glowed.

It was another miserable game, which I sat through with a now customary weak, watery hot chocolate, willing both to be over. I didn't mind not winning so much if we at least did it in style, but the matches were becoming painful to watch. In a way, I wondered why I kept coming back – the season tickets weren't that expensive, and I'd been to a lot of matches – but I was almost six months pregnant for goodness' sake, so no one would judge me if I just quietly opted out.

By the end I felt really quite despondent, as Charlton dipped into the relegation zone for the first time this season.

'Been watching on Facebook' Michael messaged me after the match. 'Hope for the best, prepare for the worst.'

'If I've caught coronavirus being here, I'll be livid,' I replied.

'I think picking up corona would have been the best thing that happened to you today!'

The season takes another dramatic turn. Well, two dramatic turns, actually

On 9 March I was on my way home from a comedy show in town when my phone buzzed in my pocket.

It was perhaps a bit daft to have gone into Soho that evening. Things were looking increasingly hairy and in Italy a quarantine, which had initially only applied to the worst-hit regions, was extended across the whole country, while people had started making noises about the possibility of a lockdown in the UK, although I still couldn't see it.

It was a bizarrely surreal thing to be talking about – I'd been in and out of Central London twice that day, and had been at a football match packed full of fans just two days earlier. Perhaps it was time to start taking this whole thing a bit more seriously, particularly as I headed into the third trimester of my pregnancy.

I looked at my phone to find a message from Michael.

'Weird stuff going on with our owner on Instagram,' he said.

Immediately clicking through to check, under a picture of the Charlton logo, Nimer wrote: 'Unfortunately I discovered that the club and its financial resources were exploited in a wrong and immoral manner, and that is why I announce that I will withdraw the club's purchase.'

The words sent me into a blind panic. What? WHAT?

'You can't just withdraw the bid after the sale has been agreed?' I replied to Michael.

Seventeen minutes later, he replied again: 'Bizarrely, an ESI statement now occupies the main page of the club's website. Strange things afoot. Never known anything like this.'

Southall, it seemed, had immediately hit back, accusing Nimer of having failed to invest in the club as promised.

'Clowns to the left of me, jokers to the right,' Michael added.

'So does Roland still own us?'

'Literally no one has a clue. Basically the whole future of the club is now in jeopardy over two wealthy bellends' Twitter beef. I'm going to hit the hay and pretend none of this ever happened.'

'Chin up,' I replied. 'We'll get through, we always do.'

Because we did always get through.

•

The next day, more posts had been made and deleted by Nimer, with further accusations hanging in the air, and Southall issued another statement via the club's website.

'Following the events of 9 March, his position is now untenable and the board has no option but to accept his resignation.'

The statement read:

'The board of Charlton Athletic and the senior management team will continue to run the club with its best long-term interests at heart.'

How could Southall be sacking the majority shareholder? It made no sense.

Shortly thereafter, the EFL weighed in on the 'concerning' developments, and seemed to confirm Southall's accusations that proof of funds had not yet been received. But an even more worrying development then came to light.

The statement confirmed news, unbeknownst to any fans at this stage, that since the proof of funds had not been provided, Charlton had also been under a transfer embargo since *January*.

'I TOLD YOU THE CRISPS WERE DODGY!' I raged at Michael.

But before we had time to reflect, Nimer was back on Instagram, this time leaking details of a flat paid for by the club, at which Southall was allegedly residing.

Nimer also hit back in a statement issued by his lawyer, Chris Farnell, citing Southall's 'defamatory' comments and added:

'We can confirm that Mr Tahnoon Nimer has not resigned nor offered his resignation. He has however instructed lawyers to investigate the financial irregularities at the club and in particular Mr Southall.

'We have been forced to issue this statement in response to Mr Southall's earlier statement and to ensure that fans are aware of the true position.'

Over the next few days, I couldn't keep up. I imagined the world looking on, licking their collective lips over the salacious gossip that Nimer and Southall's very public and very ugly fallout was generating. If I was honest, I would have been doing exactly the same had it not been my club. But *my club* – my struggling club, under a transfer embargo, and with almost all of their players about to be out of contract in June – was in deep peril, it seemed.

And then, all the while as the new, increasingly troublesome coronavirus rumbled on in the background, and with players around the world suddenly testing positive for the disease, an even less anticipated threat presented itself.

On 13 March, suddenly with our ownership under question, with 37 of our 46 matches played, and now dangling in the relegation zone just two points from safety, it was announced by the English Football Association that professional football would be suspended until 3 April at the earliest.

LIMBO

March–May: Fixtures postponed

Three days later as the situation with this new virus seemed to be getting pretty serious, it was announced that anyone considered 'high risk' in relation to it should stay at home for the next twelve weeks. 'High risk' meant anyone over 70, or with certain health conditions, or who was pregnant – especially those in their third trimester. I was *livid*. Not only was I going to be shut in my flat until I gave birth, but they'd also previously told me it was all right to go out, and that I was at no particular risk, and I had been out and about all over the place.

If I'd been worried about missing out on anything over the next twelve weeks, seven days later on 23 March, the situation was sufficiently bad that Prime Minister Boris Johnson announced that the whole country would go into national lockdown. People would only be allowed to leave their homes, he said, to go food shopping, attend medical appointments or for daily exercise; all other shops, bars and restaurants would close; and people would start saying 'unprecedented' with alarming frequency.

We were not told how long the lockdown would go on for, but by this point the summer's Euros *and* Olympic Games had been postponed – royally messing with my maternity leave. It felt optimistic at best that league football would resume again in ten days' time.

With no one to distract me other than the person I was growing in my uterus, I threw myself into worrying about the fortunes of Charlton Athletic.

What was going to happen to football? Would the leagues finish now? How would they decide who'd won and who'd lost? WHAT ABOUT LIVERPOOL? On the cusp of winning their first ever Premier League title in a runaway season, and they could have it taken away from them? No one could let that happen, surely?

Deciding on a points per game score was stupid, I thought, though if I was honest, I mostly thought this because Charlton would still be relegated under this calculation. If we couldn't finish the season, someone was going to lose, so you had to decide, would it be the teams about to get promoted, or those at risk of relegation who took this on the chin?

It transpired, however, that this wasn't completely unprecedented. In fact, Michael informed me, there was the Football League War Cup, which ran between 1939 and 1945. In the 1944 final Aston Villa and Charlton Athletic were the north and south finalists, respectively, who met each other at Wembley Stadium to draw 1-1 in the overall final. With the threat of bombing ever present and difficulties travelling around the country, it wasn't logistically possible to replay the match, and so the title was shared that year. With Aston Villa and Charlton now facing relegation from their respective leagues, perhaps it was only right that they be the joint beneficiaries of an unforeseen delay in play?

But Charlton had already been touched by the pandemic in more tragic ways, it transpired, as it was announced that one of our own had sadly become a casualty of the pandemic. The man I had seen at the Charlton Athletic museum, apparently only a little bit older than me, at 38, had died. His name was Seb Lewis.

As families up and down the country began to feel losses

of their own, when you talked about a football family, Seb was – the club said in their tribute to him – 'the heart and soul'. He had attended every single game, home and away, since 1998, his record standing at 1,076 fixtures.

'He was a *legend*,' Michael told me when I broke the news to him. 'I can't believe you *met* him.'

•

Towards the end of April, we were growing genuinely concerned by the stalemate between the directors. With no ticket sales in the club's coffers and Nimer refusing to put money into the club until Southall was out of the picture, it seemed a genuine concern that money for wages would run out sooner or later. Around this time it was revealed that far from having bought the club 'lock, stock and barrel', in fact the club had been bought for £1 on the understanding that the stadium and training ground would be bought – and paid for – at a later date. *£1.*

On an almost daily basis, Michael would send me a link to a tweet by some regular on the Charlton fan forums, or local South East London journalist who he believed to be well connected. A different theory or rumour was circulating almost every day about what was to become of us, or, more accurately, who might be in the frame to buy us. Very few of them looked like options we would have wanted.

'Why doesn't Southall just *fuck off*?' I would reply, exasperated, before going on to tweet an impassioned plea for someone – *anyone* – to step in and save us from this nightmare.

The only thing keeping anyone going was assistant manager Johnnie Jackson's isolation soundtrack which had become something of an internet sensation, along with Arsenal legend Ray Parlour's efforts to play keepy-uppy with a pint of beer.

It was around this time that Michael suggested we join the Charlton Athletic Supporters' Trust, the organisation set up to represent fans and hold the board accountable in an era of an increasing number of football clubs finding themselves in financial difficulty. Michael thought the club might genuinely be one pay day away from going into administration and it later transpired that he had not been alone in those fears. He thought we should get involved now, lest there be some kind of bid for ownership by fans, in this worst-case scenario.

CAST, as I had discovered in my discussion with Richard, were indeed a bit more the ballot to the bullet of the Campaign Against Roland Duchatelet, or CARD. Their vibe was more: 'We'll send a set of questions each week for directors to avoid answering properly' than 'We'll jettison missiles onto the pitch to irritate the board members'.

It would cost us £5 each to join – a figure they definitely could have doubled, I thought – and for that we would get ... Well, I wasn't entirely sure if the truth be told, but I was willing to find out.

'You sacrifice all that because it's what you do' – Karen and the price of women's football

Of course, as well as the men's team, Charlton Athletic was also the home of a women's team. One-time high-flyers in the women's game, recent results had been patchy. Although I had been to women's football matches in the past, it was with some embarrassment that I had yet to attend a Charlton Women's game.

In recent years, there had been a few high-profile cases where women's teams had called foul play on their overlords. Crystal Palace women's team, for example – not to deliberately pick on Palace, you understand – had been bailed out by men's team star striker, Wilfried Zaha in 2018. Coinciding with a lucrative new deal with fan's favourite Zaha, it had been revealed by the *Guardian* that the club's women players had been told they must each raise £250 either in sponsorship or from their own pockets, or may no longer be able to represent the club. Just a day later, the club announced that Zaha had made a 'substantial financial contribution'* to the ladies' team, who themselves lauded his 'stunning gesture'. Still, we couldn't all earn a reported £130,000 a week – especially not if we happened to be women.

In all fairness, the gender pay gap in football was *a bit* of a lazy criticism in football, I thought. In 2019, the BBC reported

....

* https://www.theguardian.com/football/2018/sep/05/wilfried-zaha-donation-crystal-palace-ladies

that crowds at women's top-flight football matches had aver-aged 4,112 attendees per match.* This figure had been bolstered massively by high-profile, big-ticket stadium matches recently held to help promote the women's game, and for many of them tickets had been available at a fraction of the cost of tickets to a men's football match at the same stadium, or even free. The strategy was very much bums on seats. The figure was consid-erably higher than the average of 1,000 the previous year, but it was still a long way off selling out Old Trafford – or even The Valley – week in, week out. You simply could not expect players to earn the same amount of money when the revenue they brought in was so hugely disparate – I bought into that argument. It also ignored the staggering variation in wages between even different Premier League clubs, let alone those lower leagues of the football pyramid.

For me, the argument lost potency a little bit when it came to representing your country – that was surely the same job? *'But women can't fill stadiums!'* became every single answer by red-faced men on Twitter, regardless of what the question had actually been. They seemed to seek you out so they could tell you they weren't sexist, but women really ought not to get involved in debates about football, almost as if they had funda-mentally misunderstood the concept of 'sexism'.

'The men's team don't even get paid for their England appearances!' they would shout at you, which wasn't even true. The men's team *did* get paid for England appearances, but were remunerated so handsomely in their day jobs that they could afford to donate those fees to charity – it was just loose change, pretty much. Was it not then, I thought, a little perverse that

* https://www.bbc.co.uk/sport/football/50308454

England's men's top-flight footballers earned so much that they could *literally afford to give their international fees away*, while clubs had only been obliged to offer their women's players a measly sixteen hours of contracted time per week since 2018.

In fact, since January 2020, the match fee for England's male and female players had been the same* – a figure of around £2,000 per match, it was widely understood. However, the bonuses received by men's and women's teams were still vastly different, because of the huge disparities in prize money awarded by major tournaments. Until the 2018 World Cup, the England women's team's success outstripped the men's, but the money they received for their efforts was considerably less.

The England team was far from alone in terms of this disparity. Perhaps the most famous and controversial case of this was the US women's soccer team, of which 28 past and present members had even gone as far as to take legal action against their employer, the US Soccer Federation. The case was initially brought in 2016 by just five players – Hope Solo, Carli Lloyd, Alex Morgan, Megan Rapinoe and Becky Sauerbrunn – arguably some of the biggest names in the game, who had filed wage discrimination action on the grounds that they earned less money than their male counterparts, despite vastly superior results.

Five years later, at the time of writing, the legal battle went on, having been thrown out by a district court judge in 2019

---

* https://www.theguardian.com/football/2020/sep/03/england-womens-and-mens-teams-receive-same-pay-fa-reveals#:~:text=England%20women's%20and%20men's%20teams%20receive%20same%20pay%20%20FA%20reveals,-This%20article%20is&text=%E2%80%9C The%20FA%20pays%20its%20women's,in%20place%20since%20January%202020.%E2%80%9D

on the grounds that the women had *opted* for salaries rather than per-game bonuses – they actually earned more than the men, he countered. Well, of course they'd earned more, came their response – they'd won two World Cups in the time period covered by the lawsuit, and the men had failed to qualify for any.

Though the case continues, in the most recent twist in the tale, in the summer of 2021, the US men's national team had come out in favour of the women's team's legal action; damn straight, they agreed – they *should* get paid more than them. In an official court filing, the men's team said that 'for more than 30 years, the Federation has treated the women's national team players as second-class citizens'.*

They added: 'A woman's rate of pay is not equal to a man's if the woman must consistently achieve better outcomes merely to get to the same place.'

You could argue the toss about equal pay in countries where men's football was – historically speaking – more popular, and had ergo made more money. This was simply not the case in the US where, according to figures published in 2019, attendance of the women's team's matches was 8 per cent higher than the men's† – the women were the breadwinners here.

If I was honest, I didn't particularly like the US women's team. I couldn't deny that I agreed with almost every single one of the values People's Princess Megan Rapinoe espoused, but I found her 2019 anti-Trump stance singularly underwhelming.

....

* https://www.independent.co.uk/sport/olympics/soccer-men-women-equal-pay-b1894050.html

† https://worldsoccertalk.com/2019/12/25/uswnt-average-attendance-8-greater-us-mens-soccer-team-2019/

She was an openly gay woman in a male-dominated profession – she would be *absolutely mad* not to detest everything about him. The US women's soccer team talked a good talk about fairness and equality and respect, but they'd pissed me off with their tea-drinking celebrations when they beat us in the same World Cup, and I couldn't see anything very sportswomanlike about their continued celebrations as they put thirteen goals past footballing minnows, Thailand, earlier in the tournament.

For all my disdain, which I knew was at least in part just a case of sour grapes, it was impossible to reason that their assertion that they deserved to earn more than their male counterparts – or at least have the *opportunity* to earn more than them – was unjust. It simply would not happen this way – it *did not* happen this way – for men.

Whatever my feelings about the way the US women's team had been treated, or Crystal Palace, or West Ham, or any number of other stories, I didn't have to look far from home for another example of when a women's team had been treated like second-class citizens.

Many of the English women's football teams we knew of now had not started their lives attached to men's clubs. Doncaster Belles, for example, had been a group of Doncaster fans who wanted to play football. Charlton Athletic Women were no different, having begun their life as Bromley Borough, formed by a group of former Millwall Lionesses players, including Hope Powell, who went on to manage the England women's team for fifteen years. After initial success winning the National League Division One South by a comfortable margin, the team rebranded as Croydon Women's FC, entering the top flight of English women's football in 1994. In fact, they did not become affiliated with Charlton Athletic until 2000, as the men's team returned to the Premier League having won the Division One title that year.

Karen Hills joined Charlton in 2001 after stints with Watford and Wembley Mill Hill.

'A good friend of mine, Justine Lorton, who was a big player within the England team, was actually playing at Charlton and lived locally to me where I was in North London/Hertfordshire,' Hills explained to me, from her living room.

A petite woman, with her dark hair cut in a sharp bob, Hills had an air of seriousness as she spoke with a native London twang about her playing career. She had been looking to return to football at the highest level after sustaining and recovering from a knee injury, she told me, when Lorton suggested she meet then Charlton Women's manager Keith Boanas. After a successful meeting with Boanas, Hills was happy to make the move.

Joining the team had initially been a little daunting, Hills told me – Charlton Ladies, as they were then known, had been a big deal in women's football at that time, and Hills was training with some impressive players. It took a while, she said, to find her feet and get used to the professionalism and speed of the game, but it ended up being a very successful period of her footballing career.

In the six-year period Hills spent at the club as a player, Charlton and Arsenal had been the two most consistently successful women's teams, and the alumni was pretty much a who's who of stalwarts of the women's game. During her time with the club, Hills played with the likes of Pauline Cope, Casey Stoney, Fara Williams, Katie Chapman and Eni Aluko, to name a handful.

While she was with Charlton, the team enjoyed its most successful period, winning the FA Cup in 2005 as well as making the final in 2003, 2004 and 2007. They won the Community Shield in 2004, and the League Cup in 2004 and 2006, as well as being runners-up in 2005.

It was a good time – an exciting time – she said, and Hills relished the opportunity of playing against some of the best in the business at Arsenal, Doncaster Belles and Leeds, the big guns of that era. They had a good team spirit, she said, great coaches, and were able to use the men's training facility at Sparrows Lane, where both the men's and the women's teams still train to this day.

At the time, it was rare that a women's team would be able to access such facilities, and the halcyon 'one club' approach had only really been adopted comparatively recently by a handful of teams, including Manchester City, whose women's team even played on the same campus as the men's team. It was a big deal and, along with some good people at board level like Steve Sutherland pushing the women's game forward, it was one of the major reasons for the team's success, Karen thought.

They had been a long way off the modern game's Wembley FA Cup final days, but additionally they were playing in some decent stadiums like Loftus Road, Selhurst Park and Upton Park, and had even been on a couple of pre-season tours.

'It was a big thing and there was a really big following,' she told me, speaking about those big-ticket FA Cup matches. 'I think it was up to 2 million people watching, and so it felt like everything was geared up for the season to pretty much try and get yourself into those showcase games.'

Not all of Karen's memories of the big matches were entirely happy. The FA Cup final, she said, always fell around the first bank holiday weekend in May – her birthday weekend.

'The first one I played in, unfortunately, I think I scored an own goal, which was something that will always stick with me,' she chuckled, adding, 'something that Pauline Cope will always remind me of on my birthday, every single year. Yeah, thanks for that.'

For the most part, Arsenal seemed to have the edge over their South London rivals, but Charlton were pushing, and Hills believed, getting closer. Ultimately, she said, the situation was taken out of their hands.

Charlton's men's team were relegated from the Premier League at the end of the 2006/07 campaign, the same season after they lost Alan Curbishley as the manager, and quite suddenly and unexpectedly, the club cut its funding of the women's team – they could not, they said, afford to run the team any more.

'I think it was through the pre-season,' Hills recalled. 'We'd finished the season and done what we needed to do, where everyone's going away, and it was quite a surreal sort of moment, I guess, because you were always gearing up to come back and planning your off-season programme, what you were doing, and then to be told that the team wasn't going to be supported was probably quite disappointing.'

The news came late to the team, and suddenly some of the biggest names in the game at that time were left without a club, not knowing what they were going to do or where they were going to go. For Karen, in her early thirties at the time, retirement seemed the sensible option, though as she recalled the story to me now, it seemed more like it had been a quiet, reluctant resignation at the end of a long, and by today's standards, unrewarding slog. Because despite their successes, and the professionalism that Karen remembered, professional they were not.

'In those days, you obviously had to work full-time as well,' she reminded me. 'We trained in the evening, two times a week. So I had to make the commute over and then obviously play the games on Sundays.'

Travelling over to Charlton from Hertfordshire took a lot of time and effort as well, getting home at midnight, only to get up for work again the next day, and then only earning a nominal match fee for their efforts – around £100. If for whatever reason they didn't play – say they were injured – then they didn't get paid at all. Those women truly played for the love of the game.

'The amount of sacrifice you make through the weekends,' Karen reflected. 'It took your whole weekends up, you missed so many different events that happen in your life outside of football, such as christenings or birthdays, or Mother's Day, Father's Day. And you sacrifice all that because it's what you do.'

When the team was disbanded, Karen took a bit of time out to consider her next move.

'I guess it was a bit of a shame to limp-finish my career in that way. So I sort of took a little bit of time out. I know there was a lot of media coverage around it, I just stayed away from it and focused on what I needed to do next.'

Having played for local club Watford previously, Karen ended up having conversations with the management there and going along to the pre-season training, but it didn't feel right, she told me.

'I just felt like my heart wasn't in it any more, and I don't know why that was – I hadn't fallen out of love with the game,' she mused. 'It was just that commitment and to get to know people again, to build those relationships with your teammates.

'I probably felt a little bit exhausted by it if I'm honest,' she admitted. 'So that's when I decided to move away from my playing career.'

Without a club, or any decent, consistent level of media interest in the day-to-day business of women's football, or social media to control the narrative in the way that modern players are able to, there was no fanfare or even announcement of Karen's retirement. She just, she said, 'drifted away' from the game, before returning as a coach a couple of years later.

Karen's recollection of events had been pretty measured – depressing, no doubt, but nonetheless measured. It would be understandable, I thought, if she or other players had felt less measured about it. It was insane to me that the team had been disbanded on financial grounds, given how insignificant those costs must have been, compared to running the men's team, with players who had just come from a stint in the Premier League.

In my day job for the *Standard Issue Podcast*, I interviewed Eni Aluko in 2019 about her auto-biography *They Don't Teach This*. Eni had played for Charlton at the time of their disbandment, coming in from Birmingham City and commuting *from Birmingham* twice a week for training. In her book she wrote of the sense of unfairness that the women's team had been instantly ditched, despite their comparative success.

At the eleventh hour, the women's team were saved and taken over by the Community Trust as part of its programme, but it was too late as most of the team's players – like Karen and Eni who got a call from the Women's MLS in the US to play professionally over there – had gone.

'I think a lot of players felt quite disheartened with it and quite disappointed with how it was done,' Karen told me when I asked her about the ill feeling.

'There was no communication that came through; it was just "this is happening". And you do question it. Why? Why us? Especially when you understand the reason a little bit around the men coming out of the Premier League. They obviously sold Darren Bent for £16 million that year to Spurs, and you're thinking, "Well, why are we getting penalised for that when we have been probably the most successful team at that time?"

'It shouldn't have been accepted,' Karen sighed. 'I think a lot of the players now look back and probably reflect; even now I think it wasn't done in the right way. But at that moment in time, we were just a bit numb with it.

'It hit a lot of people really hard,' she admitted, adding that this was actually compounded by the success they'd enjoyed at the time.

'You could understand if the team was poor, performing poorly, or we were just not painting the club in a good light. But we actually were. We had some fantastic supporters, and we were making a name for ourselves, and to have it all taken away was very disappointing.'

Within the next ten years – even five – the popularity of women's football grew exponentially, helped in no small part by the inclusion of a Great British team in the London 2012 Olympics. Such a team had never before existed – in fact women's football had only been introduced to the Olympics in 1996, but politics between the football associations of the respective home nations had prevented a team from coming together. Finally a British women's team was on the TV, broadcast into the nation's homes, with matches that spectators could actually go to – and swept up in the glory and enthusiasm of those wonderful home Olympics, they actually *wanted* to go.

However, looking at the modern game, it seemed to me that as much as it had moved forward in leaps and bounds, some aspects of it had changed very little. In that 2019/20 season, the FA WSL and Championship had been sacked off almost immediately – it had not been important to see them out – along with the lower leagues, once Covid-related suspensions began. All the while, politicians earnestly involved themselves – amidst a deadly global pandemic – in the business of the resumption of the top two English men's leagues. These were, after all, the money-makers.

Ironically the pandemic ultimately impacted on Charlton's men's and women's teams very differently, with both suspended in the relegation zones of their respective leagues. The women's team were granted a stay of execution when it was decided that no team would be relegated from the Championship.

While I'd like to think that a 2007-type situation could never happen again to a women's team, if you looked at that season end alone, there was sufficient reason to think that it might. How far had we actually come, I wondered?

'I would always say women's football is a very delicate sport,' Karen admitted. 'You think about football as a whole, and you look at the amount of capital and money that's invested in the top division, but then obviously it doesn't really get trickled down to the lower divisions.'

This echoed the sentiment of a freelance colleague of mine, Dr Carrie Dunn, a journalist and researcher, and the author of a number of books about women's football, including *The Roar Of The Lionesses*, and the subsequent *The Pride Of The Lionesses*, about the England women's team.

Carrie had been doing her PhD research on the experience of female football fans at the time of the Charlton women's team disbandment in 2007 and had interviewed the chief exec. She had asked him, she said, why the decision had been made, and he'd apparently told her that the club had to cut costs and the women's team was the easiest thing to cut.

'Fair enough,' Carrie said, pragmatically. 'But the money you put into your amateur women's team is going to be less than one of your men's players earn in three or four weeks.'

'I feel bad for a lot of these clubs, like Charlton women,' she continued. 'Because you're so dependent on goodwill ... What happens if the men get relegated again? Is the same thing going to happen again?

'If you're looking at women's football,' Karen told me, 'it's probably on the same sort of par as your Division Ones, in terms of the resources.'

Women's teams were a long way off equality, she said, which to be fair was patently obvious. But it was important for women's football to make its own identity. Reading not wildly far between the lines, I got the impression that Karen didn't think the women's game was managing this terribly successfully, and that it was to its detriment.

'When you look at how women's football has catapulted in the last four or five years, well, the WSL has been going for ten years, but it's only really been the last sort of three years that it shot up in terms of transfers for players and money that's coming into it. Now, the resources, the types of players that we're attracting to this league – it's not ever been this successful.

'But it's still very delicate,' she went on. 'I think for some teams, because of how quickly some of them are growing, the rest of them maybe can't catch up for finances. But then you're looking at the men's model, and thinking it is probably looking like it is going that way a little bit. Is that the right thing? My opinion is I'm not sure.'

Karen's reasoning for avoiding the men's model was a little different to most of the arguments I'd heard, and to be fair, as a woman who'd been involved in the elite women's game for over twenty years, I was happy to trust her judgement on this.

'I'm not sure because is that going to help us further down the line with the England teams? Are we going to be able to give the younger players opportunities to play at the highest level?' she wondered.

'If you look at the average age now, 25 to 28 in the WSL, a lot of those are world-class players. These younger players, there's only very few that ever break into it, similar to the men's game. You're looking at short-term contracts as well now, which are year to year, and the money that they're getting isn't sustainable to then be able to live on after, so women's footballers still have to think about dual careers.

'I think that's a really big piece that needs to be thought of, because they need a second job. They need to be educated.'

While I knew that, unlike in times gone by, a lot of female footballers in the two upper leagues were now employed full-time by their clubs, I also knew that they earned only a fraction of what their male counterparts earned. Nonetheless, it hadn't occurred to me that their salaries might be OK *for now*, but definitely wouldn't sustain them through their retirement from professional football.

Back in the day, the game had been completely amateur, though as of 2018, WSL clubs had been obliged to offer their players a minimum contract of sixteen hours per week. Prior to this, there had been high-profile players with second jobs – such as Eni Aluko, in fact, who had also been a lawyer. These days there are a lot of full-time professionals who get paid to spend their days training, as do the men, though it is not uncommon, Carrie thought, to find women players at clubs who train for their sixteen contracted hours, and are then employed elsewhere in the club, doing football in the community work, for example. There are also younger players who were still in education at university. It is only really in the last five or six years that any clubs – Chelsea and Manchester City had been the first to adopt this and, coincidentally, were among the wealthiest of the clubs – have made their women's teams full-time professional.

Endless comparisons were made between the men's and women's game, which were interesting to me, from a feminist perspective as much as anything else, and I was completely torn in terms of where I stood on them. On the one hand, I genuinely wondered, did we really have to keep making them? Did we have to tie ourselves in knots over the so-called 50-year ban on women's football and the absence of equal pay between male and female footballers? Or should we just accept that they were different products, and so much the better?

With the levels of investment that Karen had highlighted, clearly came much change. That money was coming in, I suspected, because brands were starting to realise there was money to be made – young girls to sell shirts to, as well as young boys, broadcast rights, ticket revenue, even just ticking a few Corporate Social Responsibility boxes. I highly doubted that much of it had come from an altruistic belief in the equality of men's and women's sport. But hadn't money ruined the men's game? Wasn't that why we liked the women's game?

I couldn't disagree with this sentiment, watching the twice-yearly dick-swinging contest play out between the royal families of Abu Dhabi and Qatar with each passing transfer window

– but I felt genuinely conflicted that the world seemed to think women were too fundamentally morally "good" to exhibit the same behaviours.

'I did a research project when I was out in Canada in 2015, for the Women's World Cup,' Carrie told me. 'And so many English football fans who follow women's football were like, "I used to follow men's football, but it became too money-orientated. I like to follow women's football now, because it's not like that – it's like how the men's game used to be."'

'There is this kind of Corinthian ideal of what women's football is like: "It's not driven by money, women don't dive, they're much fairer, etc, etc, etc." You get that even in commentary,' she added.

'If you listened to any of the commentary during the Tokyo 2020 Olympics, and it was like, "Oh, it's not often that you see diving", "It's not often that you see a professional foul in the women's game" – for God's sake.' Carrie rolled her eyes.

Carrie and I had spoken in January 2021 – during the third and in many ways most emotionally laborious Covid lockdown in England – about a group of WSL players who'd been panned by the press, and indeed society, for sneaking off for a holiday in Dubai, and justifying it by arguing it had been some sort of 'business' trip.

It was understandable, I thought, that people were upset by this – we had, after all, just been told we couldn't go home and see our families for Christmas at the end of a frankly terrible year, and here were these young women, disregarding the safety of others, because they felt entitled to a *holiday*? What I had found more difficult, however, were the not very subtle undertones that we expect this kind of behaviour from male footballers, the selfish pricks that they are, but that we somehow think *female* footballers are morally *better* by default.

'There is this kind of expectation,' Carrie began, 'that women are just essentially less selfish than men, that they're just better behaved, that they're not driven by the same mercenary ideals.

'It's interesting,' she told me, referencing a book about the history of women's football that she was currently researching, *Unsuitable for Females*, for which she was speaking to a number of women's players from the 1980s and '90s.

'They're kind of like, "I know that I could play now if I'd been born twenty years later; I think I'm good enough. But I'm glad I played in the '80s and '90s, because we played for the love of the game."'

'That's not to say that the girls today don't love it,' she continued. 'It's just there's other stuff that goes with it. It's the media commitments, the sponsorships. It's the whole public profile part of it. It's being a Nike athlete, being an Adidas athlete, being a Puma athlete and getting your boots and all that kind of thing.

'I think there has been this expectation that does sound a little bit patronising that women's football has good qualities that men's football used to have and now doesn't. And I think there is a concern certainly among perhaps some kind of old school, women's football fans, possibly some women's football players, that it's not the same as it used to be because of professionalism coming in.'

But money *was* going to change the game, wasn't it?

'Let's face it, women's football is not going to be professionalised unless it gets sponsorship,' Carrie reasoned.

'Women aren't going to be able to play football unless there's money coming through the till somehow – and it's not just about attendances because men's football isn't just about attendances.

'The ticket income for men's clubs is now a tiny, tiny percentage of their general income. It's about merchandising, it's about TV deals, it's about overseas fans. It's not about your old school, going through the turnstiles and getting a season ticket book scanned,' she continued.

This was an interesting point, I thought. For a start, the 'WOMEN CAN'T FILL STADIUMS' argument was, technically speaking – as I'd long suspected but never really interrogated or made the connection with the men's game in this way – sort of bollocks. But it was also interesting because at this point in time, those *were* the things that a functioning league system in the men's game depended on. We'd certainly heard it enough during the pandemic.

One thing was pretty obvious, said Carrie; if you loved how women's football was now, and hated how men's football was, you were probably in for a disappointment, because it certainly *looked* as if this was the road the women's game was going down.

'However,' she continued, 'the fact that women can play football professionally and get paid for it and make a living from it, and not have to rip up their legs on an absolute cow field or on a plastic pitch on a Sunday, then have to go to work the next day, or use all their paid holiday to go and play for England; I mean, I know that was the olden times, and people are certainly nostalgic about it, but I don't think that was particularly great either, to be honest. I don't think it was particularly fair that amateurs were treated like that when they're going to represent their countries.'

I did not disagree with her.

Of course, professionalisation of the women's game also meant that fans could now watch it from home, with increasing levels of coverage over the last few years culminating in the first major broadcast rights deal.

In March 2021 the FA announced that they had agreed a three-year deal with BBC and Sky for the rights to broadcast the Barclays FA Women's Super League, with Sky set to show up to 44 and the BBC 22 games per season, effective from the start of the 2021/22 season. The remaining games not selected by Sky or the BBC would be shown via the online platform, The FA Player. The deal was worth an estimated £8m, according to reports,* the biggest broadcast deal for any professional women's football league in the world – but still some way off the £5bn deal for UK broadcast rights for the men's Premier League.

Part of the revenue from the WSL rights deal would go to clubs in the league, with part also distributed to Championship clubs in order to aid development, the FA said.[†]

The money – at this stage – didn't seem to me to be an enormous concern, but the trajectory might be. Surely the only possible outcome – in the way that we had seen in the men's game – was that the gap would inevitably widen between the top and second tier clubs? The little clubs were bound to be pushed out to the peripheries? And the way that had worked out in the men's pyramid was that the lower league clubs had just become feeder clubs for the Premier League.

....

* https://www.theguardian.com/football/2021/mar/22/a-huge-step-forward-wsl-announces-record-breaking-deal-with-bbc-and-sky

† https://womenscompetitions.thefa.com/Article/Broadcast-announcement-20210322

'I think we're already seeing that we've got a big three essentially or a big four in the women's game,' Carrie agreed. 'But then that's partly because of the men's clubs that are funding them and the budget that they're being given.'

But it was hard to imagine this wouldn't have an impact on the teams in the Championship?

'That was one of the concerns when they announced the Barclays sponsorship deal [of the WSL] in 2019,' Carrie agreed.

'The WSL was saying then, we're looking for a title sponsor for the Championship, so they'll get their own money coming in. That still hasn't happened. So it will be interesting to see whether Championship rights do get sold, whether they do get their own title sponsor, because if we end up with a system where it is the top flight with all the money coming in, maybe with parachute payments, or we're going to see what we see in the men's game where you get the boinging backwards and forwards, but there's really no opportunity for the others to get promoted because they haven't got that financial boost.'

There were no easy answers, it seemed, and progress inevitably had to come at a cost – but surely these were things we could at least *think* about in the design of the women's game.

Karen Hills had not just been a player, of course. She began coaching at Tottenham women in 2009 and remained there until 2021, when she was taken on as the new manager of Charlton Athletic Women. Karen was a full-time professional head coach on the women's team, and her players were now also fully professional. A pioneer of the women's game, she was now reaping the rewards of the system, albeit not during her playing career.

I wondered how she felt about the constant comparisons between the men's and the women's games, having watched them develop over the last twenty years?

'I don't think women's football should be treated any differently because it is just football at the end of the day,' she said, matter-of-factly. 'I think we've got our own opportunities to create something, and I just think that people will eventually see women footballers just as the norm. It will become normal to turn on the TV and there'll be a men's game or there'll be a women's game, and then it's down to the preference of that person who they want to watch.'

There was a specific way that football managers spoke, I thought, a very straight-down-the-line, didn't waste their words, kind of style. Well, not all football managers, but a lot of them. I presumed this was some sort of media training, but I actually quite liked it. Karen was no exception.

'I think I'm happy with where it is,' Karen added. 'And I want Charlton obviously to keep pushing – to be at the forefront of that – as well.'

Perhaps it was an inevitable part of football that so many people ended up coming back to their former clubs, or remaining tied to them in some way – perhaps if you looked after your club, your club looked after you. A professional playing career was short-lived after all, and there were only so many clubs and so many ex-players. But it was nonetheless reassuring to me that it seemed to work the same way in the women's team at Charlton as it did the men's, that people like Karen also came back. Former Charlton midfielder Paul Mortimer – another Valley Pass regular – had also spent time managing the women's team. Kim Dixson, Karen also told me, a former player who had risen up through the academy ranks, still worked at the club, now as the head coach of the under-21s.

'That connection piece is still really there,' Karen agreed. 'And players who've got that history and that link with Charlton are really important to continue that legacy of where we were. We've got a lot of people within the structure now who have that connection with Charlton Women through a number of different periods of their success.

'Charlton is very much a community club, and I think, once you're in the Charlton bubble, you end up wanting to stay there, because there's been some tough times, but there's also been some good times for Charlton. I think we're all in that bracket now wanting to get back into the good old days,' she added.

So how realistic was that, I wondered? The women's team were again already – though in fairness this was as much down to luck as anything else – more successful than the men's, given their place in the second tier of English women's football by a comfortable margin. With a fully professional team, now brought back from the community side under the club, surely the future was bright for CAFC Women?

'Absolutely,' Karen said – as if she had been going to answer in any other way.

'It's going to be hard work, and it's going to be a journey – we're at the start of a new journey.'

The 'one club' approach was in full effect, Karen said.

'It's an exciting time for Charlton Athletic as a whole,' she said, as she landed a final hostage to fortune. 'I can only see it being more successful.'

The Covid Contract Conundrum

In mid-May, the government announced that it was 'opening the door' for the return of professional football in England, and soon we had a date: the season would restart on 20 June. PROJECT RESTART WAS ON – and it was a massive problem for clubs and players for any number of reasons, not least the thorny issue of contracts.

Contracts generally ran to the end of a season, usually the beginning of June, which had meant anyone whose contract was up on 1 June technically wouldn't be obliged to finish the season with their current club. Due to the mismanagement of the Roland era, fifteen of our players were on short-term contracts including six loanees, many of which had already been extended by one season after our promotion the year before. Presumably, getting key players to sign longer-term contracts was something a board which actually had some money would have sorted, but I wasn't even sure we had an *owner* at this stage.

It was fine, said the leagues, offering the opportunity for players to sign temporary extensions with their clubs, which was all well and good if your players still wanted to play for you. Fortunately for us, most of our players were *at least* prepared to finish the season. What would happen after that, one assumed, would be down to whether or not we were able to stay in the Championship.

Chris Solly deciding he would not stay on for the end of the season, to be honest, I could live with. OK, yes, he was Charlton through and through, but in the last season he'd only made fourteen appearances and had he actually added much value in them, I wondered? David Davis was another – apparently he was on loan to us, but I wasn't even sure who he was.

But there was a bigger problem.

'Taylor's not going to finish the season!' Michael messaged me on 1 June.

'Predictable,' I replied – and it was.

He'd been making noises in recent interviews which sounded as if his contract was already up. In one, he had spoken of the threat of Covid, which at the time, for reasons unknown, seemed to be more deadly for black and Asian men, particularly. I could understand these reasons for not wanting to play – we still didn't know enough about the virus to know if a fit young man such as Lyle Taylor was safe from its impacts.

What I found harder to stomach was a player refusing to play for a club they were *morally* obligated to finish a season with, and under any other circumstances would have, deciding to put their planned move to a new club above that obligation. It absolutely stank.

Speaking on the radio station talkSPORT about the situation, Lee Bowyer had confirmed the news.

'That's tough for me as a manager,' Bowyer said of Taylor's decision, adding, 'Lyle has said that he's not going to play because of risk of injury.'

To add insult to Taylor's potential injury, we wouldn't even make any money from Taylor's departure, given that he was out of contract.

I could understand Taylor wanting to leave for a better contract elsewhere, but this disloyalty enraged me. What was the point anyway? He was almost 30, past his prime and had never played above Championship level – we'd bought him from *Wimbledon* for fuck's sake.

'He's going to get a life-changing move,' Bowyer had said.

'No transfer fee, proven goalscorer – he will be getting paid by *someone* on 1 July,' Michael commented.

The Striker

L ike him or loathe him, it was impossible not to acknowledge that Lyle Taylor had been a fundamental part in the recent history of Charlton Athletic.

Lyle had started his professional career at Millwall in the under-18s, progressing to the club's reserve team, back in 2007. He joined Charlton in the summer of 2018 on a free transfer from AFC Wimbledon after three seasons at the club, during which he'd helped them secure promotion to League One. He was undeniably a huge contributory force in Charlton's promotion to the Championship, as well.

At Charlton, he'd scored 33 goals in 66 appearances, 22 of which were in the 2018/19 season and had been adored by fans, though the relationship had temporarily soured, and perhaps never quite been repaired, after it looked as if he might leave the club before the 2019/20 season as Brentford made a play for him. However, I suspected fans would have got over it pretty quickly had Taylor replicated the success of his first year at the club.

Having left under fairly controversial circumstances at the end of the 2019/20 season, I didn't think he would have much to say to me when I initially approached his agent for an interview. When I nudged them for a reply a week later, by that stage I was just going through the motions. So I was surprised to receive a reply that Lyle would be happy to talk to me, instructing me to contact him directly.

I was nervous about speaking to Lyle. I had largely made up my own mind about him over the course of the last season and the conclusions I'd drawn were for the most part negative. Still, I wanted to be fair at least and give him the opportunity to give his side of the story, and at face value he was polite, affable and he was *talking* to me – he did not *need* to do this, I reasoned.

'Hello Jen,' he greeted me with a wry smile, as we began our chat. Even at what I considered was probably a half-strength smile, and one almost accompanied by a half-sigh at that, it was a pretty dazzling one.

During his time between Millwall and Wimbledon, Taylor had played at a massive twelve clubs on various long- and short-term loan agreements and permanent contracts. It was a lot of clubs by anyone's standards, attributed in part by Lee Bowyer, when I spoke to him, to the difficulty of managing Lyle – not that he himself had found it problematic.

Lyle seemed to me, from his public persona at least, to be something of a law unto himself. But it sounded as if he'd enjoyed a fairly close relationship with Bowyer.

Bowyer had wanted to meet Lyle before he signed him at Charlton, apparently because of a reputation he had earned himself as 'a problem in the dressing room', Lyle told me.

'Was there any truth to those criticisms?' I asked him.

'No, the criticisms were bullshit,' he said dismissively, adding that he was a person who spoke his own mind and that this wasn't always welcomed in football, a point Marvin Sordell had also made.

'The problem is, in football, there is a hierarchy,' he began.

'When you're an eighteen-year-old kid you don't speak out, you toe the line – you do as you're told. But I've always been opinionated, and I've always thought for myself and I haven't ever changed.'

He certainly seemed opinionated on social media, I told him, laughing nervously. I had not intended to steer the conversation in this potentially controversial direction so early, but it was where it had gone, and much like Lyle, I was pretty opinionated myself.

'Always,' he responded to my observation. 'Because for me, at the end of the day, I have an opinion the same as everybody else.

'Everybody else has their opinion and tells me their opinion *every* single time I step on the pitch: "You were crap today; you were brilliant today." And look, sometimes the opinions are good to hear, sometimes they're not, but no matter what, that is someone's opinion and that is valid in their own life, in their own eyes.'

I got the sense that Lyle was perhaps a bit fed up with having to defend his right to an opinion.

'I'm allowed an opinion the same as anyone else,' he commented, 'So I don't see why I should hide away from that and not speak, I suppose, what I deem to be my truth. You don't have to agree with me – and that's the beauty of it. We can have a debate, or we can have a conversation about it, but the problem in the world now is that if your opinion doesn't conform to a certain set of people's beliefs, then you're the worst person that's ever lived.'

He hadn't said it yet, but I felt I knew where he was going with this, on the basis of things I'd seen him tweet previously. Perhaps it was a little defensive on my part, and certainly the left were as guilty of it as the right, but I felt it necessary to point out to him, straight off the bat, that it was not just *one* group of people trading in the currency of outrage. The notion that only left-wing *snowflakes* were offended by things was, as *Daily Mail* front pages would consistently testify, utterly ridiculous.

'No, you're right. You're right,' he said. 'It's not a one-way thing at all. But what I have noticed in the last, probably over a year to eighteen months, is that if you don't agree with the – let's say the not-so-liberal left – OK, you're a fascist.'

'And I think that's the issue,' he continued. It's that we can't be left-leaning or right-leaning; that you are either *so* far left or you are *so* far right. I think that's half the problem in this world now, is that nobody really respects or wants to *hear* anyone else's opinion or wants to even debate about it. You just get shouted down.'

Wait a minute, I thought to myself, Lyle Taylor is a *centrist*?

'Now, if we could have a debate one to one without every Tom, Dick and Harry getting involved, because we can actually sit and have a conversation,' he continued. 'But the problem is on social media, it's not one person ... It's not even a debate, it's an argument you're having – you're having an argument with 200 people.

'And the next thing you know, you're labelled – as so many people have labelled me – "You're a Tory,"' he said.

'No, I'm not,' he continued, slightly indignant. 'Because I do *genuinely* believe that Boris Johnson is a fucking inept idiot. But I just don't feel that Corbyn was any better.'

I had gone into this feeling quite sure that if Lyle *did* want to talk about politics, he would say something that would piss me off fairly promptly, but I couldn't disagree with *anything* he'd said, thus far – although at one point, I had considered myself a fully paid-up Corbynista, until the stakes had got, frankly, too high.

I got the impression that Lyle sometimes put his political beliefs out there for effect. Would it be fair to say he was a bit of a wind-up merchant?, I asked him.

'I am a *massive* wind-up merchant in every sense of the word, in every aspect of my life,' he laughed, telling me about the pranks he'd been playing on the kitman earlier that day. In football, he said, players were kept very young, in the dressing-room environment.

Bowyer had told me, of Lyle, when we discussed him later, 'He just can't help himself,' laughing.

'I've stepped away from Twitter now, for about eighteen months, because Twitter is the most negative and horrible place, and I just don't ever really want to go back to that, to be honest,' he said.

He was right, I thought. I had to use Twitter for work, I would argue, but I definitely felt calmer and less *constantly* enraged when I stayed away from it. Sometimes I could go days without saying anything remotely positive on Twitter – probably weeks, if I actually looked at it. Only very occasionally would I feel a pang of regret about this. Why would any of us willingly sign up to such a joy vacuum, I wondered to myself?

The focus of our gripes were all wrong, Lyle thought.

'We've got massive corporations and the groups that run this country, taking the *piss* out of the people of the country,' he said, before starting a rant about the health secretary Matt Hancock's unlawful Covid contracts* and the accusation, recently levelled at him, that he was an 'anti-vaxxer'.

He was pretty spirited, and I certainly didn't agree with everything he said, but I *was* enjoying the conversation.

....

* https://www.bbc.co.uk/news/uk-56125462

Since we were talking about politics, I wanted to know more about his recent comments on Black Lives Matter and why he didn't want to take the knee.

For perhaps the first and last time in our conversation, Lyle looked *slightly* uncomfortable. He explained that it wasn't anything to do with the statement itself – of course black lives mattered – but that he was not at liberty to go into further details on this subject.

I didn't *agree* with Lyle on his thoughts on the Black Lives Matter movement, but I respected the fact that he felt he had an informed opinion on the matter. It also occurred to me that the vast majority of people I'd seen slating him on social media for his views were, in fact, white, left, liberal people. It suddenly dawned on me that perhaps as a white person, it wasn't really *my* place to decide what Lyle, a man of mixed heritage, should think about this.

That said, I did wonder how he felt to be held up as a sort of poster boy by the likes of Nigel Farage and other right-wing 'commentators', knowing the damage that could potentially do.

'It is not something I ever wanted,' he told me.

He wasn't a fan of Farage, he told me, he hadn't voted for Brexit and he thought that people who were aggrieved by immigration had effectively made the entire problem up in their own minds.

'Immigrants built this country,' he said. 'My grandparents, on my dad's side, are from Montserrat. So, I suppose I'm an immigrant. If you ask the likes of Nigel Farage, I've got brown skin, so *I'm* not English.

'I think a lot of the issues that people have in this world are dreamt up from their own insecurities in their own minds, and people like him tap into that,' he added.

Again, I agreed with him – on everything.

I had been chatting to Lyle for twenty minutes and we'd not even really touched on football. I was expecting a charm offensive and robust defence of his character, but that was not what I was getting. Perhaps it helped that I agreed with *most* of the things he'd said, thus far, or perhaps I'd just spent far too much time locked indoors with an eight-month-old baby, but I was enjoying his zero-fucks attitude.

'I say it as I see it,' he said. 'And that's lost me a lot of support and a lot of opportunity over the years.'

Did he regret that, I wondered?

'No, not at all,' he responded defiantly. 'I'm not going to change who I am so that other people go, "oh, no, I quite like him".'

'I had an hour's debate with the club doctor yesterday,' he told me. 'And basically ended up saying to the doctor, "You know what, fuck it, I'm going to try and get into politics after I finish football."'

Speaking of football, because that was what we were here to discuss, I reminded him. Though I had enjoyed our chat, I wanted to know more about his time at Charlton.

'It was great for a year,' he began. 'OK, it was great for two, actually. Even at the end where it went tits up, it's not a time that I think, "It went tits up, now I fucking hate it." The first year was *unbelievable*,' he reminisced, with a smile on his face.

The jump in the quality of football between Wimbledon and Charlton had been massive, he said, and it took him the whole of the pre-season, and a couple of weeks beyond, to get up to speed. And then it was brilliant. It was the second-best year he'd ever had in football, he said – second only to the promotion year he'd had at Wimbledon, purely because it was so unexpected.

'The people around me were amazing, and my teammates were amazing. The manager was brilliant with me, the fans were unbelievable, and arguably the most dedicated and fiercely loyal fans I've ever come across in football.

'It's that same fierce loyalty that kind of spun on its head for me when this pandemic turned up,' he added.

'I knew we were going to go up,' he told me. It was a sentiment that Bowyer echoed when I spoke to him.

'Even when we went one-nil down,' he said, referring to Naby Sarr's clanger of an own goal at the play-off final. 'It was like, we need to score because if we don't score from this, we are right up shit creek – we need to score quick.'

But it was a setback, he said. They'd turned up at Wembley knowing they were better than Sunderland, he reckoned. In fact, he said, he was pretty sure they'd have gained automatic promotion had they not lost Karlan Grant to then Premier League side Huddersfield in the January transfer window.

It was a big loss to the team, and Duchatelet had form for taking the money for big players, but never reinvesting it back into the squad.

Once we'd been promoted, Lyle said that his representatives began having conversations about a new contract – he was one of many on short-term contracts at the club. This was partly because, as I was told, Duchatelet had been trying to sell the club. It made sense to have players on short-term contracts, lest a new owner take charge, with a new manager who wanted to bring in his own players.

There was no doubt that Lyle had been an integral part of the team's promotion effort, and so he'd been 'pissed off', he said, when he was told that he wasn't getting a new contract because he'd received a pay rise as a result of the promotion.

He'd scored 25 goals for the club across all competitions that season – 21 in the league which, for context, was the same number Sergio Agüero had scored at Manchester City in the same season.

'That pissed me off,' he said. 'Because it was like, hang on, I've got 25 goals. And my reward for scoring 25 *goals*, and helping this team get to the Championship is, "Well, you signed your contract, so?"'

I was pretty sure I'd been aware that money was an element in all this – it was well known that Charlton had the lowest budget in the Championship that season. In fact, Bowyer had told me, the second lowest was Luton Town, and even then, they had an extra third on top of Charlton's budget. What I perhaps hadn't appreciated in my rantings and ravings, was that Lyle might actually *want* to sign a new contract at Charlton. His starting point, he told me, was that yes, he wanted more money, but also a longer contract.

'When I stop playing football, it will be easier to talk about numbers,' he said.

Bowyer confirmed that Lyle wasn't being paid anywhere near what he should have been, and that under those circumstances, it was completely reasonable that he'd wanted to go elsewhere.

The transfer window arrived, and Lyle, not having negotiated a new contract at Charlton, wanted to know what he was valued at instead. One and a half million, his representatives were told. It was way higher than he'd expected or thought fair, he said. At the time, he was approaching 30 and he'd never played at Championship level before. He felt, he said, that he'd been overvalued and was concerned it would put other clubs off buying him.

Nonetheless, Brentford *were* interested in him. They were '*desperate*' for him, Bowyer had told me, and they matched the price, only to be told the price had increased to three million. They matched the three million, and it went up again, and again, but Brentford kept coming back.

The terms were eventually agreed and Lyle was waiting to go. It was deadline day – a Thursday – and he'd already played the first game of the season, against Blackburn, scoring the winning goal. The team were due to play Stoke on Saturday, though he expected to be gone by then. Until he received a call telling him that Brentford had pulled the plug – the club wanted five million, and this time they couldn't, or wouldn't, match it, and Lyle was furious.

'There was a lot of anger from me,' he admitted. 'I aimed it at ... let's say, the hierarchy.'

There was only so much he could say about it, he told me, but he felt enormously let down. It had been a life-changing opportunity, and he had been denied it.

The whole squad knew what was going on – most of them were on short-term contracts themselves, and he said he'd had a long conversation with Jason Pearce while sitting in his car in a Tesco Express car park. Then he called Chris Solly and the pair managed to talk him down 'off the ledge', he said. His initial reaction had been that he would never play for the club again, but his teammates managed to persuade him that this wasn't in his best interests if he wanted to move on. His contract was up in a year, so he wouldn't have to wait very long.

He went in to training the next day and had words with the manager. He'd not trained the previous day as he didn't think he'd be playing at the weekend, but he told Bowyer, he said, he was here, he was training, and he was *playing* on Saturday.

He walked into the changing room and Macauley Bonne, who'd signed in the summer from Leyton Orient, said to him, 'Oh, for fuck's sake. I'm not playing now, am I?'

Lyle played on the Saturday, the first home game of the season, against Stoke, and he said he received 'an interesting reception'. But his 25th-minute goal seemed to do the trick and the fans remained very much behind him. I told him about the text I'd received from Michael stating that 'all was forgiven', and he laughed.

I felt kind of bad for my previously held views on Lyle Taylor and the situation revealed how at odds players and clubs often were. From Duchatelet's perspective, it made good business sense to try and hold on to his star striker after promotion, especially if he was selling the club and wanted it to be an attractive prospect to potential buyers – Lyle was an 'asset' said Bowyer.

Bearing in mind how few players – and managers – spent their entire careers at one club, it felt as if, in many cases, one party was always going to lose out.

'In terms of the decision [Duchatelet] made for Charlton Athletic, he made the right decision. In terms of caring for my career, yeah, he fucked me,' he said.

The season went on, and we were six games unbeaten. The first loss came against Birmingham City, by which point Lyle was already injured. After a while, I'd had my suspicions that something more sinister was going on – that Lyle's absence was one of protest, but the injury was far worse than anyone initially anticipated.

He expected to be back within eight weeks, he said, but his injury wasn't responding to the treatment he was given and he ended up being out for over thirteen weeks. He came on as a sub in the two miserable games I'd seen against Huddersfield and Hull, in December, making his return to the starting line-up against QPR.

It was a struggle, he said, and he wasn't training very much because he physically couldn't.

'I would play a game, and then the next day I'd barely be able to walk,' he told me.

It took a while to figure out what the problem was – essentially, where his knee was weak, his other muscles were overcompensating, and would eventually just lock out.

'When it locked, I couldn't straighten my leg – I couldn't bend my knee, it was literally just stuck,' he said.

It would take a few days to settle, then, he said, he was living off anti-inflammatories, such as Diclofenac. This was pretty normal within football clubs, he said. Alarmingly normal, if reports were to be believed.*

I was not a doctor, but the basic principle of playing through pain seemed a worrying one – did it not worry him, I asked?

'We are pieces of meat,' he told me, matter of fact, returning to my previous comments about a flawed system being set up for one or the other to do well.

'You're right,' he said. 'And we have no control, no power, because there are so many footballers who the clubs can get for cheaper than they pay for you. They'll just do that and you get tossed out. They don't care.

'I'm not referencing Charlton here,' he explained 'I'm referencing football clubs in general, because this is how it is in football.

---

* https://www.independent.co.uk/life-style/health-and-families/health-news/pain-game-sports-stars-risking-their-careers-7818047.html

'We are all pieces of meat, and when they're done with you, they get rid of you. You're gone.'

It was normal, he said, at most clubs, for players to take painkillers or injections just to get through a match because they were needed.

'Because we are expendable, we are pieces of meat,' he repeated. 'We are only here to serve at the behest of our masters and our bosses, and our masters are the football clubs.'

This was interesting to me, I told him, and it reminded me of some of his comments prior to the announcement that he wouldn't be playing out the rest of the season after Project Restart – that he wasn't sure if it was *safe* to return to football.

Troy Deeney, the Watford captain, had decided not to play either,* given the disproportionately high impact Covid was having – for unknown reasons – on black and Asian men. I had thought it was a reasonable point, and one that I had some sympathy with. It was a bit like Colin Kaepernick in the NFL, and the Black Lives Matter conversations in England, I thought, in that we – the audience – were happy to be entertained by these black and mixed-race men, but they'd better not have any opinions – they'd better not take a stand.

I thought, in that particular way, I said, that sport was a bit exploitative.

'You're right, it is,' he said.

'We are performing monkeys,' he said, explaining that he did not mean this in the context of race, adding, 'Until they get bored of us. And then you're out, you're out on your ear.'

At the point of Project Restart, he *could* have claimed he didn't feel safe enough to play, he said, but he had been honest

---

* https://www.bbc.co.uk/sport/football/52721397

about it. He'd not trained in three months and coming off the back of the injury he'd just experienced, he simply couldn't risk it. He'd worked his arse off since he was eight years old to get to where he was, and he couldn't risk losing out on any opportunity he might now get. It was, he indicated, a *very* big pay rise.

I didn't think anyone could begrudge him that, I told him, but it was what they perceived to be disloyalty over the final part of the season.

'And I do understand that,' he told me.

Spoiler alert – at the end of the 2019/20 season, we would be relegated by one goal, in the end – that was all it had come down to, and I had heard people say that Lyle could easily have scored one goal in those last matches. Even in my previous state of irritation at his actions, I'd known this wasn't really a fair assessment – it had been a complicated set of circumstances we were dealing with. Perhaps if we'd had another good striker; perhaps if other players had had a better season; perhaps if we'd not had the big break in the season; perhaps if we'd not been under a secret transfer embargo; perhaps if we'd not been involved in a toxic ownership battle.

Any number of factors had conspired against us that season, and it hadn't really seemed fair to lay the blame for our relegation solely at his door, but I did wonder if there had been any bad blood between him and the manager or other players?

'None, none at all,' he said.

In fact, other players had told him he *shouldn't* play, he told me. The manager was disappointed, but he understood.

'I understand because I became a Charlton fan through my association with the club. And even now I check on the results,' he told me.

'Even now I speak to the manager [Bowyer] – I speak to the manager probably every couple of weeks. I speak to Jacko [Johnny Jackson, the assistant manager] and I speak to the boys that *are* there, and I speak to the boys that *aren't* there any more.

'Charlton became a massive, *massive* part of my life, and I never, *ever* wanted Charlton to go down, and never wanted Charlton to go down because of my decision.

'Now, did my decision contribute?' he asked. 'Yes, it did.

'I didn't ever want to be part of any contributing factor,' he said. 'But the fact of the matter is, let's say I had torn my cruciate in those last nine games, and there was no deal on the table at Charlton – there was no contract on offer.'

I wondered if he wished that Charlton's eventual owner at the end of 2020, Thomas Sandgaard, had bought the club sooner. Would things have been different for him?

'I do wish he'd come eighteen months sooner and saved Karlan. Can you imagine if he'd saved Karlan, managed to buy [Krystian] Bielik, brought [Josh] Cullen back on loan? The team we had in League One, in my opinion, was better than the team we had in the Championship,' he told me.

I told him of my initial excitement when the ESI takeover was announced. Of my dreams for Premier League glory, and how I felt able to square the moral circle of being 'the next Manchester City'. He laughed.

Lyle was brutal in his three-word assessment of Matt Southall, so I wondered at what point he realised that everything was going to shit?

'I had Matt Southall's number before even November, when I was told the interest started, and his name was linked to Charlton,' he said.

It was hard to find out how Southall had come to be involved in Charlton, with ESI, or even in football. Press reports at the time suggested he was a football agent, though there was no obvious evidence of this. He was secretary and director of Sports Media Consultancy Ltd., according to Companies House records,* a company that previously went under the names of Sports Investment Group Limited, and HFCUK Ltd. – though it was difficult to find out any further information on what these companies did or how successful they were.

An eagle-eyed Addicks fan, posting on Charlton Life forum, had also found a Facebook page for *Matt Southall Media*, specialising, it said, in 'fitness shoots both in the gym and in the studio'.† Anyone wishing to book a shoot should contact him, he said. The Facebook page had 21 followers, and his last post, which had two 'likes', had been in July 2019.

It was an astonishing change in fortunes, I thought, to go from this to having agreed the purchase of a football club, less than six months later.

The madness that had gone on in those six months was not particularly shocking to Lyle, he said – because he was used to the slightly chaotic order of things by that point.

'I was in Barcelona when Roland relieved Bow of his position,' he said, referring to a bizarre statement issued by the club, less than a month after the play-off final, explaining that a new contract agreement had not been met, and that Bowyer was set to leave.

....

* https://find-and-update.company-information.service.gov.uk/company/11645603

† https://www.facebook.com/mediabyms/?ref=page_internal

'It was like … are you fucking shitting me?' he said. 'There's no way I'm coming back to Charlton – if Bow's gone, I'm out of here.'

The matter was, however, resolved within days.

'Imagine that this is the backdrop to me having the best season of my career and having opportunities that you can't say no to?' he said.

'People will take each individual thing on its own, and they will say, 'OK, well, Lyle did this and Brentford did that …' But all of these things were building up,' he said.

The fact that half the team had left as well – it all contributed, he said, to his mindset.

He was offered a new contract by Duchatelet in September, he said, while he was housebound with his injury and watching the Ashes on TV.

'I get a call from my agent. "This is what Roland's offered you," and I just laughed. I actually laughed at him down the phone and went, "He can go fuck himself. Absolutely no chance,"' he laughed.

'No one ever spoke to Roland,' he said, 'But I got Roland's number and called him to say, "I want you to accept this offer [from Brentford] so I can leave, please."

'Nobody got Roland's number, *nobody*. But I managed to get hold of it and it wasn't from any of the staff and it wasn't from anyone at the football club. I had managed to get hold of his number and called him – blindsided and basically just had a go at him down the phone.'

I imagined, from what I had heard of him, that Duchatelet would not have reacted so well to something like this.

'Well, he was blindsided,' Lyle said. 'Which was the whole point for me. I wanted to blindside him, and I wanted him to know that this wasn't just the "Oh well, I've got a chance of playing in the Championship for this club." It was "This, with any luck, will change my life." And nobody really understood that either.

'Every football fan thinks that their club is the best club in the world, and that is why we are doing the job and we get paid what we get paid,' he began.

'Football fans think – they *believe* – that their football club is the most important and the best in the world because it has some sentimental value to them.'

I certainly felt that, over the course of this conversation, Lyle had expressed more than a little fondness for his time at Charlton, but he continued.

'It's very difficult as a footballer to have any sort of sentimentality towards a football club when you are a piece of meat. And I was a piece of meat at Wimbledon. I was a piece of meat at Sheffield United, I was a piece of meat at Scunthorpe, I was a piece of meat at Partick Thistle, I was a piece of meat at Millwall, I was a piece of meat at Charlton – and I'm a piece of meat at Nottingham Forest, because that is what we are.'

'And we accept that,' he said of himself and other players. 'But the football fan never accepts that. And if the football fan decides they don't like a player and they don't think a player is worthy of playing, they say whatever they please until that player is gone. But God forbid, if a footballer turns the tables or has the *opportunity* to turn the tables and ends up in the position I found myself in where I could wear the trousers and make the decision for myself – that's forbidden and that's not allowed.'

Lyle was born in Greenwich and grew up in New Cross – South East London was home to him, he said.

'I would never have wanted to leave if the people at the very top had shown the same ambition that I showed and the manager showed,' he told me.

And that was the point, I supposed, a big part of the problem – through his failure to invest in Charlton, Duchatelet had shown a lack of ambition for the club. And to be honest, who could have had any idea *whatsoever* what the intentions of ESI's ragtag conglomerate were?

One thing seemed pretty certain to me: that Lyle felt as let down by Charlton as the fans did by him. I had been furious with him, regarding his decision not to return for the end of the season, but talking to him now, none of it seemed unreasonable at all. And if his manager and teammates hadn't been annoyed with him – and let's not forget that the club's relegation from the Championship had *huge* personal implications for many of them – I felt much less within my rights to think ill of Lyle.

I had spoken to Sachin Nakrani, about the nature of fandom, and how tribal football was. It was odd to me, having talked to Lyle about his acrimonious ending at the club, that I could have ever felt so strongly about it.

Sachin thought there were some things, as a footballer, that you couldn't do. You couldn't play for Spurs and defect to Arsenal, for example, although as a fan you ultimately looked a bit silly if you rocked up at White Hart Lane waving a piece of A4 paper with 'Judas' scribbled on it.

'Players come and go. Managers come and go. And you really shouldn't get too attached to them or get too worked up when they leave,' he said.

'It's nonsense. It's all an absolute load of nonsense,' he told me. 'As a fan, I think it's really important in your quieter moments just to step away from it all and accept that.

'But within the theatre of being a football fan, I also absolutely get it. And I just think it's part of the dance as well.'

It was also important, he thought, not to cross the line – either in person or on social media. He didn't tweet footballers, for example, he told me – partly because it just looked a bit daft when you were twenty years older than them. I cast my mind back, quickly: I was *fairly* sure I'd only ever tweeted anything semi-abusive at Tory ministers.

Ultimately, the drama of fandom was part of the appeal, Sachin thought.

'I love the theatre of tribalism,' he said. 'You know, when your passions are running that high, it's kind of exciting and thrilling.

'It's lovely to feel strongly about something,' he told me, echoing what he had said before about the appeal of football. 'Unless it's like Nazis or something.

'What you need to do as a football fan,' he said, 'If you are like, "My club's brilliant – they're absolutely perfect; and your club's crap, and all your players are crap …", is if you find yourself in that mode, it's unhealthy. And what you need to do then is talk to opposition fans.'

I was a pretty reasonable person, I thought. I thought cancel culture was daft, and I didn't really, in any other part of my life, believe in the idea that people were good or bad. I mostly thought we were all idiots muddling our way through life and that we were largely redeemable – our entire legal system, and indeed society, was built on that premise. I wondered how I had felt so *wronged* by Lyle Taylor, a man who I had never even spoken to, before today.

In terms of the club's future, Lyle thought perhaps a return to the Premier League was a little *too* ambitious.

'I'd love to see Charlton as a sustainable Championship football club, and I think a lot of fans would love it if Charlton were a middle-of-the-road Championship club that every now and then had a run at the play-offs or run at promotion. I think the fans would absolutely love that,' he said, and indeed, it was pretty much what Richard and Alan had both said to me.

The Championship wasn't a bad ambition at all, I thought. It wasn't nearly as sexy as the Premier League, and it was hard to remember sometimes, that in 2018 it was found to be the third biggest league in the world, in terms of match-day attendance figures. This was above Spain, Italy and France's top tiers.

Lyle obviously felt a fondness for Charlton, its fans, and his time at the club in general, from the stories he told about his experience there, the atmosphere at The Valley, and the *noise* generated by their faithful, travelling away fans.

I asked him what he would say to them, given the opportunity.

'I'm sorry that Charlton were relegated and I'm sorry for the part that I played in that, no matter how small or big, depending on your viewpoint,' he told me. 'But I'm not sorry that I put myself first.

'So, saying sorry is really difficult,' he added. 'Because I suppose it could be seen as being disingenuous, and I'm not being disingenuous because I fucking *loved* it – I absolutely loved it.'

'I almost wish …' He trailed off. 'Maybe that I could come back one day. But I think there'd be so many opposed to that.'

I personally thought football fans were pretty fickle, and for the most part, if they were winning, they were able to forgive an awful lot, but who knew, perhaps that was more than Lyle could realistically hope for.

'I don't wish I'd been, I suppose, waved off as a *hero*,' he told me. 'Because no matter what, no one can take what I did and what I achieved at Charlton away from me. But I do wish that what I did at Charlton could be looked back on with a smile.'

Perhaps it was easy to look back on everything I had experienced with Charlton that year with rose-tinted glasses. It had been stressful, after all, and two grown men had fallen on top of me and actually physically scarred me for life at Wembley, but as Sachin had said to me previously, being a football fan was about *feeling* something. The play-off final was probably, after the birth of my daughter – the actual moment she was placed in my arms after I gave birth to her, and related to that, the moment my epidural had begun to kick in – the most euphoric I had ever felt in my life. I couldn't really feel angry with someone who had played a large part in giving me that.

In normal times, I told Lyle over Zoom, at the end of our hour-and-45-minute chat, I would have asked him for a selfie. So, if it was OK with him, I was going to screenshot us smiling – the Covid equivalent of a selfie, for the 'gram, I told him.

'You get to start the abuse early,' he joked.

On the basis of this interview, I told him, I had nothing bad to say about him.

A New Supporter
Joins the Ranks

I messaged the family WhatsApp group after my final trip to the hospital on 3 June.

'Induction booked for Monday night.'

'WOAH!' Michael replied immediately, 'Shiz just got real, and if all is to be believed, this is also the day for the Charlton ownership announcement.'

Over the days that followed, Michael had several suggestions as to how I might spend the first few days with my soon-to-be newborn child.

'Presumably the second thing you do with a newborn is sit them down and run through *Star Wars*? The most recent one is actually quite good.'

We had watched the final instalment together the previous Christmas. It had been something of a raucous viewing experience, leading Michael to assert after it had finished, that the people sitting behind us had ruined the last 30 years of his life, though the film had had plenty of other issues, he thought.

'Technically, there should only ever be *one* dark Sith Lord,' he'd told us.

I had to assume he was over this faux pas now.

'First thing,' he continued, 'obviously being a run-through of the '98 play-off final?'

'Do we know if we'll be able to watch the matches?' I asked, 'because it's going to be a baptism by fire for our newest CAFC recruit. These are going to be some tense early weeks of her life.'

'Imagine if they pull off the sporting coup to end them all?' I pondered, having still not learned to expect the worst.

'Without Taylor, it really is a huge ask,' he replied.

●

On the evening of Monday 8 June, I was preparing to go to the hospital for my induction, but had time for a quick call from my brother. We had a light chat about my will, lest anything terrible happen during childbirth, and whether or not it was right to pull down statues of slave masters and dump them in Bristol Harbour, as had happened a few days previously. We agreed that, on balance, we were fine with it before we were interrupted by my friend Nicola who had arrived to take me to hospital.

A few moments later my phone pinged again with another message from him.

'Sorry, know you've got a lot on – got wrapped up talking so didn't get round to saying good luck 🫤'

●

Over the tense, painful 44 hours that followed, the occasional cat picture found its way to me via the family WhatsApp group, as I regrettably responded that while labour was extremely long and arduous, I remained in a position to reply to their messages.

I reported intense pain at around 8.30pm on 9 June, and told Michael that I was waiting to go up to the labour ward before I could receive the necessary drugs.

'She'd better not be an idiot,' I added.

'At least 50 per cent of her genes will edge her that way,' he replied.

●

At 1.13pm on 10 June I let them know that an epidural had at last been administered and things were moving in the right direction.

'Obvs of vital importance – Charlton takeover has been announced and unravelling as we speak – just to cheer you along! ☺' Michael informed me.

'I'll tweet the relevant links at you so you can go through them at a more convenient time,' he added.

Exactly two hours and 49 minutes later, at 5.02pm, and after 36 hours of considerable effort, I gave birth to my baby girl, Lyra.

'She is perfect – I'm super proud,' Michael said, responding to the first flurry of photographs.

•

In the days that followed as I waited on my own, with no visitors on the Covid-compliant postnatal ward, I was entertained by the warm, fuzzy oxytocin high I was experiencing after birthing Lyra, and, of course, the family WhatsApp group.

'I'm excited about introducing Lyra to her life of misery on the twentieth – it's character building,' I told Michael and our mum a couple of days later, referring to the upcoming restart of the season.

Michael hadn't been taking the piss when he'd said he'd send me links to the relevant tweets, either. When I eventually checked, it was all there.

We'd just been sold to a 'businessman', Paul Elliott, but it seemed as if there was more to this than immediately met the eye, and we knew that even though the sale had apparently been made, the new owner had yet to be approved by the EFL's Owners' and Directors' Test.

'I actually feel sorry for her, but at least she'll never know life under Matt Southall,' Michael replied.

'That poor child!' Mum chipped in. 'She'll feel about Charlton like you lot feel about steam trains, probably.'

She was referring to a lifelong passion of our dad's, which we were as children forced to endure.

'I quite like steam trains,' I replied.

'I'm fed up of *I didn't understand. I didn't know. I wasn't sure*' – Troy Townsend and Kicking Racism Out of Football

In recent years, the discussion around racism in football seemed to have become more prominent. There were almost weekly incidents being reported by the point of the 2019/20 season, and indeed, Charlton was no exception to this. In February 2020, Leeds United goalkeeper Kiko Casilla was handed an eight-match ban for racially abusing Charlton forward Jonathan Leko.

Troy Townsend, head of development at football's anti-discrimination charity, Kick It Out, was a busy man, it seemed. Having worked with the charity before, I knew it was a small organisation, and one that was increasingly called upon for comment in press pieces after yet another racist match-day incident was reported. Troy was often the person within the organisation to provide that comment and it took me a couple of weeks to pin him down to talk about the issue.

'As long as the football world is peaceful,' he told me as I attempted to arrange the first of three proposed Zoom meetings.

Born in the UK, the child of Jamaican immigrant parents, Troy's son Andros was also a successful Premier League player, having spent time at Spurs, Newcastle, Crystal Palace and now Everton.

Troy had worked at Kick It Out for ten years and his current title was head of development, though that was due to change imminently to director of player engagement.

His role was in delivering education to, predominantly, people in the academy environment – the under-9s and under-23s – for staff and parents as well as players, around the issues of racism and discrimination more broadly. There had, however, been more of a focus on racism in recent years, which was what the charity had initially been set up to focus on, in 1993 when it was known as Let's Kick Racism Out of Football.

The organisation was founded by former chair, Lord Herman Ouseley, Troy told me, because there had been no real conversation about the racism which was undeniably present in football, and consequently, there were no real support systems for the victims and no real understanding of its impact. The charity created a space, he said, for people to feel that they could be supported and that they would get outcomes to the victimisation they'd experienced.

I personally didn't remember the establishment of the charity – I was only ten at the time and discrimination probably took a fairly secondary role in my consciousness after trolls and Take That, back then. I did, however, remember a famous advert in 1996 starring Les Ferdinand and Eric Cantona. The latter had famously kung-fu-kicked a Crystal Palace fan at Selhurst Park the year before, after he allegedly told him to 'fuck off back to France, you French motherfucker!'

Many years later, in an ITV documentary *Out of Their Skin*, Arsenal legend Ian Wright, now outspoken about the abuse he faced as a player – and still continues to receive from some quarters, as a pundit – said he had been 'jealous' of Cantona.*

....

* https://talksport.com/football/449618/arsenal-ian-wright-manchester-united-eric-cantona-kung-fu-kick-crystal-palace/#:~:text=Ian%20 Wright%20has%20spoken%20out,between%20himself%20 and%20his%20teammates

He added: 'Every black player had ten times more reasons to kung-fu-kick a fan.'

It was pretty depressing to think that perhaps not that much had changed since then. Hence the need for organisations such as Kick It Out, sending Troy to have these conversations.

He also worked on a mentoring programme called 'Raise Your Game', which helped people from under-represented groups get a foothold in the industry – be that in coaching, as an agent or in the media. The media was one of the industries called out by Manchester City and England winger Raheem Sterling* in 2018 after he was subject to racist abuse at Stamford Bridge when his team played Chelsea in the Premier League. It was hardly surprising, he said afterwards, that racism existed in the terraces, when the media helped 'fuel' it, referring to a slew of unflattering reports written about him by the right-wing tabloid press between 2014, after a dire performance by England in the World Cup that year, right up until this incident.

And it was true, from what I had seen. I had worked with a couple of sports journalists of Asian heritage, but prior to Sterling's comments, no black sports journalists at all. After this event and the hand-wringing of left-wing news outlets that followed, there had been a push for more diversity and one of the places I freelanced took on a young black sports journalist through the very mentoring programme Troy was working on.

What's more, there were practically no working-class people in journalism as a whole, it being an industry you were largely expected to work in for free, at least for the beginning bit

....
* https://www.instagram.com/p/BrKYvF3gH9e/?utm_source=ig_embed

– and a lot of people simply did not have that luxury. Secondly, on the few sports desks I'd experienced, besides me, I had only actually worked with one other woman – the brilliant Carrie Dunn.

One of the problems that the media – and society – still had, was that it had not yet grasped that diversity was more than a box-ticking exercise, and that it was actually *useful*. For a start, it seemed to me that many of the societal clangers dropped by individuals or brands in the public sphere – the kind that caused 'Twitter storms' or 'public outrage' in left-wing snowflakes, such as myself – could have been avoided if there had just been some more people, and different types of people, in the room, at a decision-making level.

Despite huge numbers actually playing football – and consuming it as fans – there were still disproportionately low numbers of black people in positions of power in the industry. In fact, the sacking of Chris Powell by Roland Duchatelet in 2011 had left just one non-white manager in the top four tiers of English football, at the time. In the decade that followed, only a handful more had joined Chris Hughton.*

In 1997 the organisation changed its name to a simplified Kick It Out and broadened its remit to include all forms of discrimination. They covered all 92 clubs in the top four tiers of the game, the non-league side, grassroots and community, and while other groups such as Women In Football, Level Playing

....

* At the time of writing, the only non-white managers in the top four English leagues were Chris Hughton (Nottingham Forest), Darren Moore (Sheffield Wednesday), Jobi McAnuff (interim head coach Leyton Orient), Jimmy Floyd Hasselbaink (Burton Albion), Hayden Mullins (Colchester United), and Nuno Espirito Santo (Wolverhampton Wanderers).

Field, Football v Homophobia and others had emerged, Kick It Out was still, he said, a pivotal part of that battle. Football had a 'mobbish' culture, he said, and if you weren't part of the mob, you might feel you weren't welcome – Kick It Out was there to provide a space where they felt valued and wanted.

Troy had started his work with Kick It Out as a volunteer, with a background in teaching and business management. He'd been a non-league manager, a coach, worked in an academy structure, and had bags of experience, but said he wanted a change and to influence football in a different way. He happened across the organisation by chance at an event, and just felt that he could help. Since then, he said, he hadn't looked back.

I felt it was highly likely that Troy, as a black man in the UK, would have experienced racism in his time, which presumably made the work he did feel very personal. But I wondered if having a son who was at the front line of that increasingly hostile environment made it all the more personal, still.

'Unfortunately, the theme of racism has been part of my life. You know, it's been part of the journey I've been on in regards to football and in regards to just life in general; you know, that different colour skin, that perception that's out there,' he agreed, adding 'but mainly in my footballing journey is where it's probably had the biggest impact.'

Andros had a few experiences in his professional career, Troy told me, one of which he hadn't actually known about at the time, when he had been taking a corner at Selhurst Park and had been racially abused by an Everton fan. While Andros was oblivious to what was going on behind him, the stewards had spotted it and the perpetrator was in court six months later. In that court case, Darren Chadwick was convicted of racially aggravated assault, fined £1,050 plus ordered to pay £625 in costs and banned from attending football matches for three years.*

Another experience, however, overshadowed his England debut in 2013 – a debut which had seen England qualify for the 2014 World Cup, and in which Andros had scored.

The incident in question involved then manager Roy Hodgson – who was at the time I spoke to Troy, Andros' manager at Crystal Palace – who made a joke during the half-time break about a monkey and an astronaut.[†] Andros had thought nothing of it – and indeed came out in defence of the manager afterwards – as had at least the majority of his teammates, though the comments were leaked to the press and became front-page news.

Hodgson had denied any offence had been intended and said that perhaps 'some of the younger players may not have understood the reference to the monkey in space'.

Troy did not think the comment had been racist, rather it perhaps underlined some ignorance by Hodgson of racist language. It was doubly unfortunate, Troy thought, because this became the focus of the press, not the achievement of Andros and his teammates.

Andros himself had said at the time: 'The manager just told the players to give the ball to me, so that's a compliment.'

---

* https://www.cps.gov.uk/london-south/news/everton-football-fan-convicted-hate-crime

† https://www.mirror.co.uk/sport/football/news/read-england-boss-roy-hodgsons-2461245

Adding: 'Everyone should be focusing on England qualifying for Brazil [the 2014 World Cup] – not on negative silly news.'*

'I'm not for one minute stating that Roy Hodgson is a racist at all,' Troy said. 'But now, obviously, we've all got to get up to speed with that language and terminology and realise that, in the day and age that it was – and still is – that it wasn't acceptable.'

I didn't remember this particular incident, which – despite the headlines at the time – seemed to have been fairly innocuous, from what Troy said and from what I went on to read about it. Perhaps more surprising to me, reading from a contemporary perspective, was the *tone* of what had been written about it at the time.

Then the BBC's sports editor, David Bond, referred to it as 'one of football's most bizarre controversies', which on the scale of bizarre incidents in football, just wasn't even nearly true, either.

In a separate article he had written: 'It's interesting how febrile the issue of race is in football. I think certainly in football after the John Terry–Anton Ferdinand case, people can be very sensitive to race issues. Raising awareness is a good thing, but are we being overly sensitive about these things?'†

It was astonishing to me that these views were published *by the BBC* only eight years ago. In 2021, for a white sports editor to have been so roundly dismissive of an alleged racist incident, worse still, imply that black people would have had *no right* to take offence at something, just would not fly.

---

* https://www.bbc.co.uk/sport/football/24577352

† https://www.bbc.co.uk/sport/football/24563131

In the last season at Charlton, I had overheard one troubling comment, but it had seemed more indicative of ignorance rather than malice, in my opinion, and part of a private conversation rather than directed at a player or fan.

'Who's that coming on?' a man behind us had asked his friend as a substitution was being made. 'I can never tell if it's [Deji] Oshilaja or Chuks [Aneke].'

It was an utterly ridiculous statement, given how completely different the two black players were in appearance. For a start, Aneke was *significantly* taller than Oshilaja. It was genuinely harder to tell two of the team's white defenders, Tom Lockyer and Jason Pearce, apart, even at close range.

It was hard to know what to do with a comment like that, which was indicative of a more pervasive kind of racism, without feeling able to ask the perpetrator 'are you fucking mad?', or perhaps something more polite. But of course, it meant that this attitude – and probably many more of a similar sort – would go unchecked.

'There's no more excuses anymore,' Troy told me when I asked him if intent was important – not regarding this specific incident, but in general – when it came to racism. 'I'm fed up of "I didn't understand. I didn't know. I wasn't sure."'

'There should be accountability for everything that comes out of anyone's mouth. You know, if I post something on a social media platform that has any kind of connotations around discrimination, I would expect to lose my job. If you start blurring the lines, you give people get-outs.'

But just because this was the only comment I'd heard, it didn't mean there weren't others, around the stadium.

In a season which had been cut significantly short, in terms of fans' physical attendance at matches, discriminatory incidents across the professional game in 2019/20 that had been reported to Kick It Out had increased by 42 per cent. The year before, they had risen by 32 per cent.*

I had seen, frequently, on social media, for example, non-white people expressing some understandable scorn at the surprise of white people when racist incidents were reported in the press.

'We have always experienced this,' the message seemed to be. 'You just haven't been paying attention to it.'

I wondered if this was the case in terms of the increasing reports. Were the number of incidents increasing, or were systems for reporting better?

'For the last eight years, reports of discrimination have been on the rise and racism has been a real focal point of that,' Troy told me.

'Reporting mechanisms are better – there's no doubt,' he continued. 'We've got a reporting app that's available and that if you're in a ground, you can report discrimination to us anonymously. So if you know your seat number and you're aware of the row and the seat number of someone who's spouting their ignorance, you can actually tap that in directly. So that means that we can home in exactly on the individual, and work with the football clubs in doing that.'

The different leagues also had their own reporting mechanisms, as did a few other organisations, he told me. However, the focus now, with fans having been largely absent from stadiums from March 2020 up to the end of the 2020/21 season, had shifted to social media, where racism was flourishing.

'But if you work in this space, you kind of know that,'

* https://www.kickitout.org/pages/faqs/category/reporting-statistics

he told me, explaining that this online problem wasn't new. Additionally, he said that the focus online was detracting attention away from the increasing number of incidents in stadiums – an increase we currently had no reason to think wouldn't continue once fans were back in stadiums.

'People have forgotten the fact that there were still many, many situations where players were being victimised on football pitches that were not being dealt with appropriately, that were very challenging and it was showing that football still has a massive problem in this space,' he told me.

'So I would probably say that this is just a continuation of what's always existed and has never been dealt with effectively or appropriately.'

The perpetrators of these incidents were not being dealt with appropriately, Troy thought, and I had to agree, that the punishments for those found to have racially abused players were nowhere near harsh enough – perhaps a huge part of the reason that the problem did not seem to be improving. In the case of the Everton fan who had abused Troy's son, for example, why was he only subject to a three-year ban?

And that was if the incident *was* recorded as racially motivated. There were others, which were not, Troy said, giving the example of a Spurs fan who had thrown a banana on the pitch at the Emirates Stadium after Pierre-Emerick Aubameyang scored for Arsenal during the 2018 North London derby, but denied it had been racist. The incident had been recorded as a 'missile', and he was not charged with a racially aggravated public order offence.

'If that was abroad, we would have absolutely gone to town on it, but it happens in England and we call it a missile,' he said to me, understandably frustrated.

It was a fair point, and one that any number of public figures had made in recent years – when complaining about the treatment of black players abroad, we often failed to acknowledge the mess that had been going on at home. It was classic English exceptionalism again, in the same way that we would argue we didn't have a race problem because we weren't *America*.

'That's not a coin. It's not a bottle – and I'm not condoning those things, by the way,' he continued. 'But I'm saying that this banana has a direct correlation with the history around black people and what they've been called for many, many a year.

'The press called it a missile when the gentleman – *gentleman* I've called him – went to a court of law,' he chuckled, as he corrected himself.

'He was *charged* with throwing a missile,' he continued. 'He got a four-year banning order because it was a *missile* and he got an extra £100 on his fine *just in case*, as he was throwing that banana, he had some thoughts about racism.'

We both shook our heads.

'The football process, the media process, the law enforcement process – none of them called it racism,' he went on. 'So if we're not going to call it racism at that point when it's blatantly obvious and in our face, when are we going to decide and who is it that decides that it is racist or not? I'll tell you for now, that it is.'

The banana *was* a missile, but I found it hard to believe that a football fan would fail to understand the specific connotations of throwing a banana on the pitch. I supposed, though, I told him, as a counter-argument, that from a legal perspective at least, it would be quite hard to *definitively* prove intent. Though the police had charged the perpetrator with throwing a 'missile', the court did find there had been a racial element to the 'targeted' gesture.*

'I understand, of course, that whenever we discuss racism, there's always a legal point of view,' Troy began. 'And you can talk to me and talk to people that have been victimised like me, our discussion around racism always comes from a legal perspective.

'It's been presented to me on more than enough occasions – my experience is not a legal case,' he added.

And this was a big part of the problem for those who experienced racism or other forms of discrimination within that culture of exceptionalism – it was one that I could relate to as a woman, certainly. Perhaps you couldn't always pinpoint *precisely* why something was sexist or racist – although in this case it was abundantly clear – but if you'd experienced it, you just *knew*. Why, then, were there swathes of people ready to tell you that you had misunderstood your own experience when you spoke of it?

Marvin Sordell, who I had spoken to about his experiences as a footballer, also cited racism as a contributory factor in his decision to retire at the age of 28. It was, he said, also a contributory factor to the poor state of his own mental health. It was a commentary that ran throughout society, and his football career, he said, and it was so much deeper than just words and phrases.

Football had probably changed quite a lot in the last few years Marvin had thought, in this respect particularly, but in

....

* https://www.standard.co.uk/news/crime/tottenham-fan-who-threw-banana-at-arsenal-s-pierreemerick-aubameyang-fined-ps500-after-magistrates-ruled-it-was-racist-a4020606.html

his time, it was what he called an 'old school' environment. He had endured racism at the hands of coaches and fellow players alike, he said, and by no means just the people shouting on the terraces or on social media. The insidious nature of the discrimination he suffered here, he said, was particularly damaging.

'When we talk about stereotypes,' Marvin said. 'These things can alter how somebody sees themselves, as well as the way you see them. If you tell someone something enough, they'll believe it.'

In his own mind, he said, he was constantly battling the perception that others had of him, and what he began to feel about himself.

'It takes a lot of energy when people are saying you're this, you're that, and I'm having to overexert myself in proving that I'm not these things, outwardly as well as inwardly. That's both damaging and exhausting.'

As an example of the kind of attitude he'd come up against, he told me it could be something really innocuous, like wearing a tracksuit – essentially the uniform of a footballer.

He could have been wearing exactly the same tracksuit as anyone else, he said, and of course, very often, he *was*. But, for example, when it was raining and he had his hood up, someone had joked 'Careful – he might rob you!'

That wasn't even a microaggression so much as it was an outwardly racist joke, but it was this and other similar experiences that built up, that weren't necessarily easy to pinpoint, but constantly took up headspace in negotiating. This was the stuff that I frequently saw other people on social media claiming wasn't a real problem. For the most part, I didn't think it was malicious, it was more because people who hadn't actually experienced it couldn't identify it in the same way that Marvin, for example, could.

'It's fine to not understand it,' Marvin said. 'You still need to show empathy. If I had a collection of women saying to me, I've said something and they find that harmful, then I have to listen to that because regardless of what I think, sometimes you need to unlearn what you think you already know. I think that's so important for football and for society as well, because we can't move forward unless we correct the mistakes of the past.

'If we think we know something about a certain demographic and that demographic collectively tells us that is wrong – we have to listen to them.'

Another one of the problems in the game, Troy thought, was that the conversations were always about the perpetrators. To some extent that was fair, I reasoned, if we were ever going to get to the nub of why it was happening and how we could stop it, but it invariably meant that there was less conversation about the victims of these crimes.

'We talk far too much about what I'm going to do, what you're going to do, what we're going to do. And, you know, they're not doing enough, FIFA are not doing enough – whatever they're doing,' Troy began. 'But what about the victims in all of these processes who are now being discussed in so many different circles publicly? But not with any kind of appropriate empathy, I would say.'

He also thought that not enough consideration was given to the impact these incidents had on the families of players. Families who also had to live through it, in the public discourse around the events.

He highlighted one incident in particular, the European Super Cup final, played in 2019 by Liverpool, as the Champions

League winners that year, and Chelsea, the Europa League winners. Liverpool won the match on penalties after Chelsea's Tammy Abraham missed in the shoot-out, and consequently Abraham received a torrent of racist abuse.

'Tammy was like, "I don't read it, it's fine, not a problem,"' Troy told me. 'Then he spoke to his mum and immediately the first thing she said was, "Why are people talking about you like that?"'

Because it was on the news, and everyone was talking about it, even if Tammy Abraham's mum *hadn't* seen it, someone she knew was going to have seen it, and bring it to her attention, he said.

'I think a lot of it is also fuelled by the lazy narratives and tones that have existed in our media circles for far too long,' he continued. 'One minute it's a story, the next minute it's not a story.'

Again, I couldn't argue with him. Certain factions of the press were always going to cover the incidents in Europe when England played, or the huge public uproars when Raheem Sterling or another player at a top club was *actually pictured* receiving abuse on our screens. However, those very same publications were going to continue to fuel hatred among a divided public, or hound public figures, for no apparent reason other than their skin tone.

In his time, according to the press, Raheem Sterling had been too 'bling', too lavish, not lavish enough, had glorified gun crime, and much, much more. Perhaps they couldn't do it to Raheem Sterling any more; after he'd called out the press attention he'd received as racist, and the public had roundly backed him. But they were sure as hell going to do it to someone else.

In fact, in 2015 the United Nations Human Rights Commissioner Zeid Ra'ad Al Hussein called out UK tabloids specifically, and urged authorities to tackle hate speech published by them, in the wake of an article for *The Sun* written by former *Apprentice* contestant Katie Hopkins, in which she referred to migrants as 'cockroaches'. *

Sterling, Abraham and their peers were high-profile victims, for the most part, but what about the people sitting at home watching? There had to be a level of transferred trauma for those witnessing the abuse of people who looked like them too, right? It would be upsetting, I assumed.

'Listen,' Troy began. 'I think it would be upsetting for most human beings to be totally honest, no matter what their background.

'People who have been educated to understand and appreciate difference and the contributions of everybody to society will see that and know the impact, and will be impacted *by* it because they will first and foremost be feeling it for the individual or group of people who it's targeted at.

'But the thing I'm saying is, if we can't get the first bit right, how are we ever going to deal with the fallout, the rest of it? I don't think football has the capacity to deal with it or even appreciates it enough to.'

Another area where the victims were not big names was in the grassroots game, over which Kick It Out also presided. It was the section of the game that was most like natural society, he said, and it was 'like the Wild West'.

---

* https://www.bbc.co.uk/news/uk-32446673

'It's a free for all,' he told me. 'And in it being a free for all, the damage that it does to the people on the end of whatever kind of victimisation is almost irreparable.'

With the incidents in the public eye, I thought, you could at least put pressure on groups to effect change and embarrass the likes of the FA or FIFA, or the league bodies. With a lot of issues of discrimination in society, one hoped that with the passage of time, things would incrementally improve, and that was probably either a pessimistic or optimistic view, depending very much on your own life experience. But I wondered how you could realistically effect change for a ten-year-old boy in Essex, for example, who'd been racially abused on a Thursday evening at an after-school football club?

'That is the tough one, isn't it?' he mused. 'Ultimately this is a hate crime. So if you've been victimised, it's a hate crime. But I understand if you're in a football environment, how do you report that? *Do* you report it? Does that bring more hatred towards you and then maybe extend it to your family?

'But. In terms of football's responsibility, football needs to be stronger in the sanctions and the way that it deals with individuals and groups of people, and if it was, then maybe the message will be stronger that it's not allowed in our game. It will *not* happen in our game, regardless of whether you're a young person, boy or girl, you know, trying to live out your dream and become the professional or whether you are a seasoned pro.

'The sanctions and the actions in regards to how we deal with these incidents have never been appropriate,' he added.

Press aside, it was hard not to look at the world around us and present various hypotheses as to what was driving what felt like the growing, or at least increasingly visible problem of racism. In Boris Johnson, we had a prime minister who had, prior to his premiership, publicly made overtly racist comments about Muslim women* and black people.[†] We had seen the creation of a 'hostile environment' by former Home Secretary, also later elevated to the role of prime minister, Theresa May, towards immigrants. She literally said: 'The aim is to create, here in Britain, a really hostile environment for illegal immigrants.'[‡]

We had seen an enormously divisive campaign around the Brexit referendum over the UK's membership of the European Union, from which I feared we would never recover. We had seen, in the five years from 2015 to 2020, reports of hate crimes more than double.[§]

But while he thought there was *something* to these hypotheses, after all, football didn't exist in a vacuum, Troy came back to the fact that the situation wasn't actually new.

'It's *always* been driven,' he said. 'So it's actually never gone away.'

For example, Troy could remember the very real threat of the National Front, when he was a young man in London.

'They always seem to go underneath the radar and then raise their ugly head at particular moments in time,' he continued, referring to perpetrators of racism. 'It's not a footballing issue, it's a societal issue.

....

* https://www.bbc.co.uk/news/uk-politics-45083275

[†] https://www.theguardian.com/politics/2008/jan/23/london.race

[‡] https://www.jcwi.org.uk/the-hostile-environment-explained

[§] https://www.gov.uk/government/statistics/hate-crime-england-and-wales-2019-to-2020/hate-crime-england-and-wales-2019-to-2020

'I suppose it's never feeling confident and comfortable that the political parties represent you – who we are as a community – as an English black person.

'I was born in this country, you know; my parents are from Jamaica, but I've never *been* there. I want to feel valued in the same way that anyone would, because this is the country I was born in, my children have grown up in – they were born here,' he explained.

He gave the Windrush scandal as an example. A situation which emerged in 2017 after Commonwealth citizens who had emigrated to the UK on their parents' passports and had been given indefinite leave to remain at the time ended up being wrongly detained and deported from the UK.

Members of Troy's close family friends had been affected, he said, and boarded onto planes after living in England for more than 50 years, never to return. We had heard a lot about the Windrush scandal in the press, I thought, but we didn't hear so much about the people who'd been deported and never made it back.

'Because we're very good at sweeping things under the carpet, making it go away, you know, not having it on the agenda any more,' he said, arguing that the topic of racism would periodically become 'sexy' and important, and something that people wrote about – until they didn't, any more.

'It's now no longer making the news because we've done it,' he said, still talking about the Windrush scandal. 'We've covered it. We don't need to know any more. And that's very similar to how football treats, I'll just say the black experience or the experience of black and Asian people, in our game.'

The issue of race, however, was – certainly at the moment – rarely out of the news, particularly in relation to football. In light of the killing of George Floyd, a black man, at the hands of policemen in Minnesota in late May of 2020, there had been a huge outpouring of public grief, particularly from the black community. Protests took place up and down the UK as they had in the US, and a statue of merchant and slave trader Edward Colston was torn down and thrown into Bristol Harbour, and for a moment, at least, it felt like this might actually be a pivotal moment in the progression of racial equality.

In solidarity with the Black Lives Matter movement, Premier League footballers decided to take the knee, as NFL player Colin Kaepernick had done in the US, ahead of their matches once the league resumed in June, and the other returning leagues followed suit. Kaepernick had originally taken the knee during the national anthem, which was sung ahead of NFL games, and most other sporting events in the US, because he said he didn't want to show pride in a flag that was symbolic of the oppression of black people and other people of colour.

That gesture continued into the 2020/21 season, in English football, but it wasn't universally welcomed. Of course, the 'all lives matter' brigade were out in force, arguing that the movement was somehow racist against white people, unable or unwilling to understand that there was little question as to whether or not white lives mattered, and that this was entirely the reason it didn't need saying.

Someone felt strongly enough about the issue, in fact, to hire a plane flying a banner stating 'White Lives Matter Burnley' over the Etihad Stadium for the Lancashire side's first game back after Project Restart, against Manchester City. It was impossible, for me at least, not to feel immense joy in the fact that City went on to beat them 5-0 that day. The act felt like a really extreme public commitment to being a total bellend, to me.

There were a few incidents at matches during the 2020/21 season as well, for example at Millwall and Colchester United. Booing was not, of course, in itself provably racist and certainly not illegal, and so no formal action could be taken, though different clubs took entirely different approaches to the incidents on their own turf. At Colchester, chairman Robbie Cowling told fans to stay silent or stay away, adding that they were 'not welcome' at the club.

At Millwall, on the other hand, having initially condemned the booing by fans, within three days of the incident, the club had announced instead that players would no longer take the knee. They would instead link arms. Millwall fans denied the reaction was racist, of course, and instead it was in protest to the 'Marxist' politics the movement was aligned with – a criticism that seemed to stem from one of the founders, Patrisse Cullors, referring to herself and another co-founder as 'trained Marxists' in a 2015 interview, recently unearthed.

These were not wholly unpredictable areas in which fans had taken against the gesture, I thought. Millwall's history spoke for itself, and having grown up in the Colchester area, I told Troy, I could vouch that it was not exactly what I would call the *birthplace* of tolerance. But the club's response had been strong.

'The club's response was *brilliant*,' he agreed. 'And I'll tell you what, if that response had been from a Premier League club, it would have gone all around the world.'

The reaction in the Premier League had been broadly supportive, but it trailed off in some areas as you got lower down the leagues, he said, echoing what Bhavisha had told me.

There was a lot of misunderstanding about Black Lives Matter, as far as I could tell. For a start, for most people, to align themselves with Black Lives Matter was more about aligning with a movement rather than any specific organisation.

Another central misunderstanding that many found objectionable, it seemed, was the concept of 'defunding the police'. I personally didn't want to defund the police much, either, to be honest, if it was meant in the same way that Laurence Fox and Noel Edmonds wanted to defund the BBC. The idea of a lawless, anarchic society was as unpalatable to many 'leftie snowflakes' such as myself, as it apparently was to Millwall fans. However, that wasn't really what it meant.

The concept of defunding the police was more about moving funds away from police departments that had historically added to the oppression of non-white people, and instead investing in other organisations that could enhance public safety through means such as education, youth services, social services, etc. Though admittedly, that was unlikely to appeal universally across different political persuasions.

After a while, players began to come out against taking the knee as well. Some – such as Lyle Taylor – for the reasons we discussed. Others, such as Ivorian-British Crystal Palace forward, Wilfried Zaha, said he found the gesture 'degrading', and that his parents had taught him to 'stand tall' and be proud of his heritage.* Another not unreasonable criticism was that the gesture was toothless if nothing was actually going to be done to tackle racism in the game by the relevant governing bodies and league structures.

I wondered what Troy thought, in particular about Lyle Taylor's comments which – though he had been very clear he

---

* https://www.theguardian.com/football/2021/feb/18/wilfried-zaha-declares-he-will-stop-taking-a-knee-crystal-palace

meant were political and in no way because he didn't agree with the sentiment that black lives mattered – had been picked up by unsavoury right-wing characters. The problem with this was that, as a mixed-race man saying it, it seemed to give some legitimacy to their views.

'Nigel Farage didn't jump on what Wilf said, that's for sure, but definitely jumped on what Lyle said,' he began.

'I know Lyle, as a human being, and to me that's all that matters,' he told me. 'I think sometimes when players do interviews, they maybe don't really fully appreciate the consequence of some of the words that come out and what it might do outside of their own circle.

'I just think it's a tough one, because I think the focusing in all the wrong areas and conversation around taking the knee, you know, the conversation around Black Lives Matter and putting it against a Marxist organisation or political group.

'The reason why they created Black Lives Matter in sports and in football, is because collectively as a group of players, they wanted to talk about football and how it had treated racial inequality,' he explained. 'They wanted to turn the focus back on to football and say we need to start seeing some real tangible actions because we're fed up as a group of people, as a group of, you know, players that play for all different football clubs from all different backgrounds.'

It was hard to find fault with that, I thought, especially when Troy put it in those terms. But ultimately, if no tangible actions were being taken, I wondered what he thought the point of it was?

'That point to me is to keep it in people's faces,' he told me, matter-of-factly.

'I deliver education,' he reminded me. 'So I show a clip where the whistle blows, everything goes silent around the ground, and everyone says it's the most powerful thing they've seen in football.

'It's the most powerful thing *I've* seen and continue to witness,' he added.

The beauty of taking the knee, he thought, was that on this occasion, unlike on so many other occasions when society had just moved on to the next thing, having this at the start of every match kept the conversation going.

'They can never actually get away from this if the players continue to take the knee whilst saying, "But actually, you're still not providing any action. We still feel vulnerable. We still are getting collectively abused on social media. We still don't feel we're being backed enough,"' he explained, echoing some of the sentiments he had heard, or perhaps felt himself.

'The knee is the part of the awareness – the conversation flows from that,' he added.

Marvin Sordell agreed with Troy's analysis.

'The act itself, if you completely isolate it, it's meaningless,' Marvin said. 'Somebody taking the knee doesn't do anything, it doesn't stop anything, doesn't make any difference. But what it represents is us having to have a conversation. If players stopped taking the knee, people just forget about it, they can just push it to the side and park it and they can ignore it.

'You know, the comment of "everything is offensive these days",' he went on. 'Well, for a start, it's completely subjective – what is offensive and what isn't – because it depends on that person and how they receive it. Secondly, the reason why a lot more things seem offensive these days is because people are being called out on what is and has *always* been offensive.

'These statues, for example,' he said, referring to those criticised during 2020's Black Lives Matter protests, but for much longer than that as well. The Colston statue, for example, had been the subject of a lengthy local campaign for its removal.*

'They've *always* been a problem. We just didn't have to think about it.'

I asked Troy how we could be better allies against racism, in football. He immediately put me straight. It wasn't him who should be coming up with the solutions, he told me.

'I just think sometimes everyone has to take ownership of their own space. If you feel it's important enough to have an opinion, to educate yourself, to learn a little bit more, to understand a little bit more – now is the time,' he added.

He echoed what I had heard a lot over the past year, that not being racist wasn't good enough – you had to be actively anti-racist, and you had to call it out where you saw it.

Kick It Out had recently launched a campaign called 'Take A Stand', he told me, which asked individuals, clubs and communities to take ownership. It asked the question – what would you like to see as change? And what would you be doing in your own environment to create change?

'A collective voice is so much stronger than an isolated voice, you know,' he told me. 'And I think that's what we've got to do – start creating collective voices and appreciate that people will be at different stages of their understanding on that journey as well, and see how we can go from there.'

But it wasn't all awful, he reminded me.

....

* https://www.theguardian.com/uk-news/2020/jun/14/the-day-bristol-dumped-its-hated-slave-trader-in-the-docks-and-a-nation-began-to-search-its-soul

'Whilst we're identifying the fact that there are some – what do you want me to call them?' he mused. 'Idiots might be the best term to describe people who will go and enter a stadium or go and post on social media, their absolute ignorance. We've got to remember that they're outweighed by the many, many thousands of millions who actually watch the game because of their love of it.

'But that small group of people, as they will be in the grand scheme of things, seem to have the loudest voice,' he added.

He was right, I thought. It was easy to go on Twitter for a bit and think that everyone was an arsehole, but in reality, that small number of arseholes were just incredibly loud.

'I said idiot,' he laughed. '*You* said arsehole.'

PROJECT RESTART

June:
Hull City v Charlton Athletic (P)

And just like that – much like the end of lockdown itself – football was back, the biggest anti-climax of the year, in a year where everything and nothing had happened. On 20 June at just ten days old, Lyra sat down to watch her first ever Charlton Athletic match. Or rather she slept in my arms, wearing a slightly baggy Charlton Athletic babygrow, completely oblivious to the lifetime of misery she was silently being inducted into. Of course the match day experience was rather different in this brave new world, watched on TV, with no crowds present.

Hull sat just one place above us in the league, hovering just two points from the relegation zone and today's match felt crucial. Another six-pointer, though with fewer than ten points dividing the relegation zone and fourteenth place, almost every match was a six-pointer, now.

We were to hurtle through the remaining part of the season, and without Lyle Taylor. I had been blasé about Taylor's inevitable departure at the end of the season – back then I had not unreasonably thought we were playing with Abu Dhabi riches – but this was an entirely different story. We had some promising players I thought, but not a natural goalscorer such as he had been for us.

Eighteen minutes in, Jason Pearce scored to put us ahead. We kept the lead, and I had to admit – we actually looked all right. Lyra occasionally opened her eyes, but not even my anxious shouting was enough to rouse her in any significant way.

As we edged towards the end of the first half, Deji Oshilaja senselessly gave away a free kick in a dangerous area. At the exact same time, Lyra's backside began to rumble suspiciously, and it soon became obvious that she was doing an enormous poo – she spoke for us all. Yet despite her apparent nerves, we somehow managed to clear the ball.

We maintained the lead right up until the end of the match, and my heart sank as the referee declared four minutes of added time. We'd pretty much had no less than four minutes of added time the *whole season*, and historically, this seemed to be when we were most vulnerable. *Especially when we were doing all right*. Though I could hardly bear to watch, the whistle blew without event, and we had won our first match back by an underwhelming 1-0. Suddenly, having been suspended in it for more than three months, we were out of the relegation zone.

June:
Charlton Athletic v QPR (P)

As I sat down with Lyra for our second match back in action, I was feeling pretty optimistic after our first outing. Lyra's eyes had opened up a bit more in the last couple of days and at least initially, she seemed vaguely interested in what was going on in front of her, even if it had been short-lived, and resulted in another absolute stinker by her. Nonetheless, we seemed to be playing relatively well again.

With the matches being shown on The Valley Pass – which I had watched a fair few times before it became the *only* way to watch games – match day was a slightly less slick production than many football fans would have been used to, although this way it had a distinctly Charlton feel to it and, as Charlton had come to mean to me, a more familial vibe.

The commentary team comprised of Terry Smith and Greg Stubley. Having not been around for the advent of The Valley Pass, which must have happened during my wilderness era, I wasn't entirely sure where these chaps had come from, but they were very obviously fans, which gave the coverage an endearing quality.

During this particular match there seemed to be quite a lot of admin going on – if we could hear wind, we were told, that was because it was windy. If we were wondering where the shout-outs were, these were scheduled for the drinks break – a curious Covid-related measure, the science behind which I remained somewhat unclear on.

There was some confusion and possibly displeasure relating

to the timekeeping of said drinks break. I later came to learn that this was when one commentator would routinely say they were handing over to the other, despite the fact that they both always seemed to then remain on air for the duration of the match.

In terms of the football itself, Darren Pratley had scored in the twelfth minute and that was as good as we were going to get, this match. There was, however, some decent football going on, and some great defending. I'd have been lying if I'd said I was anything other than surprised.

We kept our lead and at 88 minutes in, I feared the inevitable twenty minutes of stoppage time, but as the whistle blew, we were still 1-0 up, and we'd even withstood a reasonable amount of pressure. I hoped very much that our keeper Dillon Phillips wasn't one of the 10,000 players whose contract was up at the end of the season, because I knew we would miss him if he left, which he would have to if we were relegated.

But in that moment, relegation seemed a long way off. We had two 1-0 back-to-back wins under our belt, and once again we'd done it on much worse statistics, and much less possession. I didn't know how we'd done it, but I would take it, and Lyra woke up again just in time to witness the end.

•

By the time of Charlton's next match three days later, I found myself at my mum's house in Harwich. She had demanded my return following several tearful late-night phone calls and a projectile vomit too far, which had broken the proverbial camel's back. Vera had also come from Worthing to see me through the harrowing early weeks of new parenthood and join our little bubble, taking it in turns to hold the baby while I slept for an hour here and there.

They fell, of course, instantly in love with her, a tiny, squeaky beacon of hope in such a strange and troubling time, and cards, flowers and knitwear began to flood in from my mum's friends and our extended Harwich family, of sorts. It was times like these when you truly realised the value of family, those you were related to by blood as well as the ones you had taken it upon yourself to call your own, much like we did in football.

'The Charlton Way' – Jason on the Charlton Athletic Community Trust

The Charlton Athletic Community Trust (CACT) as it is now known, was set up in 1992, just a couple of months before the club returned to their spiritual home of The Valley. Jason Morgan, now the chief executive of what has evolved into the club's charitable arm, had worked for the Trust since it was established, originally as the community officer – in fact he was actually in the meeting in which then managers Steve Gritt and Alan Curbishley told their players about the impending move.

Jason's dad had been the sports development officer at Haringey Council, and he'd worked with him in various capacities in a sort of extended work experience programme during his school and college education. He understood, he said, and felt passionately about the role sport could play in delivering social change, and the responsibility of football clubs to use their platforms to do just that. When he left college he got his first full-time job at Redbridge Council in a similar sports development role, moving around a bit until he eventually got the job at Charlton.

Back in 1992, the Trust was known as the Community Programme, and was a partnership between the club and the Professional Footballers' Association (PFA). It came about off the back of a 1986 recommendation in the report by Mr Justice Popplewell, following his inquiry into the Bradford City stadium fire of 1985. The recommendation was cited again, along with the others it had made, by Lord Justice Taylor, in his later inquiry into stadium safety in the wake of the Hillsborough Disaster.

Popplewell's 37th recommendation set out that:*

'Players should be encouraged by the clubs to extend their voluntary public relations work in the community including personal appearances at youth clubs etc. and coaching sessions in schools with the objects of promoting the game and the concept of good sportsmanship.'

As a result, the PFA came up with the seed funding for an officer to be placed at every football club in the country, by covering their salary for three years. After that, the idea was that the community programme would become self-sufficient, or the club would fund them.

For Jason, he reckoned it was extremely fortunate that this new role coincided with the return to The Valley, and the club's willingness to re-engage with the community. In particular, the lost generation of supporters who, Jason said, knew nothing about the club.

They had obviously done a good job, because the club was now known almost as much for its community work as for its football. In fact, I had often heard the Community Trust referred to as one of the better community engagement programmes in football.

You might suppose that the Trust's work would have been impacted on by the many ups and downs in the 29 years since

----

* https://www.jesip.org.uk/uploads/media/incident_reports_and_inquiries/
Hillsborough%20Stadium%20Disaster%20final%20report.pdf, p. 102

their return to The Valley. In fact there is still some funding for the community engagement work of Premier League clubs, though Charlton lost this when they were relegated. However, having worked hard to ensure they were never reliant on only one source of funding, and to build up good local partnerships, the programme had continued to flourish.

After ten years of what became known as 'Football in the Community', lots of clubs began setting up their own charities to progress this work. The decision was taken by the board that Charlton would set up the Community Trust, under which there would be different programmes, and Football in the Community was one. Other strands included the community liaison department, the women's and girls' programme, and anti-racism initiatives set up in the aftermath of the 1993 murder of Stephen Lawrence in nearby Eltham.

Even with supporters away from matches during Covid, the club were still seeking to raise awareness of various issues, via their newly revamped Valley Pass, which had subsequently been rebranded as Charlton TV, including conversations around homophobia and men's health, for example, during half-time on match days.

Going back to Jason's belief that football could be a great force for societal change, there was a better understanding of that now, he thought, compared to when the Trust was first established, though it could be frustrating when people didn't get it.

'It's not just wearing a shirt and trotting out on the pitch,' he said.

In fact, even when the announcement was made in March 2020 that the nation was going into its first Covid-necessitated lockdown, the Trust was called on straight away by the local council, wanting to know how quickly their call centre could be scaled up as a single point of contact for the borough.

'We did that within three days,' he told me, 'and provided that much-needed support around shopping, prescriptions, comfort and reassurance on the phones.

'I'm a great believer that the football clubs are the hub of the community,' he said. 'They should be outward-facing, you know, traditionally, go back, all those years ago, football clubs play a game, shut the gates, and it's "See you in two weeks' time."'

'All of a sudden, stadiums evolved, where they became classrooms, youth schemes, crèches, you know, and The Valley was very much like that. [It was] developed with function rooms and classrooms and it's got one of our youth hubs down there, a health hub, the call centre.

'We very much adopted that stance, reached out into our local community, broke down barriers, worked with community groups to bring them together, that kind of level playing field, and we've still got that responsibility.'

The work the Trust was doing was yielding results, tracked by a monitoring and evaluation scheme in order to help them continue to successfully bid for funding.

'I suppose that's what kept funding coming to us and allowed us to continue to grow,' he told me. 'A bit of a reputational theme, a bit of longevity and partnerships, but also evidence of what we do.'

Bookended, Alan Dryland had told me, 'by the splendours of Greenwich and the other qualities of Woolwich', where he now lived himself, Charlton was historically an industrial area. The change in Charlton, said Alan, was not from gentrification as such, rather deindustrialisation.

Notably, there had been a large factory owned by German electronic company, Siemens, on Bowater Road, by the riverside. The initial factory had been completed in 1911, and added to during the Second World War, but it closed its doors in 1968 with a loss of around 6,000 jobs.* Now a Grade II listed building, the factory had long been abandoned. Alan was not sure what the latest plan for it was, he told me, probably flats.

Of course, it's where the club began, he told me, explaining there was a patch of wasteland called Siemens Meadow, where in 1905, on 9 June, 'a bunch of lads' got together and formed a football club. If she had been just a little bit speedier, in fact, my daughter would have ended up sharing a birthday with Charlton Athletic.

It was a rare formation of a club, Alan told me, as they tended to be attached to companies or churches. This was quite simply 'a group of lads'.

As was the case with much of the UK, the traditional industries in the area had died. Much of the riverside area had been built over with flats and other shops.

There was a split, Alan said, between the top and the bottom of the hill, as was so often the case, with the more 'exclusive' village area at the top.

'There have been immense changes, and of course, we're going through one at the moment with the effects of the pandemic,' Alan told me.

What didn't seem to get mentioned so much these days, he added, was Brexit, though he was 'sure' it was working negatively under the surface. I agreed.

It was a working-class area through and through, he told

---

* https://historicengland.org.uk/listing/the-list/list-entry/1468474

me, but I wondered if the reputation it had as being 'a bit Brexity', as I put it to him, was fair?

'Well, it's not so far away that we had the delights of the BNP in the '90s at Welling,' he told me.

Nonetheless, he didn't think of it as a particularly right-wing area. It was a very mixed area, he thought.

'It's incredible. I think there are over 100 different nationalities in the in the district,' he added.

I had been quite dismissive of the suggestion that Charlton had been gentrified, something which perhaps made the work the Community Trust did even more important within the local community. Though what I'd not really taken into account was the starting point, rather than where we were now, when comparing Charlton with my local Dalston, and the surrounding area. Perhaps it had not come up as quickly as fashionable Hackney, but it had, Jason said, still come up.

'I've worked in the borough, Greenwich, Bexley, tiptoeing into Kent, for quite a long time,' he said. 'So I have seen the improvements. I've seen the progress in areas: physically with buildings, improving relationships with housing associations that look at levels of security, and poverty and how that can be supported with the work that we do alongside housing developers.'

In 1992, the community programme started out with a traditional Football in the Community approach, but it evolved as the club developed a greater understanding of local issues. The work around racism was an example of that.

One of the reasons for this work was also because crowds at the club, it was felt, didn't adequately reflect the demographic of the local area, which contributed to the perception that there was a 'problem' at Charlton.

There was also a perception, he said, that stadiums weren't safe, on the back of the Taylor report, both in terms of the physical bricks and mortar environment, but also in terms of the problems of hooliganism highlighted in the report. The club worked to prove this was not the case, as well as send out a message of zero tolerance when it came to racism. In fact, in my many conversations with people involved with the club, it was clear that they were extremely proud of the work they undertook, early on in the conversation around racism in football.

There had also been a much-lauded programme in more recent years around knife crime which the Trust had worked on with the local authority, and moved towards employing youth workers and health workers as well as football coaches and putting them, he said, in Charlton tracksuits to give them a better way to reach the young people affected. This was part of the power of football.

One thing that was interesting to me was that perhaps crowds *still* didn't really reflect the diversity of the local area. Also, the idea of the lost generation of fans – there *still* weren't that many younger people in the stadium on match days. I wondered if, to a certain extent, the club was fighting a bit of a losing battle in that respect, given the far sexier Premier League clubs at the disposal of Londoners. I had myself, in my younger years, often said that I would have supported Arsenal had I chosen to support a 'good' team. Still: Charlton had once been known as the Woolwich Arsenal, so I felt I could square that circle if needs be.

The Trust had a strategy for improving the representation of youngsters at The Valley a few years ago, Jason told me. The club had, at one point, been looking to expand seating capacity at The Valley, and one of the criteria for applying for planning permission from the council for any such expansion was to demonstrate the demand. They could not have done that last season, I thought, thinking of the ever vacant 'Y' in the East Stand.

'We had a clear remit that there wasn't going to be an empty seat in the stadium,' he told me.

There were initiatives like Valley Express, which saw busloads of people coming in. There were complimentary tickets given away through football coaching grassroots programmes, and to young people as part of player appearances and the like.

There was a sound business case for it, in that an extra body in the stadium helped create an atmosphere, but also a secondary spend – programmes, drinks, perhaps something from the club shop. But also, and perhaps more importantly, if that person came along and had a good experience, they might well come back another time, and pay for it.

There was a specific drive for young fans, because you need young fans to become grown-up fans in order to sustain the club in the long term. An emotional connection with a club from a young age is an extremely lucrative asset to have in football, if you think about a lifetime of pencil cases, shirts, moving up to tickets and, eventually, the introduction of brand new emotional connections in their own kids.

One of the issues under Duchatelet's time as owner had been the unwillingness of fans to attend matches and pass on those emotional connections – fans voted with their feet, and indeed their seats.

A lot went into this drive, like summer camps in which every child was given their own Charlton shirt, and players were sent out into schools.

'Did they want to see Jason Morgan? No,' he reasoned. 'Did they want to see Carl Leaburn? Yes. Carl Leaburn saying, "Do you want to support us on Saturday? Here's some tickets," was quite a simple marketing tactic, but it worked.'

It was a smart thing to do, I thought. It's why pop bands did tours of schools, because if you were lucky enough to have your photo taken with Another Level when you were fourteen (as I did when they visited *my* school), that was the emotional connection you needed to buy their debut single when it was released (which I also did – and reader, you may judge me, but that was actually also Jay-Z's first appearance in the UK singles charts Top 10 – in many ways I was a pioneer).

Charlton may have had stiff competition, in terms of more successful London teams vying for their young, local supporters, but Jason didn't think that was it.

'What didn't wash for me at the time is, the kind of Manchester Uniteds and the Spurses, you know, young people won't go to those games. They were seeing the Manchester United and Arsenal games on the telly, but they were never going to go to Manchester or Liverpool,' he said, referring to the successful clubs of the eighties and nineties, when Charlton perhaps lost the attention of their local fan base.

Instead, the club decided being second best might have its own merits, if the local youth couldn't get to Manchester or Liverpool, or couldn't afford a ticket to Arsenal or Chelsea.

'Why not have Charlton as your second favourite team? And we would create the opportunity to go to the stadium.'

Leading the way in creating a safe, friendly environment, with a zero-tolerance approach to racism and other bad behaviour – essentially positioning Charlton as a 'family club' – was, he said, not only important, and the right thing to do, but it also created opportunities for the club.

I knew from the conversations I'd had with people at the club that there had been a very real threat to the club's existence in the last year. As fans we'd have been devastated if Charlton had gone the way of Bury or Bolton, or AFC Wimbledon all those years previously, but I wondered what the impact would have been on the local community.

'We've had our challenging times,' Jason admitted. 'The challenges that we had under Roland were tough for me personally, because previously I only knew one way of working, and that was in collaboration – the community programme was integral to the club for numerous reasons.

'I think the challenge will always be when you change ownership – especially foreign ownership – where they don't embrace the culture, they don't embrace your history and what we stand for.'

The understanding the club previously had, of its responsibility to the local area, was lost, he thought, and the running of the business and the charitable arm became disjointed.

It was often popular, I thought, to bring back familiar faces to the coaching staff at a club, such as Bowyer. Chris Powell had been another popular appointment and an unpopular sacking by Duchatelet. Did Charlton *need* that kind of connection with managers?

From the Trust's perspective, not necessarily. An unpopular signing amongst a large part of the fan base had been Iain Dowie who filled the vacant manager's role after Curbishley, fresh from a stint with local rivals Crystal Palace. But he had been extremely helpful to the Trust, Jason told me, coming in knowing the expectation that was on him and keen to replicate the relationship Curbishley had with them.

Despite the recent wilderness years, Charlton still had a reputation as a *nice* club, I thought. That was built on a lot of things, Jason told me.

'If you say to anyone, Charlton Athletic, I think if you ask ten people, probably eight of them will say "nice family club" – and that's not a bad strap line to have. But I think we've worked hard at that. I think we've had the right people at the club, we've had the right ethos, we've had the right values.'

The ethos of the club, he felt, was something instilled very strongly by Alan Curbishley, and the longevity of his tenure gave the club time to form this identity.

You only had to look at The Valley Pass, he reckoned, hosted by former player turned presenter Scott Minto, with Curbs himself as the resident pundit, and usually joined by another member of the club's golden era team's alumni, to see the pride and passion they felt about Charlton. They still loved being at the club, Jason thought. There was an expectation on players, at that time and still, that they were there to support the club and its standing in the community as well as play for it. Another part of that was knowing everyone working at the club, too.

'A player knew whoever worked in the ticket office, who was on different doors and gates on match days; that was part of it. We worked hard at that,' he told me.

It certainly *seemed*, as an outsider looking in, that he was right. Watching the old players come back and speak on The Valley Pass, speaking to Tracey, to Jason, and to other people working at the club – even just the fact that literally everyone associated with the club referred to Curbishley as 'Curbs' and

Lee Bowyer as 'Bow' – the familiarity between everyone was striking. It was telling, I thought, that so many former players were happy to maintain that connection with the club.

It was easy, I thought, to look back at those glory days, and that relatively short time we'd spent in the Premier League, and the success we saw and romanticise the club Curbs had built, but it seemed now that there were other good reasons to do so, aside from performance on the pitch.

'Because I was based here, you know, I knew the role that Curbs played as a manager, and I always applauded him for being *club* manager, not first-team manager, because he understood what his responsibilities around the club were.'

In Jason's opinion, Bowyer was much the same.

'I knew Bow when he was a kid here,' Jason said. 'Coming back here he understood Charlton and – not being corny – it's a special club, and he got it.

'You can see that he was one of Curbs' players, because he did things like Curbs, you know, he understood what was important, he said the right things and he was proactive around the club.'

To illustrate his point, Jason told me about a time, the day before the play-off semi-finals the same year, when Bowyer had been at the training ground with the team. Knowing that the Trust's Upbeats team – a team open to children, young people and adults with Down's syndrome – were playing at the ground at the time, he went and had a 45-minute kick-around with them. It wasn't stage-managed, or planned, it was just a friendly off-the-cuff gesture, and it was, he said, the Charlton way.

On the eve of the 2019 play-off final against Sunderland, Jason said he felt compelled to drop Bowyer a note.

'Not mushy,' he quickly explained. 'Just saying, "Good luck, immensely proud, you're so much like Curbs."'

It seemed to me that you couldn't get a much higher compliment in the Charlton set-up, and it may not have made Jason feel mushy, but it certainly brought a tear to my eye.

'They draped their Charlton flag on the wall and had a drink' – Andy and the pubs of Charlton

When I spoke to Andy Norman, landlord of The Rose of Denmark, as the third national lockdown drew to a close, his was one of only three pubs remaining in Charlton. The fourth, The Royal Oak, which was closer to The Valley and another home fans' pub, was due to reopen again shortly, he thought, in time for the next season.

One of those pubs was the Anchor and Hope, on the riverside. When I Googled it and had a look at the pictures, it was instantly recognisable to me as a place I had seen in a number of childhood photos. There was a particularly fetching one of me, I seemed to recall, draped around the titular Anchor, by the riverside.

It had been a hard year for pubs, and much of the hospitality industry, but he was in good spirits when we spoke, also looking forward to the publication of his first novel, *London Lottery Wars*. As he told me about his time as a publican in South East London, I wondered how many of his characters had been inspired by people he'd known in the trade.

The Rose is located on Woolwich Road, between Charlton and Greenwich, and we often walked past it on our way home from The Valley. Michael and I had tried to have a pint there once during the last season, presenting our tickets on the door as instructed, to prove our status as Charlton fans, but it had been heaving and we'd quickly moved on. Shortly thereafter I found out I was pregnant, which put an end to our post-match pints, though Michael had enjoyed refreshment there with some pals before one of the other matches.

A father of five, Andy had worked at pubs in and around the Crystal Palace area previously, and before that, when his kids were younger, he'd run a post office. He joked that he was, in this respect, the best dad ever, with a shop full of sweets when they were little, progressing to a pub full of beer by the time they'd grown up. Throw in some ponies somewhere in the middle, and I reckoned he probably would have been bang on.

He'd been the landlord of the Rose for four years and had taken over the reins during Duchatelet's regime. Andy was a football fan – though not a Charlton supporter himself.

'When I first got offered this pub,' he told me, 'a friend of mine who used to work for Greenwich Council said to me, "Charlton will be absolutely perfect for you, Andy, because in your head you seem to be living your life in the 1950s."'

I asked him about gentrification and, like Jason, he reckoned it was happening. Like a lot of people seemed to be doing in the current Covid-ravaged world in which we were living, there had been something of an exodus by older people from the area, he thought.

'The area has become very expensive to buy property, bearing in mind we've got the Tube station down the road – North Greenwich – which is one stop to Canary Wharf. So all of those people working in the City and in the banking industry are buying up a lot of property around here.'

Andy was right – I had myself been keeping a beady eye on Charlton as I was looking to upscale, with a new baby to house. I wondered if Charlton might actually still be affordable-ish, and had been surprised by the high price of new-builds on the market, though many of the older properties up for sale were still massively cheaper than Hackney.

Still, he said, there was a big Marks & Spencer now, on a nearby new retail park on the same road, and a Starbucks, and all sorts of other stuff as you got into Greenwich. There was also, as he pointed out, a Tube station now – although I wasn't really sure you could count it as particularly close, having once waddled there myself during the last season. Nonetheless, I could see it was an area of growth, or as Andy, and presumably estate agents, put it, 'up and coming'.

Having found out about the club's role in the local community from a social perspective, I was interested to know what the economic impact was as well, particularly on local businesses such as Andy's.

'Financially, it makes a huge difference to the whole area. Not just us,' he said.

As well as the other pubs, there was The Valley Café, which he thought was probably even more reliant on match-day sales than he was.

Every other week, he was enjoying what he called a 'bumper' day at the pub, while matches were played at The Valley, though it had taken a while to get there. Initially, they'd allowed away fans in as well, but he'd stopped this a short while into his tenure. This had encouraged more home fans to drink at the pub, knowing there was less risk of 'trouble' with the away fans. Now he was seeing fans in the pub before the match and again afterwards. On a match day, it was manic, he said.

'I wouldn't say without the football club we would go out of business, but let's say the football club gives us the icing on the top of the cake. It's a bit of extra turnover every couple of weeks. But other than that, it also brings in a lot of people on football day, who then get to know the pub and get to know myself and my wife, and they come back again during the week.'

As well as being loyal fans, the Charlton faithful were also loyal in their drinking habits, it seemed. There was a group of young men who would come down on a match day from Canterbury, he said, to drink in the Rose. The first Covid lockdown came with no warning, and venues had shut immediately, but when the second lockdown was announced, he said the same group came along to the pub on its last night.

'They draped their Charlton flag on the wall and had a drink, because they didn't know how long it would be before they could come back – which I thought was very, very nice,' he said. 'You know they've come all the way up from Canterbury because they like being in the area where their football club is, because they feel comfortable here and consider this to be their sort of spiritual home second to The Valley.'

While losing the match-day football crowd wouldn't put them out of business, they would have to consider diversifying without it, he thought.

'It's a very old school fellas' pub,' he said, which rang true with my very brief experience of it.

'We do get ladies coming in. They're always very welcome, but it's more of a fellas sitting down swilling lager-type pub; we don't have a lot of music or entertainment or what have you.'

He reckoned that percentage-wise, the number of women customers at the pub was probably pretty similar to the number of women at a football match. So if 5 per cent of The Valley's crowd was made up of women, it would probably be roughly the same afterwards at the Rose. It made sense, I thought. The Rose was a football pub, and in the same way that I thought some women were not massively comfortable being in that match-day environment, they might feel the same about a pub hosting people who had just come from it.

Football fans had a bit of a bad rap, I thought. It wasn't completely unfounded; after all, I had had a particularly unpleasant experience at the end of the play-off final, and could attest that some football fans were, indeed, bellends. Thinking of my own experience at Wembley, I wondered whether the culture put other people off.

'I can't really think of a polite way to say this,' I began. 'Are football fans sort of arseholes?'

'A very small percentage,' he conceded. 'But most of them are happy-go-lucky. I tend to find that a lot of people who go to football together don't see their football mates unless there's a football match. So they tend to come in, they'll enjoy their couple of pints beforehand and they always come back afterwards for a couple of pints.'

They were, for the most part, he said, nice, decent people, and if they weren't, he tended to be able to sort them out.

'I think it depends on who's running the pub,' he reasoned. 'Don't get me wrong. I'm no big hard man, but I know how to talk to people and they know when they've been told. Generally you get told once and if it happens again, you're out the door.'

'There are pubs that have a rough element, and there's the sort of pubs that are left to themselves and other decent people don't go to. Every area has got its pub where you wouldn't go on a football day. Let's put it that way,' he told me.

It was true that Charlton fans weren't exactly known for their lairiness. In fact, in the first half of the 2019/20 season,*

....

* https://www.met.police.uk/SysSiteAssets/foi-media/metropolitan
-police/priorities_and_how_we_are_doing/corporate/met-operations---
football-data---july-to-december-2019

there had been a total of four arrests of Charlton fans at home games, according to a reply to an FOI request sent to the Metropolitan Police. However, those fans and those disreputable places Andy had spoken of *did* exist. There had been a pub nearby that had ultimately closed down. Some of its customers had sought refuge in the Rose after this, but they were seen off fairly promptly, he said.

Andy had been told by various people that the first team's promotion to the Championship would be great for business, but he said it made little difference to him whether there were 5,000 or 25,000 fans present at matches, so he didn't really buy the notion that the erstwhile designated away fans' pub – the Antigallican – had been forced to close by an absence of away fans as the club hurtled down the leagues.

I had never been to the Antigallican, but was pretty sure I wouldn't have liked it, on the advice of a 'PubSpy' review on the *News Shopper** – a South East London and north Kent local paper – website.

Opening with the line '*Why would you stick magazine cutouts of topless women on the urinal wall?*', the review, which read like a spoof, went on to declare that '*walking in, it felt like the wild west*', before highlighting the 'mild peril' they had felt in the establishment. I felt like I had grown up in these pubs, in Harwich, and also in my time as a civil servant. During those years in Vauxhall, we'd frequented a karaoke night at a local pub, a patron of which appeared to bear the scars of an actual Chelsea smile. I'd enjoyed my time at all of them, despite the

---

* https://www.newsshopper.co.uk/leisure/pubspy/10493409.review-the-antigallican-charlton/

Jolly Gardener's trademark wall of mould, but I could see how an outsider might not feel entirely comfortable.

'There was always trouble there,' Andy told me in a sombre tone. 'The police would basically vet them as they were coming down from the station, and the ones who looked like trouble-makers, they put in the Antigallican. The families and what have you, they'd send up here.

'It was a horrible pub from Monday to Friday,' he added. 'It didn't have to wait for football days.'

It was unfortunate, because a bit of competition was good in his industry, he thought, adding that you didn't want to be the only pub in an area, which made sense, I guessed.

'Different people suit different pubs, shall we say,' he told me, which made me laugh. I supposed he was right about that.

The police had wanted the Rose to become an away sup-porters' pub, he told me, apparently because it was useful to be able to contain everyone in one place and know where they were, but Andy had too many regular Charlton fans already.

'Once they start going somewhere else on a Saturday, it's not too long before they start going somewhere else on the Sunday as well,' he reasoned.

In that respect, you could see how important football was to a local area like Charlton, but also how important football was in general to local pubs.

'Football is *very* important to us,' he told me. 'Not just having a club close to us, but televised football is very, *very* important. We pay an absolute fortune, for Sky and BT Sport, so we have to make sure it's paying its way.'

After the first wave of Covid and the initial lockdown, he said, there was some concern about how safe it would be to televise football matches in pubs. The idea of a bunch of people huddled together in a bar screaming suddenly didn't feel like a very clever idea. On discussion with the local council's licensing officer, he was told it was OK so long as the spectators were kept under control.

'I said, "I need to have Sky Sports on, it's just not worth me opening otherwise",' he told me, gravely. 'Without it, we would have been in trouble – a lot of pubs are the same.'

They would have survived without the local football he thought, or without televised football – either one – perhaps without both, though he didn't sound massively confident in the latter.

In terms of the club's standing in the local community, Andy had been unimpressed during Roland's tenure, though perhaps that was because he'd not needed to access any of the services provided by the Trust. He spoke, instead, from a local business-man's perspective rather than a resident's or fan's.

'When I first came here, I got nothing out of them. They weren't interested,' he said flatly.

Previously, the pub had approached the club about provid-ing a signed shirt for a charity event they were holding.

'Not even a "we'll think about it",' he complained.

In the end, some of his regulars had donated their own signed shirts to the event. But all that might be about to change, he thought, under new ownership.

'Since Tommy's taken over,' he said, referring to Thomas Sandgaard as if they were the oldest pals in the world, 'every-thing's changed. The whole feeling about the club's changed. He wants to be a local guy, mixing with locals. He's going to make a big difference to the club's stature within the community.'

The pub had, of course, been endorsed by the new owner,

who had visited the pub a couple of times, happily posing for pictures and posting on social media. Andy sounded quite proud of the endorsement, I thought.

'Have you met him?' he asked me.

Despite not being a Charlton fan himself, it was impossible not to follow the club given his proximity to it and the fact that most of his regulars – at least on match days – were Charlton supporters.

'I'm surrounded by Charlton supporters a lot of the time. They were impressed,' he told me, chuckling, 'because when Charlton are playing, suddenly my phone will go *ping*. And I'll go, "Oh, Charlton have scored!"

'I've got notifications for Charlton,' he explained. 'But in some respects, it's important to the business.'

'You must have seen some sad Charlton supporters in your time,' I pondered, only half joking.

'I wasn't aware there were any other type,' he laughed.

•

Though Jason and Andy's perspectives on the club and what it did for the community were very different, there was nonetheless an obvious common ground. For a start, the importance of the club within the local community, both socially and economically.

It also struck me that both were – though they had expressed it in very different ways, with Jason perhaps understandably taking a slightly less grim view of that time – ultimately quite negative about the impact the Duchatelet years had had on the club and its engagement with the local community.

Most of all, I was struck by what an impact Sandgaard had made in such a short amount of time on this aspect of the club's work and place in the world, and how hopeful both Jason and Andy were for the future.

'Thomas has come in and he's fully embraced what the club standard is, what its *reputation* is,' Jason had told me. 'What I've noticed is, he wants to understand and he wants to learn, and he's quite happy to dip back into people that have played their role over the years and draw on that knowledge – and that's refreshing.'

●

We missed Charlton's next match – a 0-0 draw at Cardiff – as we attempted unsuccessfully to finally nail a hot meal and a nap that did not require the chest or lap of another human, but I made sure Lyra was in her away kit, nonetheless.

'Has she pooed?' Michael wanted to know, having developed a superstition that Lyra's bowel movements were in fact good luck. 'It's a poop per goal at the moment.'

'Does a poop *on match day* count?' I asked. 'Or has she peaked too soon?'

July:
Charlton Athletic v Millwall (P)

The next match was against Millwall – our local rivals who I once again could not get excited by. Rivalries were strange. I had always felt more rivalry against Ipswich, despite not having played in the same league as them for a considerable period of time, simply because there had always been more Ipswich fans around to have a barney with over football as a teenager.

With my mum and Vera doing useful things like changing nappies and cuddling the baby, the match was playing on my laptop in the corner of the room, but did not have our full attention. If I had been watching with Michael, I was quite sure this would not have been the case.

We'd played a decent game, defensively, and Chuks Aneke had a shot on goal – I was beginning to wonder if he wasn't starting to look a bit more useful. It certainly would have made me feel vindicated if he ended up as our star striker, I pondered.

But as ever it was in the dying stages of the game when disaster struck, this time in the 81st minute, but in the absence of any crowd to alert us, none of us actually noticed for a minute or two.

I hadn't noticed in the first few matches, having been so all-consumed by the tepid sense of occasion, but this time it dawned on me how odd it was to watch a match with no audible crowd. Some clubs had been piping recorded cheers into their stadiums to punctuate a goal, for example. I didn't object to this but it was nothing like the sound of a 'real' match – there was no emotion. The absence of fans had removed a layer of the magic from football, and daft as it sounded, all you had left was a bunch of dudes kicking a ball.

There is a specific pitch – a rise and fall – matching the pace and action of a group of men jostling and shouting at each other during a football match. The slap of a ball hitting a person's skin, or the metallic snare as it fizzes off the crossbar, or a shuddering advertising board – these were all instantly recognisable sounds, but ordinarily barely audible over the noise of fans. Watching football without that noise was like watching a five-a-side match at your local AstroTurf – suddenly there was no mystery.

The match ended unceremoniously 1-0 to Millwall who had beaten us for a second time this season. We were eighteenth in the league, but we had some tricky matches left ahead of us, and only three points between us and the relegation zone.

July:
Brentford v Charlton Athletic (P)

Next up, we faced Brentford – a difficult team to play, given that they were fighting for promotion, but with us staring down the barrel of relegation to League One, we also had a lot to lose at this stage.

Michael had taken a week off work to join our 'essential childcare' bubble, which was sorely needed given the levels of sleep deprivation my mum and I were enduring. We had started a rota whereby I would stay up with the baby overnight, and either Mum or Vera would take over at some ungodly early hour so that I could get a few hours' sleep before starting the whole thing again. I had decided the optimum number of parents for a new born baby was three, and ideally none of them would have to go to work in the morning – unfortunately, Vera actually had work to do.

Michael joining our bubble meant that he finally got to meet and hold his niece, almost a month after she had been born, and I got to eat a McDonald's Big Mac while he did so. It also meant that after months apart, we could finally watch the football together again.

Eight minutes in and Macauley Bonne gave us the lead, but again, without the sound, nobody seemed to have noticed, other than Lyra, whose limbs were flailing on the towel we had laid out for her on Michael's living-room floor. For some inexplicable reason, she seemed to favour the scratchy, cardboard-like surface of the towels our mum owned which predated our own births. Michael seemed to think she was making celebratory arm movements.

There were some wasted opportunities by Charlton, and we willed Lyra to once again fill her nappy, but she would not oblige.

Still, we had kept the lead until the 75th minute when Josh Cullen fouled Said Benrahma and Brentford were awarded a penalty, which Benrahma converted easily, and the slide into malaise began. Now smelling blood, they scored again just ten minutes later and with only five remaining. To lose like this, it seemed, was very much the Charlton way.

Michael drove us back to our mum's house to fulfil his childcare duties, and stay up with Lyra for a few hours so I could sleep before taking on the early hours shift. He didn't really ever sleep before midnight, he'd said, and despite her lack of luck during the match, he'd wanted to spend some time with his new niece.

My mum had finally managed to get Lyra to accept a swaddle, or as she put it, wrapped her in a baby parcel. We left her swaddled and dozing in her Moses basket with Uncle Bantz, under strict instructions as to how to manage any wake ups.

At around midnight my alarm went off and I sleepily wandered into the living room to find Michael with an unswaddled baby, slithering down his arm. He looked up at me from the armchair with a film of sweat covering his brow and a wild look of panic in his eyes.

'Uncle Bantz is shit!' he wailed guiltily, as I swept her up in my arms.

'Michael,' I laughed, 'We're all shit.'

July:
Charlton Athletic v Reading (P)

Our next match against Reading struck me as a bit of a nothing match – they were firmly wedged in mid-table obscurity and had nothing to play for, nor anything to fight against, plus we'd beaten them 2-0 earlier in the season, so they couldn't be that good, I reasoned. But even though they were in thirteenth place, there were still only ten points between them and the bottom of the table. The bottom of the table was exceptionally tight, and consequently tense.

Lyra was once again the main focus of my attention, primarily because she was refusing to eat properly, as we awaited the arrival of new, age-appropriate bottles. Who knew you had to change them as they got bigger? I silently cursed the crappy online antenatal class I had attended as I considered the many gaps in my baby-rearing knowledge.

In the third minute Deji Oshilaja gave away a penalty which was promptly converted to give Reading the lead, but on the plus side Lyra had begun to feed furiously, albeit with a slightly odd technique which was, unbeknownst to me, filling her tiny stomach with air.

It was Chuks Aneke again who showed promise, finding the net in the 30th minute, but the referee decided the goal was offside. For all the tedious whinging I had heard from Premier League club fans this season about VAR, Michael and I both agreed we would rather have had it, for the amount of ridiculous decisions we felt had gone against us. If I were honest, I also thought VAR added an extra layer of tension which I actually quite enjoyed.

The debacle did result in a renewed effort by Charlton, however, as the shots came thick and fast leading into the end of the first half. To add to the excitement, as she attempted to dislodge the pocket of air in her tummy, Lyra brought up with it the entire contents of the bottle I had just fed her, projectile vomiting all over me. Not a drop touched the sofa, or the carpet, just herself and, to be honest, mostly me.

Noting that she had not pooped during a match for a while, Michael marvelled, 'But what does *that* get us?' before dutifully driving to my mum's house to fetch a change of clothes for both of us.

Sadly, Lyra's mega-puke got us nothing. Not even the penalty we should have had five minutes from the end when Jake Forster-Caskey was fouled in the exact same way Andy Rinomhota had been brought down by Oshilaja.

The match ended a miserable and, we thought, unjust 1-0, leaving us just one point above the drop zone as well as smelling of vomit. In his post-match interviews Lee Bowyer had been livid, as had been Michael who raged about the ineptitude of the match officials. Even the Reading manager Mark Bowen commented afterwards that he had 'raised his eyebrows' at some of the decisions.

And he had been right to – this could have made the difference for us staying in the league, but there would be no comeback for the useless refereeing we had seen today.

July:
Birmingham City v Charlton Athletic (P)

'Terry from The Valley Pass is on *The One Show* now!' Michael messaged me the day before our next match against Birmingham.

The feature was something about supporting your club during the pandemic without being able to attend matches, presumably nestled between a piece about lesser-known Lincolnshire dances of the sixteenth century with Shirley Ballas, and cheese rolling with Michael Portillo. Terry had been talking about his many years as a supporter and the family connections that tied him to the club – a common theme among football fans, and Charlton was no exception.

For home matches, Charlton had been running a scheme whereby you could pay for a life-sized cardboard cut-out of yourself (or a nominated other) *in situ* for a match, in order to support the club. It was a good idea I thought, and meant they could at least make a bit of money while there were no tickets bringing cash in. I had been tempted to buy a board with Lyra's face on it, but as Michael had pointed out, we didn't actually know who owned us, and did we want to give our money to *any* of the men in suits currently associated with the club?

•

On the day of the match Lyra and I were at Michael's again, and this time, I had at least had the foresight to bring a change of clothes with me in case Lyra projectile-vomited again, which she did. Once more, she missed all the soft furnishings and the puke was focused solely on me and down the front of her away kit, for which Michael and Kerry were grateful, though we did now know that this was not a good omen.

A win would have put us above Birmingham – who were also struggling – in the table, and the Blues were also currently without a manager. Turmoil could take a club in one of two directions, I thought – it could spur a club on to prove themselves, or it could exacerbate the chaos. Charlton had seemed to be veering erratically between both possible outcomes, but my positivity was relentless when it came to the club and I still backed them. I fancied our chances against Birmingham.

Macauley Bonne put us ahead in the 58th minute – have *that* Lyle Taylor – but beyond that, it was a mixed bag. We missed out on some chances and probably should have gone 2-0 up, but Dillon Phillips also made some really great saves, including a penalty taken by Scott Hogan in the first half. Alfie Doughty also looked pretty promising even if Naby Sarr was back to his maverick ways again.

It was going so well until seven minutes of added time was announced. *Seven minutes of added time.* We all groaned in despair, barely able to watch, and with good reason it transpired, as finally in the 93rd minute Lukas Jutkiewicz got the better of Phillips.

We took home a point. It was more than we'd scraped together in the last few matches, but it felt like defeat – not just in this match but for the whole season.

The Gaffers

Lee Bowyer started his professional career at Charlton in 1994, aged seventeen, having come through the academy set-up.

'I suppose you weren't going to matches then?' he asked me.

'No, I was a bit little, then.' I replied.

'You were little – so does that mean I'm old?' he joked.

I wasn't actually that much younger than him, I told him, but I was young enough to have been too little for football matches.

I did remember Lee from that era, however. Though he'd left the club two years later, I had written to Charlton – a letter, because emails weren't a thing then – to see if I could get a signed photo or something similar for Michael's birthday, one year. It must have been his fourteenth or fifteenth, because Bowyer was in the signed squad poster that I received in the post, in response. Top sistering from an early age, I reckoned, perhaps only bettered by the 40th birthday message I'd asked Alan Curbishley to record for him on the same day that I had spoken to Lee. Curbs had, of course, obliged, and Michael had the file saved on his phone ready to play to whoever would listen to it.

It seemed fitting, then, that Lee's managerial career should also start at Charlton, some five or so years after his retirement as a player.

He started out as assistant to Karl Robinson, who ended up leaving for Oxford ten games before the end of the 2017/18 season. Lee was appointed interim manager and initially told he had three games – the club was being bought, he was told, and the new owners would bring in their own staff. Three games became ten, when the takeover didn't materialise, and Duchatelet thought it would be silly to mix it up, and after a decent run at the end of the season, Charlton ended up in the play-offs. It didn't work out for them – they were eventually beaten by Shrewsbury Town in the semi-finals – but it was a strong start by the interim manager.

The fabled new owners were still expected, but as the summer went on, nothing happened and Lee was anxious to put a time limit on his interim period.

'I think I'm the longest interim manager ever,' he joked.

Duchatelet gave it until the end of the transfer window, and Lee ended up becoming the manager, almost by accident.

He brought in Lyle Taylor, first off, then focused on getting good, young players and developing a partnership between Lyle and Karlan Grant, who returned to the club from loan. As Lyle had said when I spoke to him, it was a strong team, and Lee agreed.

'Other teams just couldn't handle our energy,' he told me. 'Whenever we created a chance, we scored near enough every time.'

The team looked set to make it into the play-offs, but a tremendous run in the last week saw them move up from sixth to third, putting them in a better situation going into the play-off semi-finals. They played Doncaster away and beat them, only to end up in a high drama penalty shoot-out at The Valley.

'I remember Naby stepped up to take his shot, and if he scored we went through … and then he missed,' he laughed.

They came through the sudden death penalties, a euphoric pitch invasion ensuing and what Lyle had described as better than winning the play-off final.

Like Lyle, Lee said he knew they were going to win, even after the terrible start to the match.

'You were there weren't you?' he asked me.

'It was ... it was awful,' I laughed. 'I can't imagine how you felt.'

'I wasn't even looking at that,' he said. 'I was looking further up the pitch. So Naby's got the ball, we're comfortable. And I'm thinking, "OK," I'm looking at the strikers for their movements, to give him options. And then I literally turn around, I see Dillon running back into the goal. And ... what just happened??'

But he'd felt OK about it, he said – there was plenty of time left.

When Patrick Bauer scored the winning goal, he said he went back to the technical area and turned to ask the fourth official how much time was left.

'And he said six seconds. And I was like, "Wow, that was good timing,"' he laughs.

And so the team were promoted at the end of his first full season in charge, but that, he said, was when it became difficult.

Duchatelet wanted to sell the club, and the budgets came down to make the costs look as attractive as possible, Lee said. It was understandable, he thought, but the basic wage he was allowed to pay new players was low, by Championship standards.

Lee and Steve Gallen, head of recruitment for the club, did good business in the transfer window: they secured decent loans by way of Conor Gallagher, Jonathan Leko and Sam Field, but it was tough.

'Me and Steve were literally ringing up clubs and begging them to do the best deal they possibly could. I was like, "Look, please, we can only pay this; if we could give you more we would, but we can't."'

They were trying to achieve a certain standard of play in the Championship, but on the budgets they were working to, if they could afford a player, there tended to be a catch, and half of his players were made of glass.

'When you lose twelve players, and you have to sign twelve, and of the twelve you're signing, eight of them are made of glass – because that's why they're still on the shelf – you're going to get injuries,' he explained.

Lee spoke incredibly fondly of Lyle, when I asked him about the deadline day debacle at the beginning of the 2019/20 season.

'He gave everything for me. I can't really say a bad word against him,' he said.

'He gave everything to the club. He helped us get promotion. Without him, we would never have got the promotion. He was flying at the start of the season. So, the injury – I think it ruined him.

'Brentford came in for him, obviously, at the start of the season, and we turned it down,' he said. 'He wanted to leave. Of *course* he did, because what we were paying him was ridiculous for the type of player that he is, and the money that he should have been earning.'

There were clearly no hard feelings whatsoever between Lee and Lyle, from either of their perspectives.

'Financially, he *had* to leave,' Lee said. 'He has not been one of those players that have been gifted and had money handed to him; he's had to work his way even to us.'

Duchatelet moving the goalposts was frustrating and disappointing for Lyle, but also presented a problem for Lee who now had to get him to play for him, though it didn't take long.

'So he was disappointed, but once that went, then he just switched back across and said, "OK, I'm here now. I'm going to try and keep in the game." And he did.'

At the same time, he couldn't criticise Duchatelet for making the decision to keep hold of Lyle.

'There's a lot of people that criticise Roland, and that's why I always said he was good to me. Obviously, I would have liked a bigger budget to actually compete, but he could have easily sold Lyle and taken that money,' he said, adding that he'd actually had quite a good relationship with Duchatelet.

Most of what Bowyer said chimed with Lyle's recollection of events, though – perhaps understandably given their different positions – they didn't necessarily agree regarding who was in the position of power when it came to bargaining. With the tiny budgets they were working to, the club were never in a strong position to negotiate with players, he said.

It was a bit of a problem for Charlton, I thought, but across football more generally in the lower leagues, that money had made the game, in so many ways, anti-competitive. Clubs like Charlton just became feeder clubs and couldn't really ever compete unless a massive amount of money came in.

'Exactly,' Lee agreed. 'And that was the problem with Charlton that I found in the three years – near enough – I was there; each season I was losing twelve, and then you've got to try to find twelve more.

'Twelve – this is a big number,' he went on. 'That's a new team, and you've got to then get them to gel.'

Then of course, the club were still under transfer embargo for the first part of the season, and then they got hit with the salary cap that was introduced to League One. They just could not get a break, it seemed.

Back in the 2019/20 season, at one point, Lee thought they'd had fifteen injuries in a 25-man squad, and were forced to recall young players on loan to non-league teams even.

Alfie Doughty's agent, he said, had not been keen when he was recalled from Bromley, in the fifth tier of English football.

'"Leave him there. This is his development – let him learn the game."' Lee recalled the conversation they'd had with him. 'And we were like, "Sorry, but we've got no players, he has to come and play for us. This would be good for him – good experience." "Nah, you should leave him there."'

'And then, six months later, Alfie ends up getting the move to Stoke,' he laughed. 'It's crazy how football works.'

In the run-up to the January of that season, Lee could have left, he told me. A club, recently relegated from the Premier League, came in for him. But someone at Charlton pleaded with him to stay.

'Someone that works at the club, who'd worked at the club for a long, long, time, basically said, "Look, please Lee, don't go, we have these new people that are going to be taking over. They have a lot of money,"' he told me.

'He actually said they could even get Mourinho if they wanted,' he laughed, incredulously. 'That was what he said. And I was like, "What are you talking about? Mourinho? If they've got that money, they don't need me."'

The idea of Mourinho at Charlton was funny enough for me to almost wish it had been so. But Lee was persuaded to meet the new buyers – none other than Nimer and Southall. He was assured that he was a big part of the appeal, in terms of the club, and that they had money to spend on players. They told him it was a great club, they wanted to push for the Premier

League, they understood there were a lot of injuries, and they were going to help him.

'And I thought, "Great, the club that I care about; now I'm going to finally be able to try and compete." If only it had worked out how it sounded in that meeting.'

Everyone fell for it, he told me, when I explained how delighted I'd been about the takeover. How on earth had it happened?, I wondered.

'How he was allowed to come through the door?' Lee asked, echoing my thoughts.

'I was blaming the EFL,' he said. 'If you buy a house, you have to show that you've got the money – I don't just give you the door keys, say, "There you go – there's your house, just pay us later."'

'You can't just say, "Oh, there you go. Yes, Matt Southall, you've passed this test, and now you're the chairman. Tahnoon, we'll wait for you to show us proof of funds four months down the line."'

'You *can't* give them permission to walk through the door,' he said. 'But they did. They walked through the door, and maybe two weeks into January, we got put under the embargo.'

He recalled a meeting he and Steve Gallen had with Matt Southall. Southall had told them he'd spoken to a club about a player and wanted to know if they were interested in him for Charlton – they were. He'd agreed a fee, they could meet him tomorrow, and all being well, they'd sign him.

Ten minutes later, he said, Steve received a call from the club secretary, Chris Parkes, making him aware that the EFL had put the club under a transfer embargo. This news was relayed to Southall, who assured them he'd sort it – perhaps he thought he could, who knows. And so, with those assurances, the decision was made to crack on and head up north to meet the player that same day, regardless. They had a match at the weekend and, after all, maybe the deal could be done by then. So off they went. It would be fixed in the morning, Southall told them.

It all went swimmingly with the player – he wanted to come to the club, and Lee and Steve wanted him. Great. There was another player, and Southall had arranged for them to meet at the player's house.

'Me and Steve – idiots,' he laughs. 'Up to Manchester on the train, getting back in the morning.'

'Nothing ever happened,' he added.

It all got quite murky as more and more people seemed to be entering the frame, but Paul Elliott, he said, was actually the only person to put any money into the club, and before he'd arrived, the club was weeks from going into administration. As was also the case with a number of clubs during the first Covid lockdown, the players and management team agreed to defer 30 per cent of their wages, and while there were no match receipts going into the club, their money was being whittled away. The club had been awarded £7 million for their promotion to the Championship. By the time the summer came, he said, it was all gone.

Lee could laugh about the comedy of errors that had unfolded now, but he had been angry.

As anxiety grew within the club about what was going on, and with no one putting any money in as the drama unfolded between the warring directors, a meeting was held with all of the staff. Worried staff were grilling Matt Southall on the financial situation, asking how long their wages would be paid for – at what point would the club be in trouble?

Initially he had taken the line that he couldn't tell them – he didn't have the information, he said – but the players kept pushing, Lee said. He *must* know, they said.

'One of the groundsmen staff who was in there actually collapsed,' Lee said, shaking his head in incredulity, again as he recalled the bizarre turn of events. 'He's just standing there, then he just goes *whoomph* and just collapsed. It was crazy.'

The meeting finished then and there as the collapsed staff member was tended to, and Matt Southall avoided any further questions, he told me.

'He was OK. It got too much for him, I think,' he laughed, after I asked if the groundsman had been all right.

By the time I spoke to Lee, it had just been announced that he would leave the club and take up the vacant manager's position at Birmingham City, a club he'd once played at and had a personal connection with.

It felt unexpected and even more odd, after hearing him speak in a sort of retrospective disbelief about everything that had gone on at the club during his time managing Charlton. He'd gone through so much in such a short period of time, and though the season hadn't gone as well as we might have hoped – doubtless because of the hangover from the previous season – it finally looked as if we might be in for a period of relative stability. Had he always planned for his stay to be so short?

'I've been through so much, so much,' he said. 'And we've had Thomas come through the door, and great, I think he's going to be good for the football club. I really do. And I think he's ambitious. And he wants to do the right thing. Finally.

'I know it looks crazy from the outside – you finally got someone that wants to improve the place, so why would you leave?' he acknowledged. 'But I just feel like, again, I've put this squad together – me and Steve, and we've worked so hard. And how many times can you keep doing that? Because again, in the summer, you're going to lose another twelve, and you've got to bring another twelve in. It's just not normal. You can't keep sustaining that.'

He had asked himself, he said, whether or not he could realistically take the team back to the Championship at the end of the season. They were strong enough to get into the play-offs, he thought, but probably not to win them. He was improving players all the time but then consistently losing them. It wasn't just that he was losing his players, either – but he was losing his *best* players.

There had been some growing disquiet among some of the fans that season, I had noticed. It was unfair, especially given the loyalty that we all knew he'd shown us. We knew other clubs had made moves to sign him, and that he'd stuck it out to see us right. I suspected, on the basis of what he went on to tell me, that he'd been aware of the dissent amongst the ranks.

'I came to a point and I thought, I don't want to leave here on a bad note,' he said.

'I like to think that I've helped change the culture and brought the fans back to the club, because there was a big separation,' he said, referring to the fan protests under Duchatelet.

'I think I've done a hell of a lot of good, and I've got some great memories. I don't then want to overstay my welcome,' he explained.

Did he think there was a danger of that, I asked him?

'Yeah,' he admitted.

He had a connection with Birmingham, he said, he knew the fans already – had a relationship with them. They were – like

Charlton, he said – a family club, and a working-class club. Had it been another club, who knows what might have happened.

'I probably would have stayed,' he pondered. 'It was a hard decision for me to leave – I *love* the club. I love everyone that works there, and the fans and I have good relationship. And that's what I mean, I didn't want to outstay my welcome. I didn't want people to think, "You're rubbish now." I've not changed – I believe I'm good.'

When I spoke to him, he was back at home for the evening, and planning to leave extra early to get back to Birmingham for the next day, in time to watch the Charlton match in the afternoon, he said.

'I want them to do well,' he said. 'I want them to get into the play-offs and get a promotion. There's nothing more that I want. I hope that happens and I hope Thomas takes it to where he wants to take it. Because I care about the club and I always will.'

Was he sad to have left, I asked him?

'I think if you ask anyone that was actually in the meeting, when I called the meeting to say goodbye – I was choking up, I was in trouble,' he admitted.

'It was probably the hardest thing I've had to do in my football career, even as a player.'

It was sort of sad, chatting to Lee now, and, much like Lyle, he wasn't what I had expected. I was hard-pressed to find an article about Bowyer's playing career that didn't refer to the reputation he'd had, both on and off the pitch. Words like 'violent', 'thug', and of course references to the infamous 'incidents' he had been linked to. Some of it made for pretty harrowing reading.

It would be fair to say that none of my youthful exploits were anywhere near as headline-grabbing as the ones written about in Bowyer's past. But certainly, I would not want to be judged for evermore on the person I was, aged between 19 and 23. And without a shadow of a doubt, he *had* been judged – his card was marked. Articles spanning more than fifteen years raked over the same ground, with Bowyer quoted in more than one, several years apart, stating that he wanted to be judged as the person he was now.

Reading the articles again now, I felt that there was undeniably a class element in some of the column inches dedicated to his past. It was interesting to me that there were men playing in the Premier League now, global superstars accused of heinous crimes, crimes still under investigation even, over whose signing fans rejoiced rather than recoiled in horror.

Certainly the person I had read about in those articles bore absolutely no resemblance to the person I was speaking to, now, or the style he seemed to have as a manager. He obviously had very close relationships with his players. I wanted to know – what had been the difference for him? Was it age? The therapeutic powers of carp fishing in France? Or had a lot of it been, well, bollocks?

'The person you're talking to now, I like to think when we leave this call, you'll think he seemed like a nice, genuine, honest fella,' he said, and I nodded – he *did* seem like all of those things.

'I've always been that person. And the difference is when I'm playing, I *have* to win, and when I'm manager, I have to win. I'm the *worst* loser,' he told me.

'I was hungry to win and I would do *anything* to win. Sometimes I overstepped the mark, and I accept that and I made mistakes. But that was the person I was – I *am* that person when I'm playing tennis against my kids, or in a swimming race.'

It was a bold admission, I thought.

'Then when I come off the pitch, then I'm this person – I'm really laid-back,' he said.

He seemed laid-back, I thought, especially given the stories he was telling me about his time at Charlton. It would have been easy not to have seen the funny side, I thought.

When it came to work, he was necessarily demanding, he said, and that was why he'd had such good results with his players. It was his job to keep pushing, and in that respect he was still that same winner – just in a different way. The trick was, he thought, to know when a player – like Lyle – needed love.

'I didn't need love,' he said. 'I needed pushing. Like, I need more from you.'

'I needed more until I actually broke,' he joked. 'But other people aren't like that. They need an arm around them and a reminder that they're good.'

And that was how he'd done it. He'd taken Josh Cullen and Krystian Bielik, respectively wasting away at West Ham and Arsenal's under-23s, and who were now playing for Anderlecht and Derby. Karlan Grant was playing in the Premier League, Joe Aribo was at Rangers. You had to have two sides, he thought.

He obviously had a huge amount of affection for Charlton. I wondered, what did the club mean to him?

'It means everything,' he said. 'They gave me my opportunities as a player. I was only seventeen when I made my debut, and I had an amazing relationship with the fans. Then coming back now as a coach, we had that bond again.'

'My first task was to try and bring everything back together,' he said, referring to the wilderness years and the estrangement of the fan base during Roland's tenure. 'Like "Come on, this is a great club – this is not what I remembered when I left."'

'So my main aim was to bring it all back together, because that's what needed to happen – and we did.'

'Hello, Alan speaking' – at last I talk to Curbs

In the morning of my interview with Alan Curbishley, which after months of pursuit had eventually come about quite quickly, I texted Michael to let him know it was happening.

'Bastard!' he replied to me – not Curbs, obviously. 'Can't even type to you right now!' he added.

I had to remind myself *not* to call him Curbs, even though everyone else seemed to, because even though I had known him in *my* heart for many years, he obviously didn't know me.

It was not a Zoom call – just a phone call, which I had almost forgotten how to have, over the last year. I found myself conversing with everyone super loud, like a nana who couldn't hear herself, or like myself, abroad, as if widening my eyes and over-enunciating every word would somehow make it easier to understand a different language.

In my efforts to sound super professional, I made an idiot of myself immediately when Curbs answered the phone, saying something along the lines of 'Hello, Alan speaking.' Out of habit, I immediately asked, 'Is that Alan?', then attempted to style it out by promptly declaring, 'Hi, it's Jen!'

I told him how angry my brother was that I was talking to him, and he laughed, and I tried *very hard*, and thankfully succeeded in *not* telling him, that I was sort of hoping, as a conclusion to the phone call, that he might consider adopting me.

Instead, I managed to power ahead and ask him, first and foremost, about the club's identity, and if, as Richard had told me, it had been forged in the Back to The Valley campaign of his early years at the club.

He and Steve Gritt had been contracted as player-managers in 1991, taking over from Lennie Lawrence. At the time, the club had moved from Selhurst Park to Upton Park – home of West Ham – and, he said, he thought they had maybe twelve players, before they were joined by John Bumstead, who'd been signed by Lennie before he left. It was a backs-to-the-wall situation, he said.

'I think we just, we just thought, "Blimey!", myself and Steve. "We've been given a chance to become joint managers, we haven't got a ground. We've got thirteen or fourteen players, and we're playing away from home every week, at Upton Park!"'

They went about putting together an experienced squad, he said – Gary Nelson, Steve Gatting, Bob Bolder, Simon Webster, Colin Walsh – who would understand the predicament they were in.

'Not so much a situation,' he added. 'It was a predicament.'

'We felt that there was only one way forward, and that was to do well,' he said. 'So I think our attitude was galvanised.'

He wasn't sure if the club was ever really on the brink financially speaking, but on the football side at least, it felt like it was make or break.

Andy Norman had suggested to me that the club, despite its long history – The Valley had just had its centenary after all – was quite a young club, establishing itself almost as a new entity when it returned to The Valley in 1992.

It was true, he said, that all the seven-year-olds who were there when the club left The Valley had grown up and were now fourteen and fifteen, and supporting other clubs, referring to the lost generation of supporters I'd spoken to Jason about. The community work that they then started to undertake to get bums on seats in The Valley again *did* bring in a new crowd and a new club community from 1992.

'I felt for a long while that the team on the pitch were out-doing perhaps the things that were going on off the pitch. And, you know, I think my last couple years at the football club, it was even-stevens. The team was doing well, but obviously the stadium was also doing well and the community was doing well.

'Everything was on the up,' he told me.

And it had been. As Richard Wiseman had told me, Charlton had been the model club. After our stop-start when we were relegated in 1999, only to be promoted back up to the Premier League at the end of the following season, we spent six pretty comfortable years there, and one year – the 2003/04 season – we were chasing a spot in Europe, even.

The following two seasons, we looked a little stagnant, per-haps, slipping back down into mid-table obscurity, but hardly in trouble. It seemed, as it had for Lee, an odd time to leave, but it was a decision that had eventually been made for him.

He'd spoken publicly many times about being approached for the vacant England manager's job, and indeed he was one of several who were interviewed, alongside Sam Allardyce and Steve McClaren – who eventually got the job – as well as a few others.

He had a year left on his contract and was under pressure from the board to sign an extension, but he wanted to be able to make a decision at the end of his contract.

'I wanted to do the one year and let the contract run down, and then be free to decide what I wanted to do. If I signed a three-year contract, which would have been a better deal for me, I felt that I wouldn't be able to make any decisions for myself for three years,' he explained.

It was a difficult position for the board, with Curbishley wanting to bring in new players on longer contracts, but in a similar situation to the one Lee had found himself in – the board not wanting to commit if they might potentially end up with a new manager, wanting to bring in his own players in a year's time. Meanwhile, Curbs didn't know that he definitely *would* want to leave in a year; he just wanted to have the option.

He hadn't planned on leaving at all, but somehow, over the course of the conversation with then chairman, Richard Murray, that's exactly what ended up happening, in order to allow the incoming boss to have a full pre-season to get to grips with the club.

'It was an incredible afternoon,' he told me. 'It was the Friday afternoon before the Blackburn game. I was having a meeting with Richard and was talking about players I wanted to bring in, talking about the club, and by the time the meeting ended I was leaving.'

He could understand the club's position, he said, but he was upset by the turn of events, and his family, too.

'I'd done fifteen, sixteen years, I'd been a player there as well, so I'd been at the club for twenty years, really. Signing for another three years was not in my best interests, and not the right thing to do,' he said.

'You've got to have enthusiasm as a manager for what you're doing. If you start to lose enthusiasm, then you're going to lose the players and the people around you.

'That's what I was worried about – signing a longer contract, then not having the enthusiasm for it. I knew I'd have the enthusiasm for another year, at least.'

The Blackburn game Curbs had referred to was the penultimate game of the 2005/06 season, on 29 April. Less than two weeks later, he was gone. A year and three managers later – including interim boss, Les Reed – we were relegated back down to the Championship under Alan Pardew, at the end of the 2006/07 season. Two seasons after that, down we went again to League One. We'd seen it happen a lot in recent years – after managers who'd been with teams for a long time moved on, a period of instability often followed.

For the likes of Manchester United and Arsenal who'd lost their managers of 20+ years, Sir Alex Ferguson and Arsène Wenger, I didn't have a huge amount of sympathy. After all, they were still two of the richest clubs in the world and the entitlement – the feeling that they had an almost divine right to be in the Premier League's top four – pissed me off immensely. It was kind of like political parties, I thought, or the economy – cyclical. Eventually one party would run out of ideas, or the limitations of their play ceased to yield the returns they needed. You simply couldn't be at the top forever, and their fans had been at best complacent about their comparative talents, I thought, though this wasn't always a vote-winning view, I'd found.

The funny thing was, it had never really occurred to me until those managers left that this might be an actual 'thing', perhaps because Curbs had left his role at Charlton some time before those two obvious examples. I had just thought it was understandable, given the length of time he'd been with the club.

'I'll add another couple to that,' Curbs said. 'Sam Allardyce at Bolton and David Moyes at Everton.'

Indeed, both had been just shy of ten years.

'When you find a manager that has gone further than ten years, which is really unusual, there has been a dip. Man United dipped, Arsenal dipped, I think Everton dipped – *Bolton* have dipped,' he stressed, because what a dip it had been.

'So there is a view that having a manager for that long can cause a problem. I suppose,' he pondered, 'the nearest one now is Sean Dyche at Burnley, he's been there seven or eight years. Let's see what happens if he ever leaves.'

It had been great seeing Curbs back at The Valley recently, and on The Valley Pass. The reconnection with the club had been a more recent development, he told me, and came about as a result of Bowyer.

'I drifted over on a couple of occasions,' he said. 'But when Lee took over I started coming a bit more.'

'I'd known Lee since he was twelve, as a kid and an apprentice at Charlton, and I had him at West Ham,' he said, referring to the brief period he had managed the Hammers after his departure from Charlton.

'When he took over, I thought I'd come and have a look, and I was quite impressed. Well,' he added, correcting himself. 'I've said on more than one occasion, I was *really* impressed with the team in the Championship.

'I thought it looked as if it was going places, and, like a lot of others, with the people in charge at the time, I thought that was OK as well. You know, Southall and whoever. I thought the club was back on the up, I must admit.'

In the few games he'd seen, he'd been impressed by the likes of Cullen and Gallagher, and he thought there was a shot at the Premier League.

'And I thought, the fans deserve this after Duchatelet,' he told me.

It seems even Curbs had been taken in, but the Charlton he knew had been up against it in the past. When he'd first come to the club as a player, the threat of bankruptcy had loomed large.

'I think we were nearer going into administration then, because I don't think the club was as attractive as it is now, you know, the dilapidated stadium, etc., etc.,' he said, adding, 'I think Lennie went through a lot as a manager. And as I mentioned, I think me and Steve went through a lot in our early years.

'I came to quite a few games in the Championship year, also in League One, and obviously the play-offs,' he told me.

He'd come back again for the 2020/21 season because the club's new commercial director, Wayne Mumford, was someone he'd known during his own playing career, and he'd been asked by him and Scott Minto, one of his former players, to get involved in The Valley Pass shows. 'It was a shame,' he said, 'that the results had perhaps not been as good as we might have hoped, in that time.'

He was sad to see Lee go, he told me, but he understood that he'd had a connection with Birmingham, and he'd been through a lot with the club in his brief period as manager.

'As I pointed out to him a few times,' he said, referring to the £2.8 million Leeds had paid to buy nineteen-year-old Bowyer, 'when we sold him to Leeds, we built the West Stand – a big chunk of money went on that. So, you know, he'll always be part of Charlton.'

It felt sort of fitting that the week after Alan and I had spoken, the club announced that the East Stand would be named after him – the Alan Curbishley Stand.

'I've enjoyed going back. I've enjoyed seeing some of the old players,' he said. 'I think there's a theme when you talk to them, the old players, about what went on in those years, because of the way we talk about it.'

Curbs agreed that there was a feeling of family among the former players, but more so a sense of solidarity.

'I think the mentality, even when we were in the Premier League, was that we're in this together.'

Perhaps in the Premier League, he told me, players wanted to hear more about where they were *going*, than where they'd come *from*, but, by and large, they got it.

'Whenever we signed – apart from a couple – whoever we signed, I think they really understood the club, and understood where we'd come from in the early years. They all knew about the hardship and the struggle.

'I think when you get the players who are coming back, they're all saying the same thing. They feel as if they've all played a part in it.'

As it did to Lee Bowyer, and as it had to so many others, Charlton meant a lot to Curbs.

'It is a major part of my life,' he told me.

And it must have been, as one of what ended up being only two managerial positions in football, especially when you considered that in the fifteen years since he'd left, the club had seen fourteen managers take charge, plus another five caretakers.

'If I close my eyes and think about Charlton, I think of a family club. I think the fans, when I was playing and managing, were an older generation – let's say that – that were always reminding everybody about the old days, but there was nothing going on in the present day,' he told me, reflecting on Charlton's identity as a club.

'So, I always look back at Charlton as the grand old lady, if you like. The grand old club that has survived a lot of battering, but it's still there.'

I had a lot of time for a matriarch, and I loved the idea of Charlton as the proverbial battleaxe. But there was life in the club yet, Curbs reckoned.

'When I first remember Charlton when I was playing – at West Ham or wherever –they were in Division Two. They were a comfortable Championship side, but there's no reason why they can't become another Premier League side, because it's there – there's an opportunity and it's there,' he said, referring to the clubs who'd managed to make that jump in the past, such as Sheffield United and, though struggling now, at one time Wigan.

'The thing I like most about The Valley Pass,' he told me, speaking of the new owner Thomas Sandgaard, 'is that he can see the potential of the club, because he's there every time we go through the old footage, he is there. He understands that it can be done – getting back to the Premier League.'

Almost everyone I'd spoken to about Charlton understood that it was, as so many had put it, a special club. It was more than that the club had *heart* – though it did have that, for sure, and it was undeniably the fans who made it beat.

But it had a soul, too, in the history of the club and the work that Curbishley and his team, and the staff at the club past and present, had put into instilling this culture. When Lee Bowyer took over as manager at Charlton, that soul was wounded, and he'd been determined to repair it, and rebuild what those before him had worked so hard to create. From time to time, over the years, it had needed some defibrillation, but as Curbs said, it always seemed to get there in the end.

RELEGATION

July:
Charlton Athletic v Wigan Athletic (P)

Sitting down to watch our penultimate game of the season was not a task I undertook with enthusiasm. Bar the first two winning games of Project Restart, it had been a relentlessly miserable descent further towards the relegation zone and it felt like we were a hopeless cause now.

But we had two possible lifelines beyond winning one or both of our remaining games, and the hope that the few teams still below us choked. The first was courtesy of today's opponents, Wigan, who had gone into administration under slightly odd circumstances, having only just been sold. It was all deeply strange.

The upshot was that Wigan would now have twelve points deducted, as was the penalty for clubs who went into administration – even if it wasn't their fault. It was yet to be decided if that deduction would be made before or after the end of the season. It seemed counter-productive to penalise a struggling club, but the purpose of the rule was to incentivise sustainable finances at league clubs. While Wigan looked safe on paper with 57 points and thirteenth in the league, a twelve-point deduction would bring them two points lower than us and in the thick of a relegation dogfight.

I couldn't help but feel something of an affinity with Wigan – lest we forget we too might be subject to a points deduction if it was found that the East Street Investments purchase had not been above board. But the truth was, where fault lay depended entirely on how you defined a football club.

In my view, a club wasn't defined by any one of the people in the revolving door of suited pricks who came in to throw their weight around, buy bragging rights, or, worse still, strip one asset at a time. A club was its people – its fans and its staff – it was defined by its community. Why should Wigan's *community* pay the penalty for the actions of investors? Matt Southall had been right about one thing and one thing only – he had just been the custodian of Charlton Athletic.

The truth was, football was not a money-spinner for the vast majority of clubs. Only the really big ones made the fortune newspaper headlines so readily associated with the beautiful game. Any lower league clubs like Charlton – or Wigan – will always be *vulnerable* to exploitation, and the EFL's rules will not protect them.

In the case of clubs which have been bought – as it had transpired Charlton had by ESI – for a nominal amount of money, it arguably makes no odds to an owner whether they end up running a football club if they failed to pass the EFL's Owners' and Directors' Test and wind up kicked out of the Football League. They would still end up with a valuable plot of land in London or wherever else.

I had taken to tweeting aggressively and relentlessly about the unfairness of it all, tagging in the EFL and then Secretary of State for Culture, Media and Sport, Oliver Dowden. What were they doing about it? Didn't they realise that *communities* were in jeopardy, here? Or did the Tories just want to Tory and let their mates buy clubs with no money so they could take advantage of them for their own profit? Yeah? *Yeah?* Neither Oliver Dowden nor the EFL replied to me, but my brother *did* like most of these tweets.

I even signed an online parliamentary petition – the final,

futile act of the desperate. Look, if enough people indicated that they didn't want Brexit via an online petition, they were *bound* to revisit the democratic choice the public had voted for 6, 12, 18 and 24 months before. So DCMS was *bound* to consider the heartfelt pleas of football fans to 'Review the need for a statutory Owners' and Directors' Test in football'.

I was furious when, almost three months later, I received an email from the UK Government and Parliament Petitions team inviting me to agree with them via an online consultation that Premier League clubs should fund lower league clubs during the Covid pandemic. It was a surprisingly socialist principle for a government which evidently couldn't have given even part of a shit about a fairer distribution of wealth. And anyway *what the fuck were they doing about these shady football club owners???*

In fact, some time later a fan-led review of English football was undertaken by the government, chaired by former sports minister, Tracey Crouch. Crouch, herself a Conservative MP, found that the beautiful game was in need of an independent regulator to stop it 'lurching from crisis to crisis,' she said. At the time of the announcement, it was reported that Downing Street would support that recommendation, though it remained to be seen what the clubs would make of it.

Our other lifeline, although I did feel a bit guilty thinking of it in those terms when it came to Wigan, came from Sheffield Wednesday. They stood accused of deliberately concealing information around the sale of their ground, therefore breaching financial protocols, and were also likely to be subject to a twelve-point deduction, which would also see them drawn into the relegation battle. But, like Wigan – who rightly or wrongly I had far more sympathy for – when the deduction would occur was yet to be decided.

Either way, when it came to today's match, there was a lot at stake for both teams potentially. We were also going into the match fresh from a club record 8-0 win by Wigan over Hull in their earlier midweek fixture.

Certainly Wigan started with intent, scoring in the ninth minute, but Alfie Doughty followed with a great goal just two minutes later.

Still in the first half, Macauley Bonne was brought down in the box, but the referee denied the players' pleas for a penalty, and we were raging.

'WHAT IS HE DOING???' Michael half shouted, half wailed.

Again, that decision could be the difference between us staying in the league or getting relegated – that *wrong* decision. But what would it mean to the ref? There would be no comeback for him. I was sure that all football fans felt this about their own team, but I was starting to develop a bit of a victim complex about it – much like when I read the BBC's always overly negative match reports. It really felt as if decisions had gone against us *all season*.

Kerry sighed.

'You just can't catch a break,' she said sympathetically.

And moments later, Wigan scored again, five minutes before the end of the first half. This time no one made a sound, but you could almost hear the air deflating from us.

After a moment I began wittering about how it was a shame that the scoreline didn't reflect how well we'd played – we had played *all right*, but we looked like we lacked confidence. Given that we were two points above the relegation zone on our penultimate match of the season, perhaps that wasn't unreasonable.

Michael left the room in disgust to regain his composure for the second half, though Chuks Aneke came off the bench ten minutes into the second half and Michael was not cheered much by this.

'What if Chuks Aneke scores the *winning goal*?' I laughed.

Aneke looked all right – again – and Charlton appeared to have a renewed sense of urgency about them. I'd have liked to have seen this urgency five matches ago, but I would take it now. Nonetheless, in injury time we were still a goal down.

Aneke *didn't* score the winning goal, but he *did* provide the assist for Macauley Bonne's 92nd-minute equaliser, and, as the whistle blew, we were still in with a shot of staying up.

Michael immediately began ranting about the refereeing, before reeling off the various permutations that would allow us to stay up.

We were one place above the drop zone on the same points as Luton, three above Hull and five above Barnsley, though they had a game in hand, and we *still* didn't know what was happening with Wigan or Sheffield Wednesday.

Staying up was still possible. Not *likely*, but we were still in the game.

July:
Leeds United v Charlton Athletic (P)

The opening scene of *Casualty* had always been too much for me – peril lurks everywhere. The wonky ladder? The toaster with the dodgy plug? The seemingly conked-out lawn-mower? Which banal household item was going to cause the certain death, or at the very least, life-changing injury, to the affable family man and/or his wife? It was the same reason I couldn't cope with penalties – I couldn't handle the jeopardy, and that was how it felt on the final day of the season.

Our final match was against Leeds United – dirty Leeds, dirty, dirty Leeds, Lee Bowyer's former club. Leeds were at the top of the league, already promoted, nothing to prove – the victory already theirs. Surely they would want to do us a kindness? But even if they didn't, so long as Luton didn't win, we'd still go ahead of them on goal difference, and Luton were *awful*.

Barnsley had picked up a draw, but a win today would put them a point ahead of us if we lost. Hull, I rather thought, were done for. Even if they won and we *and* Luton lost, they would need to win by three goals to overtake Luton.

Wigan's point deduction would be applied at the end of the match, but if they won their final game, they might yet be safe.

No one knew what was happening with Sheffield Wednesday, with an independent disciplinary hearing hanging over them to decide. In sixteenth place, if they were hit with a points deduction this season, they could end up bottom of the table. It was hard to understand why this hadn't already been resolved, given that they had been charged in November the previous year.

It was hypocritical, but I didn't care about Sheffield Wednesday. Even though exactly the same rules applied – that it was someone in an office's doing rather than the fans or the club itself – a breach of financial fair play rules seemed to me to be worthy of punishment. But I didn't want us to benefit from Wigan's situation – it felt wrong, given how easily it could have been us in their position. It could have been any club in their position. Much like anyone was only ever two pay cheques away from being homeless – as they said – Michael reckoned the same rules applied in football.

'It only takes one person backing out of something, one manager getting sacked, one really bad season,' he pondered. 'You never believe it's going to be your team, but *any* of us could be where Wigan are.'

Michael was right, and even up until the final match of the season, I still thought we were going to get away with it. I knew now that we wouldn't and I couldn't bear to watch it play out in front of me.

With a heavy heart, I'd returned to London two days earlier, not wanting to leave my family again for who knew how long if further lockdowns were to happen later in the year, but aware that I had to at least *see* if Lyra and I could manage without their help.

Without Michael there to make it happen, I decided I'd been through enough. Lyra had been through enough in her six weeks of life as a Charlton fan. I didn't want to watch us go down, and so I didn't.

About half an hour in, I checked in on the score to find we were two goals down already.

I messaged Michael my excuse, that Lyra was 'making it impossible to watch'.

'It's all going wrong anyway,' Michael replied.

●

In the end, it was an injury-time goal by Barnsley that did for us. *Barnsley.*

An injury-time winner for Barnsley at Brentford put us down.

As our 4-0 defeat by Leeds played out, Luton beat Blackburn and Cardiff beat Hull. But with Wigan's twelve-point deduction in place, a 1-1 draw with fourth-place Fulham put them in the relegation zone too. Barnsley's 92nd-minute goal put them a goal ahead of Brentford and one point above us – even if they had drawn, we would have been above them on goal difference.

I felt bereft – hollow. It was impossible to feel like, 'Oh well, you know, we've all had a lovely time,' even though really I had, despite the disastrous outcome of the season.

The odds had always been against us, as had the results for at least half of the season, but as Michael had pointed out – no one ever thought it would be *their* team. This was, after all I presumed, how the England football team had managed to sustain any interest for the last 54 years.

The result passed without comment. Michael and I said nothing of it, and not even our mum had chipped in with a 'better luck next time', or 'well, you knew it was coming'.

No one texted, no one called, just radio silence between us until he sent me a tweet the next day – a story about former Charlton player and later boss Chris Powell.

'Chris Powell ringing around the Charlton fans he knows to check in on them melts my heart ☺'

But we didn't have time to dwell on the result …

The End/The Beginning – Thomas Sandgaard

O ver the course of the last season and our correspondence, it had seemed to me, at times, that Alan Dryland, who I had met in the museum, was distressed by what had been going on in the Charlton boardroom, and the very real – though we had not known how real – peril the club had been in. I wondered what it would have meant to him, had we gone the way of Bury or Bolton.

'Well, you have to say it's only a silly old football club – it's a silly old football club,' he repeated, a response I was perhaps a little surprised by, when I spoke to him after the end of the season. But he went on: 'Life has to go on because in terms of national tragedies, it doesn't come high up the scale. But it's born of the feelings of resentment, of frustration, anger, betrayal.'

A man of strong pro-European politics, Alan had been delighted by the takeover of Roland Duchatelet, initially, not least because of the five sister clubs it wedded us to, through Duchatelet's empire. But Alan saw a direct causal link between this and the situation that had eventually ensued with East Street Investments, through his lack of respect for the club's heritage.

'The situation with the club, if anybody outside Charlton Athletic fans were interested because it had been dragging on so long, was embarrassing,' he told me, firmly. 'Embarrassing that that could be allowed.'

'I would be very upset if Charlton had ceased to exist, but for such a pathetic reason that it just couldn't be made viable,' he tailed off.

'On the other hand, who in their right minds would ever want to buy a football club? We nearly went bust in 1923, we had to be taken over in 1932 by the Glickstein family who then kept it for 50 years, but we were never very profitable or prosperous.'

'We scratched around while we were at Selhurst Park and Upton Park. And then gradually through the '90s, which is my favourite decade, we gradually pulled ourselves up and ended up in the Premiership and with a respectable stadium.'

I could see his point, that having been through so much as a club, to have staved off disaster *so many* times, to have lost it all over half a season thanks to this bizarre bungled takeover and a mad social media barny would have been *embarrassing*. An insult to what others had worked so hard to salvage.

On 27 July the EFL issued a statement announcing that it had written to the club 'requesting further information and a meeting with the club, the current majority owner of ESI and also the proposed new owners, as it seeks to clarify the ongoing ownership issues at the club in the context of the EFL Regulations.'*

Further to this, it said it was the club's responsibility to meet EFL requirements and that it was 'aware of the consequences' of not doing so.

'This is very worrying,' Michael told me. 'Seven weeks until the season starts – we are in the shit!

'I say don't buy season tickets until this is sorted out, one way or the other,' he added. 'I hate the idea of these *scumbags* getting a penny.'

----

* https://www.efl.com/news/2020/july/efl-statement-charlton-athletic/

It was a reasonable position, I thought. At this point, not only did we not know if the world would open up again and we would actually be able to *see* any of the matches, or if a second wave of Covid would result in another dramatic pause in proceedings altogether, as it had earlier in the year. But also, we had absolutely no idea who we were effectively giving our money to, it was now so fiendishly complicated. I did not mind giving the *club* some of my money – I felt like it probably needed it, at this point – but I might have objected to handing it over to some of the names still being mentioned in connection with the club.

Less than two weeks later, the EFL announced that the club's new owners had, after a 'full and comprehensive appraisal of the relevant matters'* failed to meet their Owners' and Directors' Test.

The new season was set to start in just over a month, and if the situation wasn't resolved by then, we may not have been allowed to compete in it. Despite this, the new owner, Paul Elliott, appeared to have absolutely no intention of walking away and allowing another prospective owner – a few of whom seemed to be sniffing around – to have a crack. The way I saw it, we were quite possibly only a month away from The Valley being sold off as a development project for some 'luxury apartments'.

At the same time, a growing number of players, previously tied to the club by short-term contracts, were now inevitably jumping ship. You couldn't really blame them, but it put us in an increasingly dire situation.

....
* https://twitter.com/EFL_Comms/status/1291720647832416256

Football fans and commentators alike began to spread messages of support for the club, highlighting the many others whose fates had taken a turn for the worse in similar situations – the Burys and Boltons, and apparently soon-to-be Wigans of the world.

'Another of our great football clubs being messed with #SaveCAFC',* tweeted Gary Lineker in support of a campaign by the Supporters' Trust.

Around the same time, another prospective buyer entered the frame. A Danish-born businessman, Thomas Sandgaard, who was based in Colorado, USA, and had made his fortune in the medical technology industry, manufacturing and marketing electrotherapy devices. He'd later established the Sandgaard Foundation, aimed at 'decreasing the habitual use of prescription pain medication'. A guitar player and rock enthusiast, his Twitter bio referred to him as 'Entrepreneur and Rockstar CEO'.

'Interesting – three interviews and Sandgaard always mentions the women's team ... rarely hear that from an owner!' Michael had messaged me, sometime after Sandgaard's name had first been linked with the club.

I wondered how I could get an interview with him.

'Just ask,' Michael advised. 'Looks like he's giving pretty much *anyone* an interview.'

About three weeks later, after a short exchange via LinkedIn messenger, I found myself on a Zoom call with Thomas, slightly confused by what looked like a fully dressed Christmas tree behind him, in August, but very happy to be speaking with him, nonetheless.

I explained to him, as I did with all of my interviewees that

* https://twitter.com/GaryLineker/status/1293928935147876353?s=20

it was a friendly interview, etc., etc. Except in this case, if he ended up being like Matt Southall, it might become a bit less friendly with Charlton fans.

'I've actually made pretty good friends with Matt Southall,' he told me, laughing. I was not entirely sure if he was joking.

'I'm glad to hear that you're making friends with Matt Southall,' I retorted. 'I think he needs some friends.'

'That's funny,' he replied, laughing again.

By this point, in late August, it was not yet a done deal, but Thomas was confident he could get the sale over the line. Everyone, he said, seemed to be willing.

This was good news, I told him, and I hoped it would happen soon, not least because I wanted to renew my season ticket at the early-bird rate, but I didn't feel able to until this was resolved.

'That's interesting,' he told me. 'You're not the only one – there's probably more in that position than actually renewing.'

I thought people were genuinely worried about the club no longer being part of the Football League I told him, and didn't want to …

'Waste their money,' he interjected.

Yes, exactly.

'I'll make sure that doesn't happen,' he told me.

From what I had heard about Thomas, I felt largely positive, but it was hard not to be suspicious of *anyone's* motives when it came to Charlton right now, least of all someone coming forward at a time when the club was in *such* a pickle. Why did he even *want* to buy Charlton at this point in time, I asked him?

'If you set aside what's going on in the boardroom at the moment, the foundation for a great club couldn't be any better,' he told me, confidently.

'One of the most important things for a football club is the fan base. It's hard to find any more engaged, bigger fan bases in all of the English clubs.'

Additionally, he told me, the club had the right people in place in Lee Bowyer, Steve Gallen and Johnny Jackson to help the – albeit somewhat decimated – team achieve things, and a reasonable prospect of getting promoted straight back up to the Championship.

'It's a fantastic stadium,' he added, speaking of The Valley. 'And I think even for a few seasons in the Premier League, it'll do really well.

'Everything is right there to make this a formidable Premier League club; it just takes a lot of hard work and a lot of patience,' he told me.

He had good business acumen and was comfortable with the boardroom side of things. He expected to be heavily involved in the running of the club, he told me, though he hated micro-managing.

So far, so good, I thought.

What about the fans, I asked him, starting to feel like a protective parent sizing up their child's prospective boyfriend. As he'd no doubt have seen by now, the fans could turn, if we felt let down. Was that a daunting prospect?

He laughed.

'I don't expect that to happen, because I think what the fans want and what I have in mind is very aligned,' he said.

The fans were 'fundamental' he said, but of course we had heard all this before.

For a start, he added, it was no fun without fans, not really. But also, it was just good business to keep them on side.

'That's a large part of where you get your income from sponsorships, etc. – it depends on people watching the team and following the team.

'It's like in the music industry,' the Rockstar CEO added. 'It might be good music, but if you don't have people wanting to buy and listen to it, it doesn't really mean much.'

In terms of community, he'd already spoken to Jason Morgan, he told me. Assuming he had the chance to take the club on, the Community Trust would be very important to him, he said.

I wanted to make sure Sandgaard understood the 'Charlton Way' and that this was more than a football club, and I told him Michael's story about the woman in the ticket office who'd saved his seventeen-year-old self's bacon. As a businessman, I wondered what he thought about it?

It told him a lot about the culture of the club, he said. When his company – a very successful and large company, by all accounts – hired people, he said, he still interviewed every single person, regardless of the role. When people asked him what he was looking for in his employees, he had two answers, he said.

'One is I look for people with common sense. And I look for people that just know how to do the right thing. Because that way, we can always keep focus on the patients, which are our customers over here,' he said, referring to his business in the medical industry.

'Obviously I want to hear a story like that,' he continued, referring to the woman in the ticket office. 'That if we can have the same two qualities instilled in everybody around Charlton, common sense, and always knowing how to do the right thing – what she did, was doing the right thing. Not only do you get a fan for life, he goes a little beyond.

'And it's not like you're taking any significant financial risk,' he added.

What about the women then, I wondered, going back to the point Michael had made about Sandgaard frequently mentioning the women's team. What was he going to do with them? Was doing the right thing going to be important when it came to them, too, especially given how badly they had historically been treated?

He didn't really know what he was going to do with the women's team, he told me, honestly. He'd had more sight of what was going on with the men, though he did have a meeting scheduled to discuss them.

'I couldn't tell you yet,' he admitted. 'But I can guarantee you that I'll make something out of it that people can be proud of.'

Finally, and most importantly on my list of questions about his intentions towards the club: what about us – the fans? Would he consider the model used by the club all those years ago, and install a fan *on* the board, to help make decisions about the future of the club?

'I don't know if board presence is the right model – I wouldn't know that at this point in time,' he replied, admitting again to not having all the answers. However, he had spoken at length with the Supporters' Trust, he said, and he wanted to maintain regular meetings to ensure he knew what was going on.

'Listening to what's going on is going to be one of the key things for me,' he said.

'I rarely, if ever, make short-term decisions – my decisions are always made for the longer term. And I think that will resonate well with the fans,' he said. 'So I don't think there will be that many differences in opinion, as maybe there has been in the past.'

In our 30-minute conversation, Sandgaard had said all the right things. But then so had Matt Southall when ESI had taken over. It was easy to say all the right things, I thought, and perhaps I wasn't a great judge of character; I had been taken in by Southall, after all. But even in the wary state I, like many other fans, had found myself in, something about Sandgaard made me believe in him.

He'd admitted he didn't have all the answers yet, but he was thinking about the right things and talking to the right people and his answers had implied a realistic amount of consideration from a business perspective, as well as all the nice, warm and fluffy things a fan would want to hear. Most importantly, perhaps, for a person dealing with Charlton Athletic, he seemed to have a good sense of humour.

I told him my theory about Charlton's Premier League sweet spot, as I saw it. He laughed, but respectfully disagreed.

The first part of the journey was about stability, and the second about optimisation, he thought – but it was going to take a while.

'Once you have that stability, you've got something to build on – just look at Leicester, after they created that turnaround and actually stayed in the league,' he pointed out. Indeed, they'd finished fifth in the last season.

'I think that's a good example to look to, at least short term. If they can do it, Charlton can do that, too.'

I liked Sandgaard, and I wasn't sure I agreed that we could replicate Leicester City's fairy-tale turnaround, or at least not without a pretty substantial investment on his part, but he was right, and Curbs was right, that the model existed.

As I knew only too well with Charlton Athletic, it was the hope that killed you, yet there it was again, somewhere in the recesses of my dark, 2020-battered heart.

'Did he apologise for being late?' Michael asked of our meeting, which had been delayed by an hour.

'He thanked me for being patient,' I said, which was almost the same thing.

'You're ignoring too much recent history,' Michael told me when I said I'd agreed with Thomas' analysis that we were, really, a Premier League club, just not a good or even mediocre one.

'I feel it in my heart!' I protested. 'It's not evidence-based!'

'Your heart is ignoring a painful ten years while you were busy being a non-partisan North Londoner,' he retorted, scornfully.

Perhaps he had a point, but I couldn't help but feel that somewhere in him, there was hope, too. I often joked about how supporting a club like Charlton, you learnt to manage your expectations, but there was always hope, otherwise what was the point?

After lengthy discussions about the pros and cons of renewing our season tickets, we agreed that the club probably needed the cash, and that Charlton matches were for life, not just the second tier of English football and above (although we were a bit pissed off that the cost of a season ticket had actually increased).

With the club's future hanging in the balance, no definitive knowledge of when we would actually next be able to *go* to The Valley, and still awaiting Sandgaard's purchase, we decided to renew our season tickets anyway on 4 September.

A couple of weeks later, in the biggest turnaround of the

year so far, Michael messaged me to let me know the terrible news that Chuks Aneke had coronavirus.

'Also,' he added, 'Cat from *Red Dwarf* and the dude from *Maid Marian* – his nephew scored against us today.'

'Even worse, Charlton fans protest EFL by "occupying" Woolwich Screwfix,' he informed me.

And in those two messages, I knew neither of us would regret a thing.

Acknowledgements

For as long as I can remember, writing a book – and actually getting it published – has been my greatest dream. So please indulge me for a minute while I give due thanks to the many people who made the realisation of this possible.

They say you never forget a good teacher, and indeed, it is true. My dream of writing began at the age of around ten and was in no small part encouraged and nurtured by the brilliant Dilys Patten of Ramsey County Primary School, as it was then known. I had wanted to seek Mrs P out, to let her know that her encouragement had paid off but was sad to hear that she had died the year before. I owe so much to her encouragement, and though I regret not being able to tell her that, I also found out that apparently she had also been a regular at the Harwich and Parkeston Sunday Shrimpers, back in the day, so I think she would have been doubly chuffed to hear about this book.

I would also like to pay tribute to my GCSE English teacher, Mrs Lynch, a formidable woman who knew when a student needed a proverbial stick, rather than carrot, and much like Lee Bowyer, I was the former.

To my long-suffering agent, Louise Lamont, who apparently knew what I should be writing, before I knew it myself. Thank you for seeing the potential in a mad-cap plan and a lapsed civil servant. Whatever the endless rapture brings next, we'll always have 2012.

To Michael Sells at Icon, who also saw the potential in me, as well as my beloved club. I am enormously grateful to you for taking a punt on a football book written by a woman. It is ridiculous to be writing this in the year 2022, but it nonetheless remains true – thank you for recognising the importance of diverse voices in sports writing. Thank you also to Duncan Heath and Ian Greensill, for your efforts in helping me to hone this text.

To the contributors of this book: Lee Bowyer, John Brewin, Alan Curbishley, Alan Davies, Alan Dryland, Carrie Dunn, Gary Ginnaw, Karen Hills, Tracey Leaburn, Jason Morgan, Sachin Nakrani, Andy Norman, Bhavisha Raji, Thomas Sandgaard, Marvin Sordell, Lyle Taylor, Nick Tondeur, Troy Townsend (and to Sarah Train for helping me to pin him down!), Richard Wiseman, as well as Tom Rubashow, for your help securing so many of these contributions. This story is as much yours as it is mine, and I am hugely privileged to have been able to tell it. Thank you for taking the time to share your wisdom and experiences with me.

To Nicola, John, Katherine, Harriet, Nancy, Cariad, Stef, and Tessa, thank you for your endless support, and always making me feel like I could finish this, even when I very much felt I couldn't. To the ladies of the Knocked Up Indoors group, the best thing about being a mum (apart from, like, your actual kids) is other mums – thank you for keeping me sane over the last couple of years. To Adrianne, for your thorough and insightful feedback, as well as words of encouragement. To my colleagues at Standard Issue, Sarah, Mickey and Hannah, thank you for your patience and support while I birthed a child and wrote this book. Thanks also to Jonny, for the excellent headshots.

To Vera, for being my biggest champion/proofreader/therapist/and general surrogate sister – you are the best, and I can never thank you enough for all that you have done for me over the last 30+ years.

To Bayo, Conman, Dave, Jamie, Joel, Kerry, Sean and Steve for coming to (sometimes really crap) matches, and/or letting me use your words/private messages in this book.

Thank you to my mum and dad, for not kicking off when I announced I was leaving the Civil Service. I was right though – the pension *is* getting shitter. Thanks also for finally relenting and getting me that laptop – I told you I wouldn't leave it on the bus.

To Lyra, my proudest achievement of all – I realise that you might feel a bit weird, one day, about having your early bowel movements committed to print, but good omen or otherwise, you are the best thing that ever happened to me, and my motivation for everything. This story began before I even knew of you, but it couldn't have finished without you.

The biggest thanks must, of course, go to my brothers Stephen and Michael for sitting me down with that yoghurt pot and apple core, all those years ago, but especially to Michael, the reluctant star of this book. You have been the most tremendous sport in allowing me to tell the warts-and-all rollercoaster story of your life as a Charlton Athletic supporter, as well as being my day one best buddy, and total champion of my ridiculous life choices. I am so tremendously grateful to you for being twenty times funnier than I will ever be, and allowing me to mine your hilarity for content, even if your short-term memory of things you have said about League One footballers is, at best, patchy. Thank you for being a dickhead (and redeeming yourself) about your (admittedly not great) 21st birthday present – it worked out quite well for me, in the end.